Governance, Risk and Compliance

This book on Governance, Risk Management and Compliance (GRC) and Data Privacy is designed to equip apprentices, students and professionals across various industries with a deep understanding of this holistic approach to organizational security and risk management, quality management and regulatory responsibilities. It involves aligning a company's governance structure, quality and risk processes and compliance and data privacy activities to better enable the achievement of the company's strategic goals. It also looks at what is an Enterprise Security Architecture through the lenses of TOGAF and SABSA, which isn't about the technical implementation; think of building a house where you get an architect to design it and you ensure the construction is aligned to best practices and your goals.

Whether you are an Information Security or Cybersecurity specialist, a risk management practitioner, or simply seeking to enhance your knowledge in this domain, this book will provide you with the necessary framework and tools to excel in your current or future role. It teaches you the fundamentals of GRC, including what GRC is and why it is important; the key components of GRC; how to implement a GRC program; what Data Privacy is beyond protection; and how to use GRC to improve your company's performance.

Dr Michael Brass is a senior information security leader with 25 years of experience of Information Security, Cybersecurity and IT within the technology, manufacturing, charity, financial and public Arms Length Bodies sectors in the UK. He has a proven track record of delivering innovative and practical solutions that are business-focused and pragmatic, driving digital transformation efforts. Visit his website at www.risk-specialist.com and his LinkedIn profile at https://www.linkedin.com/in/drmikebrass.

Security, Audit and Leadership Series

Series Editor: Dan Swanson, Dan Swanson and Associates, Ltd., Winnipeg, Manitoba, Canada.

The scope and mandate for internal audit continues to evolve each year, as does the complexity of the business environment and speed of the changing risk landscape in which it must operate. The fundamental goal of this exciting series is to produce leading-edge books on critical subjects facing security and audit executives and practitioners. Key topics addressed include Leadership, Cybersecurity, Security Leadership, Privacy, Strategic Risk Management, Auditing IT, Audit Management and Leadership, and Operational Auditing.

Analysis of Threat Perceptions: NATO and Türkiye's Cyber Terrorism Policies
By Mehmet Emin Erendor

Members, Methods, and Measures: Unlocking the Secrets of IT Leadership
By Thomas E. Armstrong

Philosophy.exe: The Techno-Philosophical Toolkit for Modern Minds
By Matthias Muhlert

Guardians of the Digital Age: Securing the Future
By Elçin Biren

Ironwill 360° Leadership: A Blueprint for Level 5 Unicorn Leadership
By Douglas P. Pflug

Behavioral Insights in Cybersecurity: A Guide to Digital Human Factors
By Dustin S. Sachs

Integrated Assurance: Unified Risk Strategy
By Patrick Hayes

Preparing for Sustainability Audits: A Practical Guide for IT Sector
By Mahsa Fidanboy

Scaling Pyramids: Leadership Lessons from a Mid-Level Bureaucrat
By Christopher Stitt

Program Architecture: Fight the Good Fight
By Gideon T. Rasmussen

Operation Carder Kaos: How One Agent Penetrated the Underground Community
By Richard K. LaTulip

Digitalization and Women's Rights Women and Sustainability: Volume 2
By Muharrem Kılıç and Sezer Bozkus Kahyaoglu

Governance, Risk and Compliance: Demystifying the Risk and Data Privacy Landscape
By Dr Michael Brass

Governance, Risk and Compliance

Demystifying the Risk and Data Privacy Landscape

Dr Michael Brass

CRC Press
Taylor & Francis Group
Boca Raton London New York

CRC Press is an imprint of the
Taylor & Francis Group, an **informa** business

Designed cover image: Michael Brass

First edition published 2026
by CRC Press
2385 NW Executive Center Drive, Suite 320, Boca Raton, FL 33431

and by CRC Press
4 Park Square, Milton Park, Abingdon, Oxon, OX14 4RN

CRC Press is an imprint of Taylor & Francis Group, LLC

ISBN: 9781032890586 (hbk)
ISBN: 9781032896717 (pbk)
ISBN: 9781003543992 (ebk)

DOI: 10.1201/9781003543992

Typeset in Sabon
by KnowledgeWorks Global Ltd.

Contents

Acknowledgements

This book represents the culmination of countless hours of thought, research, writing and revision. The majority of books on the market are geared towards a technical audience. I have taken a different approach. I have been in IT since 2000, in security in various guides since 2009 and I have worked in different industry verticals ranging from charity, political, university press, technology, manufacturing and Arms Length. I have been in academia since 1996. These experiences, particularly where I have led and passed on knowledge, have informed a particular viewpoint on communication and engagement and form the bedrock of this book. I have therefore written this book for diverse audiences and removed as much jargon as possible. Students, people wanting to enter the field, juniors and seniors from other areas within and outside of Information Security will all find something of value.

It stands as a testament to those who supported me along the way. I am deeply grateful to each of you. Thank you to my wife Isabelle for your support over the years. Your perspectives and strengths have helped me see things in new ways. To all my friends, thank you for your belief in me.

To my professional mentors and colleagues: your insights, critiques and shared experiences over all this time have been invaluable. You helped me refine my thinking, test my assumptions and push beyond the obvious. You know who you are.

To my editor and the publishing team: thank you for your tireless work, your sharp eye and your commitment to excellence. You helped me find clarity in complexity and gave this book the polish it needed to reach its full potential.

To my fellow security practitioners and fellow academics: I stand on your shoulders. Your contributions to the field laid the foundation for this book.

I also need to mention mental health, something I am very big on: To the quiet moments – the early mornings, the long walks, the cycling, the scribbled notes – which is the space where clarity emerged.

And finally, to you, the reader: thank you for choosing to spend your time with this book. Whether you are here out of curiosity, necessity or passion,

I hope these pages offer you something meaningful, whether it is an insight, a challenge or simply a moment of connection.

With deep appreciation,

Dr Mike Brass

LinkedIn: https://www.linkedin.com/in/drmikebrass/

Website: https://www.risk-specialist.com

Introduction

The fields of Governance, Risk and Compliance (GRC), Enterprise Security Architecture (ESA) and Data Privacy have emerged as vital pillars of modern business operations in an era defined by rapid digital advancements, uncertainty over the direction of global interconnectedness and complex regulatory landscapes. Organisations are no longer measured solely by their financial performance; their ability to safeguard sensitive data, ensure operational resilience and comply with evolving regulations is equally scrutinised. These interconnected disciplines not only protect businesses from risks but also serve as enablers of trust, innovation and sustainable growth.

My journey into the complex world of GRC, ESA and Data Privacy is rooted in the Social Sciences, which highlights the interdisciplinary nature of these fields. I hold undergraduate, Masters and a PhD in Archaeology. I am currently an Honorary Research Fellow at the Institute of Archaeology, University College London. I am also a former global head of Information Security, Data Privacy and Business Systems, and currently serve as the Head of Security Services (GRC and ESA) at one of the UK's Arms Length Bodies, part of the country's Critical National Infrastructure.

Social Science disciplines provide unique insights into human behaviour, organisational dynamics and ethical frameworks, all of which are essential in addressing the challenges these disciplines face. Later, we will discuss the value, and I would argue the necessity, of the Social Sciences with the background and skills it brings to bear in greater detail. For now, it is sufficient to mention that Social Science principles can inform the design of user-friendly compliance training programmes, the implementation of inclusive data governance policies and the development of communication strategies that resonate with diverse stakeholders. This perspective is particularly valuable in fostering collaboration across departments, bridging the gap between technical teams and decision-makers, and embedding ethical considerations into technological advancements.

One of the advantages of coming from a different disciplinary or subject matter background lies in the ability to approach problems from unique angles. Professionals with diverse expertise bring fresh perspectives to traditional challenges, fostering innovation and adaptability. To provide an example, a

DOI: 10.1201/9781003543992-1

background in psychology can enhance understanding of user behaviour in cybersecurity, while experience in anthropology might offer insights into cultural factors affecting organisational compliance. These varied lenses enrich decision-making processes, creating solutions that are both comprehensive and contextually relevant.

THE CONVERGENCE OF GRC, ESA AND DATA PRIVACY

GRC provides the strategic foundation for organisations to operate ethically and efficiently. GRC frameworks align business objectives with regulatory requirements, ensuring accountability, transparency and effective risk management. ESA, on the other hand, delivers the blueprint for safeguarding an organisation's digital infrastructure and processes through standards. It integrates security measures across systems, processes and technologies, creating a resilient ecosystem capable of withstanding cyber threats. Complementing these is Data Privacy, a field dedicated to protecting individuals' personal information in compliance with regulations like the General Data Protection Regulation (GDPR) in Europe and the California Consumer Privacy Act (CCPA) in the USA.

Together, GRC, ESA and Data Privacy address the triad of strategic governance, digital security and regulatory compliance. This convergence enables organisations to not only defend against risks but also position themselves as ethical leaders in a competitive market. Organisations can establish a strong foundation for operational integrity, mitigating risks while simultaneously fostering innovation through ensuring alignment.

At this point there may be some people raising an eyebrow at the inclusion of data privacy, or some people may be thinking data privacy is important but limit their thinking to "protecting the data." I would like to nip both views in the bud. Data has become one of the most valuable assets for businesses. This is now recognised, for example, in the UK's 2025 Industrial Strategy where data as an economic asset is finally one of the core pillars. Security practitioners therefore must have a comprehensive understanding of data privacy laws and regulations. This knowledge is essential not only for mitigating legal and financial risks but also for fostering trust, supporting business operations and aligning security strategies with privacy principles:

1. *Ensuring Legal and Regulatory Compliance*: Data privacy laws, such as the General Data Protection Regulation (GDPR) in the European Union, the California Consumer Privacy Act (CCPA) in the United States and the Personal Data Protection Act (PDPA) in Singapore, establish strict requirements for the collection, use and protection of personal data. Non-compliance with these regulations can result in hefty fines, legal penalties and reputational damage.

2. *Safeguarding Against Data Breaches*: Many data privacy laws include specific provisions on how organisations should handle data breaches. For instance, the GDPR requires companies to notify supervisory authorities within 72 hours of discovering a breach. Similarly, the CCPA mandates timely notification to affected individuals. Practitioners must know these requirements to ensure compliance during a breach. An informed practitioner can design and implement incident response plans that align with legal timelines, reducing the risk of regulatory scrutiny and demonstrating accountability to stakeholders.
3. *Protecting the Business' Reputation*: Data privacy is directly linked to consumer trust. Organisations that fail to protect personal data face reputational damage that can impact customer loyalty, investor confidence and market competitiveness. Understanding privacy laws enables practitioners to establish robust data protection measures that reassure customers their information is safe.
4. *Supporting Business Growth*: In a globalised economy, organisations often operate across multiple jurisdictions, each with its own privacy regulations. Compliance with these laws is often a prerequisite for entering or continuing operations in specific markets. Practitioners must understand these regional laws to ensure seamless operations and avoid legal barriers.
5. *Managing Cross-Border Data Transfers*: Many data privacy laws impose restrictions on transferring personal data across borders. The EU GDPR requires that data transferred outside the EU must be sent to countries with adequate data protection standards or be governed by mechanisms such as Standard Contractual Clauses (SCCs). Similarly, laws like the Personal Information Protection Law (PIPL) in China impose strict controls on international data flows. Practitioners must be aware of these regulations to implement secure data transfer mechanisms and avoid disruptions to global operations. By understanding the legal landscape, they can work with legal and compliance teams to develop strategies that ensure secure and lawful cross-border data flows.
6. *Aligning Cybersecurity with Privacy Principles*: Modern data privacy laws emphasise principles like data minimisation, purpose limitation and accountability. These principles often intersect with security practices. Limiting data collection and retention reduces the attack surface for cyber threats, while accountability measures ensure that security practices are documented and auditable. This includes embedding privacy-by-design practices into the organisation's systems and processes, ensuring that security measures are not only robust but also compliant with privacy requirements.
7. *Navigating Emerging Privacy Challenges*: The rapid pace of technological innovation presents new challenges for data privacy and security. Emerging technologies such as artificial intelligence (AI), machine learning and the Internet of Things (IoT) generate massive amounts of

data, often collected without explicit consent. Practitioners must understand how privacy laws address these technologies to mitigate risks and ensure compliance.

8. *Enhancing Accountability and Governance*: Data privacy laws increasingly emphasise accountability, requiring organisations to demonstrate compliance through audits, data protection impact assessments (DPIAs) and the appointment of Data Protection Officers (DPOs).
9. *Mitigating Financial Risks*: Fines for non-compliance with data privacy laws can be significant. EU GDPR violations can result in penalties of up to €20 million or 4% of global annual turnover, whichever is higher. Similarly, the CCPA allows consumers to seek statutory damages for breaches of unencrypted data. By understanding privacy laws, practitioners can implement the necessary safeguards to avoid these financial penalties. A proactive approach to compliance not only reduces legal risks but also minimises the costs associated with data breaches, such as remediation, compensation and reputational repair.

For practitioners, understanding data privacy laws and regulations is no longer optional: It is a necessity. The increasing complexity of privacy regulations, coupled with the growing importance of data protection, places practitioners at the forefront to navigate the evolving privacy landscape is critical to their organisations' success in a data-driven world.

CHALLENGES IN THE CURRENT LANDSCAPE

Despite their importance, the implementation of Security and Data Privacy initiatives is fraught with challenges. Organisations face rapidly changing regulations, resource constraints and an evolving threat landscape. Data breaches, ransomware attacks and supply chain vulnerabilities expose gaps in traditional risk management practices. High-profile incidents, such as attacks on critical infrastructure or global organisations, highlight the consequences of fragmented or outdated security strategies.

Global disparities in regulatory frameworks further complicate compliance efforts for multinational organisations. While GDPR prioritises stringent data protection, other jurisdictions may adopt less robust standards, creating inconsistencies that increase compliance burdens. Overlapping or conflicting regulations can result in confusion and inefficiencies, particularly in sectors like finance, healthcare and technology. The shortage of skilled professionals in these fields exacerbates the challenge. There are numerous overlapping and conflicting reasons for this shortage which are beyond the scope of this book. Suffice to say that organisations must invest in training and talent retention to ensure the sustainability of their GRC, ESA and Data Privacy efforts.

To achieve this, there are a number of general security principles which will guide us throughout the book. Principle 1 is *Security enables delivery.*

Security is here to support the business and help keep everything running safely. Good security means business alignment, focusing on what matters and where the risks are. It's part of every plan, project and team, building secure from the start and not being bolted on later. It helps us stay safe, bounce back quickly and keep things going when something bad happens; in other words, good security supports business continuity and disaster recovery. Above all, good security needs to be simple, clear and easy for people to use.

Principle 2 is *Expect the unexpected*. We must be ready for when a breach does happen. The idea that there will never be a breach or that a breach means your programme has completely failed is wrong. At some point this will go wrong, whether it is a data leak, a break-in, or a supplier incident. How we respond should already be baked into our plans, which is where business continuity and disaster recovery planning and resilience really matter. These are not simple problems, so we need a blended response covering people, processes and technology. Run the scenarios, test the plans, learn what works and keep getting better.

Principle 3 is *Do the basics well*. Getting the basics right makes a huge difference. Start with the simple stuff: strong passwords, updates, who gets access and how we handle information. Apply these things everywhere; good security should be foundational. Mix people, process and technology as a blended setup gives better protection and backup. This way you'll stop most issues before they start.

Principle 4 is *Defend as one*. Security works best when it is blended. Do not allow boundaries between teams, partners or suppliers to slow down things. Share what we know, who is doing what and act fast when something is not right. Make sure the supply chain is secure as everything we rely on from suppliers needs to be protected.

Principle 5 is *Own your security*. Security starts with each of us. It's not just the security team's job. Daily behaviours make the biggest difference, whether you are on the front line or in leadership. If something does not look right, report it. We should never blame – we learn. Mistakes and near-misses help us get better.

OPPORTUNITIES

While the challenges are significant, understanding what security is and how to leverage GRC, ESA and Data Privacy presents opportunities for organisations. Demonstrating commitment to governance, security and privacy fosters trust among customers, partners and regulators. Trust is particularly critical in industries where the handling of sensitive data is paramount. A secure and compliant foundation enables organisations to innovate confidently, exploring new technologies and markets. Compliance with regulations and adherence to ethical standards differentiate organisations in competitive landscapes.

Businesses with strong privacy frameworks can leverage data analytics for business insights without risking regulatory penalties and can position themselves as leaders in their respective industries.

To give briefly some examples, which are taken from the security.gov.uk website for Secure By Design:

- *Prepare a Secure Service*: Identity your resources, agree roles and responsibilities, include security within the project business cases for funding in line with risk appetite.
- *Understand the Security Landscape*: Understand the business objectives and their needs, understand security's obligations, identify the supply chain.
- *Manage the Security Risks*: Document the assets and the respective importance, undertake threat modelling and assessments, examine your controls,
- *Anticipate and Respond*: Vulnerability management process which goes beyond just technology, managing observability, have defined processes for discovery.
- *Continuous Assurance*: Evaluating the impact of changes, securely retiring services and assets.

Accordingly, this book delves into the intricate world of GRC, ESA and Data Privacy, providing readers with a comprehensive understanding of these disciplines and their intersections. It aims to equip apprentices, students, professionals and decision-makers with the knowledge and tools needed to navigate the complexities of modern governance, security and compliance. The integration of GRC, ESA and Data Privacy is not merely a technical or regulatory necessity. It is a strategic imperative that underpins trust, innovation and long-term success in an increasingly complex world.

In the chapters ahead, we will explore frameworks, best practices and provide fictional case studies that illustrate successful implementations. Readers will gain insights into how small businesses can leverage Security principles to protect against threats and establish opportunities, and how data privacy initiatives can transform relationships. From building resilient architectures to fostering a culture of compliance and safeguarding data privacy, this book offers actionable insights for shaping the future of secure and sustainable organisations. You will be better equipped to drive meaningful change within your organisation and contribute to a safer, more ethical digital ecosystem by understanding these interconnected disciplines.

Chapter 1

Social Sciences and Information Security

Bridging disciplines to build understanding

Strong interrelationships between much of the Social Sciences and Information Security, in all its various guises, stretch back decades. There is much to unpick. The Confidentiality, Integrity, Availability (CIA) Triad forms the foundation of technical security operations, though in my view it is a desired output and desired state, and the CISSP certification is about assurance concepts. However, effective security goes beyond leadership principles (e.g., SABSA's) and not viewing Information Security in isolation from multiple human behavioural disciplines. Leadership and resilience in Information Security require a broader understanding of human behaviour, societal dynamics and cultural relativity.

The Social Sciences include, amongst others, Anthropology, Political Science, Psychology and Sociology. Criminology is also included under the broad umbrella of Criminal Anthropology which, like Archaeology and Cultural/Social Anthropology, is a sub-discipline of Anthropology (or first cousin, if outside of North America). In this chapter, I will use the terms Anthropology and Archaeology interchangeable for convenience. Of these, Criminal Anthropology has traditionally been most leaned on for motives, responses and how to counter cyber attackers; this is expressed succinctly in Sarah Armstrong-Smith's book, *Understand the Cyber Attacker Mindset*, and in Loiseau *et al.*'s book, *Information Security in Humanities and Social Sciences: A Research Methods Approach*. This chapter takes a step back to include the Social Sciences in the conversation and at this critical juncture of profound digital transformation, geopolitical turbulences and the inherent attendant dangers. The Social Sciences offer dynamic perspectives to aid in comprehending and strengthening information security (see the edited volume *EMTech Anthropology: Careers at the Frontier* by Matt Artz and Lora Koycheva).

THE SOCIAL SCIENCES AND INFORMATION SECURITY

At first glance, Archaeology and Information Security might appear to be entirely unrelated fields. However, both share a common approach, namely the meticulous analysis of incomplete trails to construct coherent narratives

DOI: 10.1201/9781003543992-2

and their emphasis on human behaviour. Different cultures have varying attitudes towards privacy, information sharing and online behaviour, which help provide us with a valuable perspective on security through the examination of cultural norms and practices related to technology and data privacy. Understanding these cultural nuances is critical for the development of effective security strategies in a globalised world.

Let's take a quick detour, the reasons for which will quickly become apparent. I undertake my archaeology work in Sudan. There is a long list of stakeholders: the Director and other personnel of the division of my university, Sudan's foreign Ministry, prominent individuals from the Sudanese antiquities service (NCAM), the University of Khartoum, our fieldwork team and specialists, other Sudanese scholars and journalists, local government officials and most importantly the local inhabitants who are the custodians of their heritage. The methodologies deployed in the field include but are not limited to the oversight of operational work, heritage outreach and educational activities and the director and co-director activities, which include but are also not limited to programme and project, risk and stakeholder management.

Moving down one level from strategic and programme to operations and datasets, Archaeology and Information Security share more fundamental similarities: the meticulous analysis of incomplete trails to construct a coherent narrative. Some of the core overlaps are:

1. Data analysis and interpretation: In archaeology, data analysis involves examining physical artefacts, using ethnographic methods to reconstruct the social complexities and behaviours of past societies. Similarly, information security leverages behavioural science and strategic analysis to minimise disruptions to business operations. At an operational level, security professionals analyse digital data to detect threats and vulnerabilities, constructing narratives about system weaknesses and potential breaches.
2. Pattern recognition: Both fields excel in recognising patterns, a skill critical to their success. Archaeologists identify distribution patterns in artefacts, settlements and cultural practices, while Information Security experts use pattern recognition to detect anomalies that may signal security threats.
3. Digital preservation: Digital preservation is another shared concern. Archaeologists work to preserve both physical artefacts and digital records of their findings, ensuring these are accessible for future study. Information security professionals, meanwhile, focus on protecting digital assets and data from loss or corruption, often employing similar principles of redundancy and encryption.
4. Data recovery: Both fields involve meticulous examination of evidence to uncover hidden information or work with damaged or corrupted data. Digital forensics mirrors archaeological techniques in its detailed examination of evidence. For example, just as archaeologists examine

> soil samples for pollen or other microscopic evidence, Information Security professionals analyse system logs and network traffic to identify suspicious activity. Both processes demand a careful, methodical approach to uncover hidden information and build actionable insights. Both fields involve meticulous recovery and reconstruction of data. Archaeologists often work with incomplete or damaged artefacts, piecing together fragmented patterns to reveal larger truths about ancient societies. Similarly, forensic investigators in Information Security analyse corrupted or incomplete digital information to uncover malicious activities.

In various guises, anthropologists therefore deal with vast stretches of time and space. Anthropologists delve into past human motivations, decision-making and social dynamics. This knowledge can be applied to understand the motivations of cyber attackers, their decision-making processes when targeting systems, and the social structures within cybercrime rings. Another example is that Archaeology itself is multi-disciplinary, drawing upon technology, geology, cultural anthropology, genetics, climate science and many others besides. The reconstruction of past societies necessitates understanding their climatic contexts both locally and regionally. This view of deep time for climatic change and the knowledge of the types, nature and severity of ecological changes means there are lessons which can be drawn for Environmental, Social, and Governance (ESG) frameworks. Investors are looking for companies that are not only financially profitable but also socially responsible and environmentally sustainable. Investors can potentially identify companies that are less likely to face risks associated with environmental damage or social issues, and that may also have opportunities for long-term growth.

The resulting data can also be placed within appropriate social contexts, e.g. security measures implemented in a Western context might not be readily adopted in a culture that values collectivism over individualism. Anthropology helps security professionals adapt their strategies to different cultural contexts, ensuring their effectiveness across borders. Cyber criminals may exploit differences in infrastructure, legal frameworks and digital literacy levels in those regions. Anthropology provides insights into related vulnerabilities, allowing for the development of targeted solutions and capacity-building initiatives. This point leads into the next outline: Criminal Anthropology, although it is a distinct discipline within the social sciences, draws not only on the theory and practice of anthropology, but also on sociology, psychology, economics and even biology.

Criminal Anthropology

Criminal Anthropology plays a pivotal role in security by providing insights into the minds and methods of attackers. Criminologists study criminal behaviour, motivations and trends and their findings can be directly applied to understanding cybercriminals. They can identify common attack patterns and predict potential future threats. They help construct and deconstruct knowledge about potential threat environments, behaviours, deterrents and changing contexts to influence choices. This knowledge empowers security professionals to develop targeted security measures that anticipate and deter attacker strategies. This includes the social and economic factors that contribute to criminal activity. Understanding the root causes of cybercrime – such as poverty, inequality, or lack of job opportunities – can inform broader societal interventions that may reduce the overall pool of potential cybercriminals.

Additionally, Criminology offers valuable insights into the psychology of cybercrime. Studies explore the motivations of attackers, ranging from financial gain to ideological extremism. Understanding motives allows for the development of more effective deterrents, such as targeted awareness campaigns or psychological profiling of potential offenders.

However, it is my view that we need to delve down deeper than Criminology to understand what behaviour actually is. Apart from what has been mentioned already about Anthropology, one could turn to Sahlins and de Almeida for cultural relativity, as well as Latour, Foucault and others. Sahlins' Stone Age Economics (1972) challenged conventional views on early societies, arguing that hunter-gatherers were not struggling for survival but instead highlighted how they met their needs; this has been substantially revised by subsequent anthropologists, but what is important here is that anthropologists explore economic and social structures, emphasising reciprocity, gift economies and non-market exchange systems. For modern companies, Sahlins' insights highlight the importance of collaboration, adaptability and sustainable resource management. His work suggests that businesses can benefit from fostering strong social networks, decentralised decision-making and trust-based exchanges, rather than relying solely on rigid hierarchical structures. The emphasis on reciprocity and shared responsibility can inform corporate strategies that prioritise long-term relationships over short-term gains.

We could also turn to linguistic relativity (e.g., Martin Heidegger's notion that we do not speak language, language speaks us). There is the French Enlightenment literature, which is so important. In the Anglo-Saxon intellectual world, there were and are endless debates on how knowledge and behaviours were/are culturally constructed, enacted and construed in terms of power and interactions. Other areas of the world outside of the Anglo-Saxon academic sphere also have their own interesting debates.

David Graeber is a now sadly deceased anthropologist and anarchist. Some of his broader views on technology, bureaucracy, state power and digital labour can be interpreted as relevant to security, especially in terms of its social and political dimensions. His ideas invite critical reflection on who benefits from digital security regimes, who controls our data and infrastructure, and how these systems shape the political and social order.

1. Bureaucracy and Surveillance: In The Utopia of Rules, Graeber critiques how bureaucratic systems – often propped up by digital technologies – enable state and corporate surveillance. This ties into concerns around data privacy, mass surveillance and control over digital infrastructure.
2. Anarchism and Decentralisation: Graeber's anarchist philosophy promotes decentralised systems and horizontal organisation, which can align with the ethos behind certain movements like open-source encryption tools, privacy-focused technologies, or decentralised internet protocols.
3. Technology and Power: He often lamented how modern technological innovation seems to focus more on control, surveillance and efficiency rather than liberating or imaginative possibilities (e.g., compared to the dreams of the 1960s about space travel or automation liberating labour). This indirectly critiques regimes that prioritise state or corporate power over individual autonomy.
4. Digital Labour and Control: In his "bullshit jobs" thesis, he points out how many people work in roles that perpetuate digital and bureaucratic systems without real value. That critique could extend to some security roles that exist more to maintain complex and opaque systems of control than to actually protect users.

So while he didn't write about security in a technical sense, you can definitely apply his critical frameworks to ask: Who benefits from security policies? Who gets to control data and digital infrastructure? How is digital security tied up in systems of domination or resistance? Accordingly, let's take the example of Pegasus, a state-sponsored spyware developed by the NSO Group, which has been used by governments to covertly monitor journalists, activists and dissidents. Though justified under the guise of national security or counterterrorism, such tools represent a kind of digital violence: surveillance without consent, facilitated by opaque bureaucratic systems and legal loopholes. Graeber might argue that this is precisely how modern power operates: not through overt force, but through quietly sanctioned intrusions.

This phenomenon also connects with Graeber's critique of what he called "bullshit jobs": Roles that exist not to create value but to sustain systems of control or maintain the appearance of productivity. Enormous resources are devoted to developing surveillance tools, counter-surveillance defences, threat assessments and risk mitigation strategies, many of which serve to perpetuate an arms race of digital control. These efforts, while ostensibly about safety, often serve corporate or governmental interests rather than those of ordinary people. From Graeber's perspective, such cycles of attack and defence may represent a form of "mutual sabotage", a world where entire careers are built not on solving problems, but on perpetuating them.

Furthermore, Graeber lamented the way in which technological progress has failed to live up to its emancipatory promise. Where once people dreamed of jetpacks, space colonies, or a post-work society, we now live in a world where the most advanced technologies are frequently used to monitor behaviour, enforce compliance, or extract data. Security tools, in this context, are double-edged: they can protect individuals, but they are also part of the architecture of digital enclosure. For Graeber, this represents a tragic narrowing of our technological imagination.

While he may not have written about encryption standards or network protocols, Graeber's anarchist commitments – his advocacy for decentralisation, mutual aid and horizontal organisation – resonate deeply with movements for digital privacy and open-source security. He would likely have championed technologies that empower users over institutions and criticised those that concentrate power in the hands of the few. The rise of decentralised networks, privacy-focused tools and grassroots digital activism can all be seen as aligned with his vision of a freer, more cooperative world.

Ultimately, applying Graeber's thinking to security leads us to fundamental questions: Why is it acceptable for corporations to sell military-grade spyware to governments? How did we reach a point where digital surveillance is more profitable than digital freedom? And what kind of internet might we have created if it had been designed not for profit or control, but for collective flourishing? These are questions that Graeber's legacy reminds us that we must.

Let's take another book by Graeber, this time co-authored with a colleague of mine from University College London, Professor David Wengrow. The book was published after Graeber's passing, and it is titled *The Dawn of Everything*.

Published in 2021, it presents a radical rethinking of human social evolution. Rather than portraying inequality, bureaucracy and top-down authority as inevitable consequences of civilisation, the authors argue that early societies were often diverse, flexible and highly experimental in their social structures. These societies frequently shifted between different political arrangements, including egalitarianism, temporary hierarchies and decentralised governance. This revisionist history invites readers not only to reconsider the past, but to question the assumption that our current models of power and organisation – especially in corporate settings – are the only or most effective options available. When applied to the field of information security, their framework opens up the possibility for imagining different approaches to digital governance, autonomy and collective responsibility.

Modern corporate security is deeply rooted in hierarchical logic. Information is compartmentalised, access is tightly controlled and decisions about policy, risk and compliance are made at the top and disseminated downwards. These structures reflect a worldview that sees security as control, often enforced through surveillance, monitoring and compliance regimes. While this model may appear efficient, it comes at a cost: employees are treated primarily as potential liabilities rather than trusted collaborators. In Graeber and Wengrow's terms, this resembles the "small-scale despotisms" that they describe in historical contexts – systems that function through coercion and obedience, rather than mutual understanding or shared purpose.

This dominant model is not questioned as often as it should be, largely because it has become naturalised: organisations assume that hierarchy is required for safety, that surveillance is a necessary trade-off and that compliance structures must be rigid. The Dawn of Everything challenges such assumptions. The book presents evidence that prehistoric and early historic societies frequently developed non-hierarchical systems of coordination, including seasonal shifts in power structures or pluralistic governance. Some communities even deliberately rejected permanent hierarchies, preferring instead to rotate authority or decentralise decision-making. These insights disrupt the idea that strict control is necessary for large or complex systems to function. Applied to corporate security, this suggests that alternative, more participatory forms of digital governance may not only be possible but historically grounded.

One key concept in the book is the idea of freedom as a practical condition. Graeber and Wengrow argue that in many societies, freedom was not an abstract value but a tangible experience: the freedom to move, to disobey orders, or to shift one's social identity. Rather than treating security as a collaborative process, organisations often reduce it to a set of restrictive rules designed to pre-empt misuse. This "command-and-control" approach mirrors the bureaucratic mindset that Graeber critiqued in earlier works, where systems become less about solving problems and more about reinforcing their own internal logic.

Moreover, Graeber and Wengrow's emphasis on institutional memory and social possibility provides a valuable critique of the cybersecurity status quo. They argue that societies were able to imagine and experiment with new forms of organisation because they retained a collective memory of alternatives. In contrast, corporate security policies tend to forget or exclude alternative models such as open-source collaboration, peer-to-peer authentication, decentralised identity systems or user-driven threat modelling. In doing so, they not only stifle innovation but replicate outdated power structures.

It is also worth noting that The Dawn of Everything draws attention to how narratives about inevitability are used to legitimise certain social orders. Just as past historians claimed that inequality arose naturally with agriculture or urbanisation, many in the corporate world argue that strong surveillance, internal audits and strict control are simply "best practices". This rhetoric masks the contingency of these choices and forecloses alternative futures. Yet as the book repeatedly shows, the organisation of society – like the design of digital systems – is always a political and ethical decision, not a technical inevitability.

Reimagining corporate Information Security in this light means a shift in priorities: from control to trust, from rigid policy to adaptive governance, from top-down enforcement to participatory design. Employees could be brought into the process of security creation, not simply as subjects to be monitored, but as co-authors of the systems they use. Security practices could be aligned with values of autonomy, transparency and collective responsibility, principles that reflect the kind of social experimentation Graeber and Wengrow highlight throughout human history.

Consequently, The Dawn of Everything offers a profound philosophical challenge to the assumptions underlying corporate information security. By showing that human societies have long experimented with non-hierarchical, flexible systems of governance, Graeber and Wengrow invite us to question the inevitability of current security models. Rather than accepting surveillance, bureaucracy and control as necessary evils, we are encouraged to ask: What would a liberatory, cooperative and historically conscious approach to information security look like? In a time of escalating digital surveillance and risk management, that question may be more urgent than ever.

Let's momentarily switch our attention, therefore, to another example: Critical Discourse Analysis (CDA). CDA is a powerful tool used in both Criminology and wider Anthropology to examine how language shapes our understanding of crime and social context. It provides a valuable lens for understanding the language of both crime and security. In Criminology and Anthropology, CDA examines how language constructs power structures and cultural narratives. Anthropology uses CDA to uncover hidden assumptions in dominant cultural narratives.

Anthropology also uses CDA to explore how knowledge about cultures and social groups is produced through language. This can be particularly important in studying how dominant narratives about crime and deviance are shaped. CDA also helps analyse interview transcripts, ethnographic notes and other forms of communication between and within communities. It can reveal hidden power dynamics and cultural assumptions. Finally, CDA is also useful in examining the language used during colonial periods, and the lasting impact on how certain cultures and practices are perceived, including those related to crime and what is regarded as deviance in different socio-economic contexts.

As Sarah Armstrong-Smith recounts in her book on the cyber attacker mindset, referencing specialist publications and expert conversations she held, CDA applies *inter alia* to the language used in social engineering. CDA reveals how language choices can reinforce power structures and could possibly show how certain contexts may make individuals more prone to crime, which is an alignment with Criminal Anthropology studying the cultural aspects and underpinning of crime.

In Information Security, CDA helps deconstruct the language of social engineering attacks like phishing. These attacks rely on creating a sense of urgency, authority, or trust to manipulate victims. By analysing phishing emails through CDA, security professionals can identify the linguistic techniques used – such as imitating legitimate organisations or exploiting cultural norms – and develop better detection and education strategies.

Successfully adopting these approaches requires an understanding of business goals and objectives, as outlined in frameworks like the Business Canvas Model. As a trusted advisor, a security professional must not only recognise technical risks but also understand the broader organisational context, aligning security practices with business priorities. For now, we return to briefly looking at other Social Science disciplines, starting with Sociology, which is also a cousin of Anthropology.

Sociology

Sociology examines the social structures, institutions and norms that shape human behaviour. The sociologist's perspective is invaluable because it helps information security professionals understand the social context in which security practices are implemented.

Organisational culture significantly impacts security. A culture of openness and trust can foster a more responsible approach to data security. Conversely, a culture of fear or secrecy can discourage users from reporting security incidents, hindering the overall effectiveness of a security posture. Sociology helps information security professionals create a positive security culture within organisations through a better understanding of what motivates employees (needs and desires, and incentives and rewards encouraging compliance) and understanding of how social norms can differentially influence employee behaviour both within different areas of a country and between countries. Additionally, helping identify cognitive biases that can lead to security breaches (people may be more likely to take risks if they believe they are invulnerable).

There are further aspects to consider, namely those of team dynamics, and power and influence. Sociology can help understand how to create effective teams that can work together to improve security. A culture of collaboration and trust is fostered by understanding the dynamics of group behaviour, and the values and beliefs underpinnings those behaviours. This also feeds into the next point about power and influence, whereby through understanding the distribution of power (hierarchical and heterarchical) within an organisation, security professionals can identify potential vulnerabilities and develop strategies to mitigate them.

Sociology also sheds light on the broader social implications of security practices. For example, the use of surveillance technologies to combat cybercrime can raise concerns about privacy and civil liberties. Sociology helps information security professionals navigate ethical considerations and develop solutions that balance security needs with societal values.

Psychology

Psychology plays a crucial role in information security in terms of human behaviour and decision-making. Understanding how users interact with technology, their susceptibility to social engineering attacks, and their awareness of security risk is critical for developing effective strategies. This helps information security professionals create user-friendly security solutions that do not hinder productivity. Research in behavioural science can be used to develop training programmes that encourage secure practices and raise awareness about common threats.

Political Science

Political science examines the role of government in creating and enforcing policies. Information Security is increasingly becoming a matter of national security, with governments playing a crucial role in developing and enforcing cybersecurity regulations. Political science helps Information Security professionals understand the legal and regulatory landscape surrounding data privacy and security. This knowledge allows them to develop security practices that comply with relevant regulations.

Additionally, political science sheds light on international cooperation in Information Security. Cyber threats are often transnational in nature, requiring collaboration between governments to effectively combat them. Having an understanding of international relations and the political dynamics of security cooperation is crucial for developing effective global security strategies.

Science and technology studies

The interdisciplinary field of science and technology studies (STS) is focused on the creation, development and consequences of science and technology in historical, cultural and social contexts. STS scholars come from various backgrounds such as sociology, anthropology, history and philosophy. They explore how science and technology shape societies and how societies, in turn, shape science and technology. The emphasis is on the interconnectedness of science, technology and society in their historical, cultural and social contexts. In other words, STS scholars investigate how science and technology are produced and how they interact with and are shaped by society.

While criminology directly informs Information Security, STS plays a more nuanced role. It examines the social and cultural factors that influence practices. STS can help illuminate how organisational cultures, user behaviour and societal attitudes towards privacy impact security decisions. It sheds light on how technology itself can create new opportunities for crime. It also considers how social media platforms might be used for cyberbullying or how online anonymity can facilitate criminal activity. As technology advances, STS facilitates an examination of the ethical implications of new security measures related to surveillance, privacy and potential biases in security algorithms. It challenges the idea that technology is neutral, supporting the value of Anthropology in understanding societal and social context.

Both STS and Anthropology challenge the idea that scientific knowledge or technology is objective. They emphasise how social, cultural and political factors influence their development and use. Anthropologists' extensive use of fieldwork, where they immerse themselves in a culture or community, provides valuable data for STS scholars studying the social implications of science and technology. STS draws on anthropological concepts such as power dynamics, cultural relativism and the importance of local knowledge to understand the development and impact of science and technology in different contexts. STS scholars often use anthropological methods such as fieldwork and participant observation to study scientific communities and technological practices. STS broadens anthropological perspectives by promoting consideration of the broader social, political and economic forces shaping technology.

For the purpose of illustration, consider a simple analogy: Imagine Information Security as a castle. Criminology helps shed light on who might try to attack the castle and how they might do it. STS, drawing upon multiple intersecting disciplines, helps reveal the social dynamics within the castle (morale of the guards, vulnerabilities in the walls), the tools available to defend it (weaponry, training) and the ethical considerations of defending it (avoiding civilian casualties).

TRANSFERABLE SKILLS ACROSS DISCIPLINES

The intersection of the social sciences and information security highlights numerous transferable skills, which are critical in both fields and beyond. These include:

- Project management: Coordinating complex, multi-phase operations.
- Understanding societal contexts: Interpreting the interplay between human behaviour, societal structures and systems.
- Strong communication skills: Conveying complex ideas effectively through writing and speech.
- Analytical skills: Conducting research, interpreting evidence and challenging assumptions.
- Collaboration: Engaging with diverse groups, from local communities to business leaders.
- Problem-solving: Applying evidence and logic to develop practical solutions.
- Adaptability: Managing diverse projects in dynamic and unpredictable environments.

These skills underscore the need for diverse perspectives and interdisciplinary approaches in information security. A rigid, one-size-fits-all approach rarely works. By integrating multiple perspectives from varied backgrounds, organisations can address security challenges more effectively.

DISCUSSION

Let me briefly highlight one particularly relevant intersection between the social sciences, Information Security and business, namely that of ESG, which has significant implications for organisations and society as a whole. ESG, a framework used to evaluate a company's performance in ESG dimensions, has gained prominence in recent years due to growing concerns about sustainability and ethical business practices. As covered above, the Social Sciences provide valuable insights into human behaviour, group dynamics and culture. They help in designing educational campaigns that correct misconceptions, fostering a more realistic assessment of security risk. Educational psychology suggests that interactive and practical training sessions are more impactful than passive learning. Tailoring content to accommodate different learning styles – visual, auditory and kinesthetic – can also improve the retention of security protocols. These disciplines can help us understand how people interact with technology, how they perceive and manage risks and how they respond to security threats.

As organisations increasingly rely on technology to conduct their business, they are also considering the environmental and social impacts of their digital activities. A good ESG programme not only addresses these challenges it also helps to enhance their reputation, attract investors and improve their overall performance. Such a programme would consist of good governance and processes, capacity planning, reproducibility, interwoven strands of support and delivery/service, alignment amongst multiple stakeholders, economies of scale, contractual compliance and grasping changing contexts. These are all skills also either grounded in or leveraging skillsets which practitioners from the Social Sciences can and do leverage in Information Security.

Additionally, social networks have transformed the way information is shared and introduced novel security vulnerabilities. Studies of how groups behave online can inform strategies to combat social engineering attacks that exploit trust and relationships within social networks. When users trust the entity that handles their data, they are more likely to share information. However, this trust must be earned and maintained through transparent practices and respect for user autonomy.

The formulation of security policies and regulations benefits greatly from a social science perspective. Ethical considerations, societal norms and legal frameworks must be balanced to ensure that security measures do not infringe upon fundamental rights. Public policy research can guide the creation of regulations that are both effective and socially responsible.

It is at this point that I wish to start homing in further on governance specifics. ISO/IEC 38500 is an international standard that provides a principle-based framework for the corporate governance of information technology (IT). It is used by many organisations as an overarching digital governance framework, inclusive but not limited to security. It is designed primarily for boards of directors, company executives and senior management, guiding them to understand and fulfil their legal, regulatory and ethical obligations. Rather than being a technical manual, ISO 38500 focuses on high-level decision-making and leadership responsibilities, ensuring that digital systems are used effectively, efficiently and responsibly to support organisational goals. The standard outlines six key principles for good governance:

1. Responsibility: Individuals and groups within the organisation must understand and accept their responsibilities in respect of both the supply and the use of IT. They must have the authority to meet those responsibilities.
2. Strategy: The organisation's business strategy must take into account the current and future capabilities. Conversely, strategy must support the organisation's business strategy.
3. Acquisition: Acquisitions must be made for valid reasons, based on appropriate and ongoing analysis. All acquisitions must be made with a full understanding of the costs, benefits and risks.
4. Performance: They must be fit for purpose in supporting the organisation, providing the services, levels of service and service quality required to meet current and future business needs.
5. Conformance: They must comply with all applicable legislation and regulations. Policies and practices must be clearly defined, implemented and enforced.
6. Human behaviour: Policies, practices and decisions must respect the human element, including the needs of all people in the process and the impact on their work and wellbeing.

For companies, ISO 38500 encourages board-level oversight and strategic alignment with business objectives. It moves digital governance out of the realm of technical specialists and into the broader corporate governance framework, where accountability resides with senior leadership. This is especially important as digital transformation, security and data protection increasingly influence organisational success and stakeholder confidence. The standard helps organisations make better-informed decisions, weigh up opportunities against risks and ensure that digital investments are justified, transparent and aligned with business needs.

The framework promotes a lifecycle view, encouraging oversight of systems and services from planning and acquisition through to operation and eventual retirement. This approach ensures that IT continues to deliver value throughout its lifespan, while also enabling organisations to adapt to change and manage obsolescence more effectively.

In the context of Governance, Risk and Compliance (GRC), ISO 38500 plays a crucial role. For governance, it provides a high-level model that aligns digital oversight with overall corporate governance structures. It ensures that security supports business goals and that responsibilities are clearly assigned. In terms of risk, the standard promotes structured analysis and risk assessment around IT systems and initiatives, helping organisations mitigate operational, financial and reputational threats. Regarding compliance, ISO 38500 ensures that digital activities adhere to relevant laws and regulations such as the UK GDPR, the Companies Act 2006 and sector-specific frameworks. This also strengthens audit readiness and supports external assurance processes.

Ultimately, ISO 38500 helps organisations treat digital not merely as a technical function, but as a strategic asset. By applying its principles, organisations can build a governance culture where IT enables innovation, drives value, protects against risk and complies with both internal and external obligations.

I'll end this section with an example from Toyota Corporation, the Japanese-headquartered car manufacturer. The Kanri Nouryoku Program (Kan-Pro) was a pivotal management development initiative launched by Toyota in 1979. The term "Kanri Nouryoku" translates to "management capability", and the programme was created in response to a growing concern that Toyota's management culture was becoming complacent. In the decades following the postwar boom and the development of the Toyota Production System (TPS), Toyota executives noticed that managers were no longer acting as proactive leaders. Instead, they were becoming passive executors of routine tasks, leading to a decline in problem-solving quality and strategic alignment.

One of the major issues was the inconsistent application of the Plan-Do-Check-Act (PDCA) cycle, a cornerstone of Toyota's approach to continuous improvement. Additionally, the use of A3 reports – a structured problem-solving and communication tool – was deteriorating. These reports were increasingly being used retrospectively, simply to document completed work rather than to guide strategic planning or facilitate real-time decision-making. Toyota also observed a growing disconnect between the company's high-level goals and how those goals were being implemented on the shop floor and in middle management.

To address these issues, Toyota launched the Kan-Pro programme, a two-year initiative involving around 2000 managers across various divisions. The programme was designed to reinforce essential management skills and instil a disciplined use of strategic planning tools. It emphasised the importance of the PDCA cycle, the development of clear, measurable goals and the proper use of A3 thinking to support real-time, evidence-based decision-making. Participants were also trained to align their departmental objectives with broader company-wide goals using a method known as Hoshin Kanri (policy deployment).

Another key feature of the Kan-Pro initiative was its commitment to on-the-job coaching. Senior leaders were directly involved in mentoring participants, encouraging a culture of accountability and continuous learning. Managers were expected not only to improve their own capabilities but also to become responsible for developing their teams. The programme encouraged a hands-on approach to problem solving, rooted in the Toyota principle of "go and see" the actual situation on the ground.

The impact of Kan-Pro was profound. It revitalised Toyota's managerial effectiveness and restored a strong culture of leadership and accountability. More importantly, it ensured that tools like A3 reports and PDCA were not just formalities, but embedded practices that supported strategic thinking and operational excellence. Today, Kan-Pro is often cited as a model for companies seeking to develop robust internal leadership programmes that align with Lean or Agile practices. It serves as a reminder that no matter how effective a system or tool may be, sustained success ultimately depends on the wisdom and discipline of an organisation's leaders.

CONCLUSION

There are multiple entry points into information security. The traditional career trajectory in information security often involves starting in a helpdesk role and progressing upward or transitioning laterally within the IT department. However, this is not the only route to success in this critical field. Many disciplines cultivate strong analytical thinking, problem-solving abilities and a keen eye for detail, which are all essential qualities for information security professionals. Individuals from diverse backgrounds can leverage these transferable skills to thrive in security careers, bringing unique perspectives and innovative approaches to security challenges. This can lead to more effective solutions and a richer understanding of the ever-evolving threat landscape.

The intersection between academia in the Social Sciences and Information Security presents a powerful opportunity to build a more secure digital future. By integrating insights from Criminology, Psychology, Sociology, Anthropology and Political Science, amongst other disciplines, Information Security professionals can develop holistic strategies that address the multi-faceted nature of security threats.

Moving forward, the continued fostering of collaboration between social scientists and security experts is crucial. Social science research can inform the development of new security solutions, new practices, training programmes and awareness campaigns. Conversely, security professionals can provide real-world data and case studies to enrich social science research on cybercrime and human behaviour in the digital age.

This interdisciplinary approach is not just about fortifying digital systems, but also about fortifying the human element of security. Addressing the social, cultural and psychological factors that contribute to cybercrime is as important as developing robust technical defences. An understanding of the motivations and methods of attackers, the vulnerabilities of human behaviour and the broader societal context of data security will contribute to the creation of a more resilient information ecosystem.

However, the path forward is not without its challenges. Bridging the gap between academic research and real-world application can be difficult. Information Security professionals may struggle to translate complex social science theories into actionable practices. Similarly, social scientists may lack access to the data and resources needed to conduct robust research on cybercrime.

One of the fundamental but often overlooked concepts underlying this book, which may help you digest this information more easily, is the presence of diverse cultural traditions within any society, whether at the level of a town, village, or broader community. The same principle applies to companies, where variations in culture exist across corporate divisions, departments and functional areas. These cultural dynamics are not merely tied to physical structures; they are constantly evolving. Consider how shifts in social networks, business operations and organisational boundaries shape interactions and influence decision-making. This continuous movement can be visualised as distinct orbits, each varying in its degree of separation, overlap and impact. In other words, these orbits have fuzzy boundaries and they shape our understanding of the activity we're involved in. In agile companies, these orbits can be dynamic and fluid. They also foster a feeling of community – think of a close-knit team or department, providing identity and a sense of belonging – and therefore multi-textured environments within companies.

Overcoming these challenges requires ongoing dialogue and collaboration. The creation of interdisciplinary research centres focused on information security can foster communication and knowledge exchange between social scientists and security experts. Furthermore, promoting open-source intelligence (OSINT) initiatives can provide researchers with valuable datasets for analysing cybercrime trends and attacker behaviour.

The Social Sciences equipped me with essential skills such as critical thinking, analysis, research, learning, absorption, condensation and articulation. These abilities are indispensable in navigating the dynamic and evolving landscape of our field. Ultimately, security is a collective effort. Harnessing the combined power of social sciences and information security expertise will make it possible to build a digital world that not only secures technology but also fosters trust, privacy and responsible behaviour in the online sphere. As the digital and information realms continue to evolve, an understanding of the human element in security must evolve as well. An interdisciplinary approach offers a roadmap towards a more fortified future, where information security serves not as a barrier but as an enabler of progress in the digital world.

Chapter 2

The importance of governance, risk and compliance in modern business

Information Security touches every facet of an organisation. Far from being merely a technical concern, it serves a similar purpose to the brakes on a vehicle: it enables the business to take calculated risks and manoeuvre safely. At its core, it is both a quality management and a risk management function, which are flip sides of the same coin. It involves preventing, managing and mitigating risks that could expose, alter or deny access to critical data. While technical explanations abound, practical perspectives illuminate its broader scope, in some companies the Chief Information Security Officer (CISO) role is a Chief Security Officer role incorporating physical and people security. In small-medium enterprises (SMEs), you may also find elements of the Data Protection Officer (DPO) under both Legal, HR and the CISO.

The rapid pace of technological innovation and the evolving threat landscape have made governance, risk management, compliance (GRC) and data privacy critical components of modern organisational strategy. As businesses expand into global markets, they face a myriad of challenges, including regulatory changes, security threats and operational disruptions. These factors necessitate robust frameworks to ensure organisational resilience and sustained growth.

GRC and data privacy frameworks are not merely a set of isolated processes but a comprehensive approach that aligns governance structures, risk management practices and compliance mechanisms. They enable organisations to make informed decisions, enhance operational efficiency and foster a culture of accountability. In this chapter, we explore their intricate interplay in fortifying organisational operations. By delving into foundational concepts, we unravel how these elements collaborate to drive not only security but also business resilience and growth.

INFORMATION SECURITY: A STRATEGIC IMPERATIVE

Information Security's roots trace back to the early 20th century, evolving alongside technological advancements. In the 1960s, the National Security

DOI: 10.1201/9781003543992-3

Agency (NSA) pioneered methodologies to secure routing protocols, setting the stage for modern practices. Milestones such as John McCumber's 1991 model and the Information Assurance framework of 2001 have shaped contemporary approaches. See Dr Mansur Hasib's book *Cybersecurity Leadership* for further particulars.

The evolution of Information Security is marked by a shift from reactive to proactive measures. In the early days, organisations focused on perimeter defences, such as firewalls and antivirus software. However, the rise of advanced persistent threats and sophisticated cybercriminals necessitated a more holistic approach. Modern practices integrate predictive analytics, behavioural monitoring and artificial intelligence to anticipate and neutralise threats before they materialise. This evolution underscores the dynamic nature of Information Security, as it adapts to an ever-changing threat landscape.

Though often conflated, cybersecurity and Information Security represent distinct domains. While cybersecurity addresses threats emanating from cyberspace (e.g., hacking, malware and phishing attacks), Information Security encompasses all threats, internal or external, electronic or physical. Cyber risk forms a subset of the broader Information Security landscape, underscoring its criticality in today's digital ecosystem. A robust cybersecurity framework will deploy firewalls, intrusion detection systems and encryption techniques to safeguard digital assets. However, broader Information Security measures will, for example, include secure physical storage for sensitive data, policies for employee access control and contingency plans for business continuity. Both domains must work in tandem to protect an organisation holistically.

The definitions of Information Security coalesce around its purpose: preserving the confidentiality, integrity and availability of information as an outcome and helping the business go about achieving its objectives without malicious interference. Dr Hasib describes it in his book *Cybersecurity Leadership* as "the mission-focused and risk-optimised governance of information, which maximises confidentiality, integrity, and availability using a balanced mix of people, policy, and technology while perennially improving over time."

This strategic outlook extends beyond technical measures. Information Security and data privacy significantly influence key business priorities, including product success, innovation and customer trust. Robust frameworks demand a nuanced understanding of an organisation's operations, value chain, risk appetite and regulatory environment. They incorporate policies for data privacy, information management systems, technical systems, physical systems, business continuity and compliance with diverse regulations. Moreover, in today's digital economy, sound strategies contribute directly to the organisation's brand reputation, market credibility and operational efficiency.

THE BACKBONE OF BUSINESS STRATEGY

Governance serves as the foundation for an organisation's decision-making processes, ensuring alignment with strategic objectives and stakeholder expectations. It aims to unlock the delivery of defined business value. It encompasses oversight mechanisms, policy frameworks and leadership directives that guide operations and foster transparency. Effective governance also promotes accountability and facilitates the integration of risk management and compliance initiatives into the broader organisational strategy.

These structures are shaped by the leadership. Executive mandates and board-level oversight provide the strategic direction necessary to address emerging risks and capitalise on opportunities. Governance committees, comprising cross-functional representatives, ensure that decisions are informed by diverse perspectives and are aligned with business objectives and regulatory requirements.

Policies and procedures form another critical aspect of governance. These documents outline the organisation's expectations for employee behaviour, operational practices and risk mitigation strategies. On the latter, one example may be the need to comply with regulations such as the General Data Protection Regulation (GDPR) if entering the EMEA market for the first time.

Governance frameworks also enable organisations to monitor and evaluate their performance against established benchmarks. Performance metrics, such as compliance rates and risk mitigation effectiveness, provide valuable insights into the organisation's operational health. These mean that leaders and managers can identify areas for improvement and implement targeted interventions.

Ideally, the establishment of oversight mechanisms means key roles such as the CISO, or equivalent, oversee organisation-wide Security governance and operations. Other examples could be a DPO tasked with compliance in data-intensive sectors, ensuring adherence to data privacy regulations. There needs to be a Security Steering Committee comprising senior executives who guide investments, policies and technical priorities. Lastly, internal auditors provide assurance on governance efficacy and recommend improvements.

RISK: NAVIGATING UNCERTAINTY

Risk has been a word repeatedly used. What then is Risk Management? Risk management is the art, governance and process of identifying, assessing and mitigating potential threats to an organisation's assets and objectives. This helps businesses unlock and deliver business value without interruption from unwanted adversarial friends. Its core principles include risk identification, which involves recognising vulnerabilities and threats, whether financial, operational, strategic or compliance-related, and working out how to keep the business' operations working without disruption or with the ability to keep core functions ticking over (resilience). Risk analysis follows, assessing the likelihood and impact of risks through qualitative and quantitative methods, aided by tools like heat maps and risk registers. I know there are strong views on heat maps and quantification methods, which are sometimes diachronically opposed; we will address these in a later chapter. Finally, risk mitigation involves employing strategies to avoid, reduce, share, or accept risks while continuously monitoring their efficacy.

Proactive risk management transforms potential vulnerabilities into opportunities for innovation by embedding risk management into the decision-making process. An organisation that identifies supply chain disruptions as a risk can implement predictive analytics to anticipate delays, ensuring continuity. Similarly, financial institutions can mitigate credit risks by employing advanced machine learning algorithms to assess borrower profiles.

Moreover, risk communication plays a pivotal role in effective management. Organisations can secure buy-in from stakeholders, aligning risk mitigation efforts with overall strategic priorities by articulating risks in business terms. A robust risk management framework enables organisations to prioritise resources, implement effective controls and respond proactively to emerging threats.

The risk assessment process begins with identifying potential threats, which may include cybersecurity attacks, natural disasters and operational failures. Once identified, these threats are analysed to determine their likelihood and potential impact. Quantitative methods, such as risk matrices and Monte Carlo simulations, can provide valuable insights into risk exposure and inform decision-making. As part of assessing, analytics is here to stay. It enables organisations to find their way through noise to better anticipate potential risks and implement pre-emptive measures.

We need to stop thinking of Information Security as a technical problem. We can only measure some of it using traditional means. Business problems require business-centric metrics: how the behaviour of people work and operate. References to Standards and IT architectures are great, and we explore them in more detail later; however, businesses can still be compromised through misconfigurations and a myriad of other reasons. Ask yourself, what are your business' indications which can lead to deliberate or inadvertent behaviour harmful to a business? This is what has to be understood in order to put the brakes under what is ultimately a silent killer to the economy and society.

The subsequent risk mitigation strategies must therefore be tailored to address specific threats and vulnerabilities, with vulnerabilities not limited to digital technology. In addition to internal threats, organisations must address external risks posed by third-party vendors and supply chain partners. Conducting due diligence and implementing robust contractual agreements can mitigate these risks. Suppliers should adhere to strict quality control standards and provide regular compliance evidence.

COMPLIANCE: BUILDING TRUST AND CREDIBILITY

Compliance involves adhering to legal, regulatory and ethical standards that govern organisational operations. It serves as a cornerstone for building trust with stakeholders, including customers, investors and regulatory authorities. Effective compliance programmes demonstrate an organisation's commitment to accountability and integrity, enhancing its reputation and market position. Such programmes involve internal audit assessments, which provide an opportunity to evaluate the effectiveness of controls and identify areas for improvement. The other compliance assurance mechanism involves external audits validating compliance with industry standards and regulatory requirements.

These compliance requirements vary across industries and jurisdictions, necessitating a tailored approach. In the USA, for example, healthcare organisations must comply with regulations such as the Health Insurance Portability and Accountability Act (HIPAA) to protect patient data, while financial institutions must adhere to anti-money laundering and know-your-customer regulations.

To sustain compliance, organisations must invest in training programmes that educate employees about relevant regulations and their role in maintaining compliance. Leveraging compliance management systems can streamline processes and ensure timely adherence to regulatory requirements. Additionally, compliance programmes should incorporate mechanisms for monitoring and reporting, enabling organisations to detect and address non-compliance promptly.

A HOLISTIC APPROACH

The integration of GRC and data privacy programmes creates a cohesive framework that aligns organisational objectives with operational practices. This holistic approach enables organisations to anticipate challenges, adapt to change and achieve sustainable success.

Through enhanced decision-making, companies can prioritise initiatives that align with their strategic goals by rephrasing or reframing risks in business terms. Cross-functional teams comprising representatives from various functions ensure that initiatives are aligned and mutually reinforcing. An example is that a pharmaceutical company may establish a cross-functional team to oversee its product development process, integrating risk assessments, regulatory compliance and ethical considerations.

Such integration also fosters resilience by providing a comprehensive view of vulnerabilities and controls. This visibility enables organisations to address weaknesses proactively, reducing the likelihood of disruptions. A logistics company may identify and mitigate risks in its supply chain, ensuring continuity of operations during adverse events.

OVERCOMING CHALLENGES

Despite its benefits, implementing appropriate frameworks can be challenging. Common obstacles include resource constraints, resistance to change and fragmented systems. Addressing these challenges requires a strategic approach and sustained commitment from leadership. As this book repeatedly stresses, securing executive buy-in is critical for overcoming resistance to change. Leaders must articulate the value of GRC and privacy initiatives in terms of business outcomes, such as improved efficiency, reduced risks and enhanced reputation.

Technology plays a pivotal role in enhancing the effectiveness of these initiatives. Advanced tools and platforms streamline processes, improve data accuracy and enable real-time monitoring of risks and compliance activities. Cloud-based platforms can provide centralised access to governance policies, risk assessments and compliance reports, facilitating collaboration and decision-making.

Another key strategy for overcoming challenges is adopting a phased approach to implementation. By piloting initiatives in specific departments or regions, organisations can identify best practices and address potential issues before scaling the programme enterprise-wide. This approach minimises disruption and builds momentum for broader adoption.

CASE STUDIES: LEARNING FROM SUCCESS

Three hypothetical studies highlight these points. Zikki, a control manager at a small factory, implemented cross-functional workflows and digital tracking systems with the aim of streamlining operations, enhancing compliance and reducing risks. Zikki's proactive governance and risk management practices not only improved efficiency but also bolstered stakeholder trust.

Similarly, a global firm faced significant challenges in aligning its security practices with its rapid expansion. It established a centralised governance framework and embedded security into its innovation processes. The company achieved remarkable results, including a 25% reduction in downtime and a 30% increase in customer satisfaction scores.

A financial services company offers a final compelling example. It faced regulatory scrutiny and increasing cyber threats. The company invested in an integrated platform that unified its compliance, risk management and audit functions. This initiative led to a 15% reduction in compliance-related costs and significantly improved the organisation's ability to respond to emerging threats. The company not only enhanced its resilience but also strengthened its competitive position.

CONCLUSION

Security GRC and data privacy measures are indispensable for navigating the complexities of the modern business environment. Building appropriate business-aligned frameworks not only protects organisational assets but also enables innovation, aligning operational practices with strategic objectives. It integrates governance, risk and compliance to enable sustainable growth, build stakeholder trust and ensure regulatory adherence.

Moreover, the role of leadership in setting the tone and demonstrating a commitment to these principles cannot be overstated. Leaders who prioritise transparency, accountability and proactive risk management create an environment where employees feel empowered to contribute to security initiatives. Similarly, leveraging technology and adopting tailored strategies ensure that organisations remain agile and adaptive in an ever-changing landscape. As the business environment becomes increasingly dynamic and interconnected, their importance will only grow, making them a critical enabler of success in the years to come.

Chapter 3

Business-related security governance and culture

Modern organisations function in complex and dynamic environments where governance, risk management, data privacy and culture interweave to determine the efficacy of both business operations, privacy and security frameworks. Organisational culture is the collective behaviours, assumptions, values and norms. It acts as the lifeblood of a company, influencing "how things are done" across all levels. This culture is not a static construct; it is shaped by leadership, policies and practices that evolve over time. In turn, these factors shape the mechanisms of governance and risk management, aligning the structure of the business with its strategic objectives.

The cultural fabric is inevitably disrupted when businesses undergo transformations, whether through mergers, management changes, or expansion. These transformations such as integrating a newly acquired company or adapting to regulatory shifts have the potential to introduce stress points into organisational structures. These stresses can manifest as misaligned expectations, duplicative processes and inconsistent communication channels. However, these disruptions also present opportunities for recalibrating governance and enhancing risk-aware mindsets. The challenge lies in ensuring that structural realignments maintain a cohesive cultural identity while fostering resilience. This chapter explores these interconnections, delving into how governance frameworks and cultural practices intersect to create robust, security-conscious organisations. First, however, we need to establish a common lexology and understanding.

BRINGING TOGETHER STRUCTURE, GOVERNANCE AND CULTURE

Business reporting relationships, whether centralised or federated, dictate how teams interact and collaborate. Centralised models foster uniformity but may stifle innovation. Decentralised models promote flexibility but risk fragmentation. Striking the right balance ensures that cross-hierarchical interactions flourish, enabling innovation and inclusivity.

DOI: 10.1201/9781003543992-4

Effective governance encompasses risk oversight, compliance policies and codes of conduct, which establish boundaries for decision-making and accountability. Governance ensures that decision-making processes are transparent and aligned with organisational values, fostering trust among stakeholders. When governance mechanisms promote diversity, egalitarian work designs and equitable incentives, they create a fertile ground for positive cultural experiences.

Businesses that implement cross-functional committees to address governance issues often see improved integration between diverse teams. These committees act as platforms for discussing shared goals and challenges, thus mitigating the risk of miscommunication. However, businesses often develop blind spots, particularly as they grow and diversify. Companies risk fostering "cultural islands," which are pockets of resistance where localised hubs or new departments fail to integrate with the broader corporate framework. Any disconnect not only hinders collaboration but also compromises long-term security by introducing vulnerabilities in governance.

During periods of rapid expansion, local offices may adopt practices that deviate from headquarter's standards, creating inconsistencies in governance and cultural expectations. A company expanding into new markets may face resistance from local teams that perceive governance measures as bureaucratic. This resistance can lead to fragmented practices and inefficiencies. Addressing these blind spots requires proactive measures such as regular audits, open communication channels and tailored governance structures that accommodate regional distinctions. Regular leadership visits to local offices, combined with cultural assimilation programmes, can bridge these gaps effectively.

The interconnected nature of governance and culture becomes particularly significant during crises. Consider the COVID-19 pandemic, which forced organisations worldwide to adopt remote work models. Companies with robust governance frameworks and adaptive cultures were better positioned to adapt. Businesses that previously emphasised cross-functional collaboration and transparency found it easier to implement remote operations without sacrificing productivity or employee engagement. In contrast, companies with siloed structures and rigid governance faced greater challenges in adapting to the new normal.

OVERCOMING CULTURAL CHALLENGES IN GOVERNANCE

Reshaping legacy cultures to align with evolving business needs is a daunting task. Changing deeply ingrained attitudes requires patience and persistence. Establishing direct feedback channels with leadership ensures that employee voices are heard and addressed effectively. These platforms also serve as valuable data sources for identifying recurring themes and challenges within the organisation.

Governance frameworks must also be updated regularly to account for technological advancements and shifting business landscapes, ensuring policies reflect new regulatory requirements, emerging risks and innovations. Updating frameworks often involves collaboration across multiple departments; otherwise, the risk is run of the changes not being comprehensive or indeed implementable. Rewarding behaviours that emphasise ethics and integrity, while being sensitive to risk, aligns the workforce with organisational values. Incentive programmes such as recognition for adhering to security protocols reinforce positive behaviours and motivate employees to adopt best practices.

It is vital to have executive leadership backing for cultural initiatives, including training and communication. Leaders must demonstrate their commitment to a security-first culture. If a senior executive publicly champions security and privacy practices, it signals to employees that these initiatives are a priority. Such cultural reinforcement is not a one-time endeavour. It requires the continuous interlinking of formal controls with governance structures to create an environment where risk awareness thrives. Leadership's role in reinforcing this integrated approach cannot be overstated, as it sets the tone for organisational priorities and behaviours. The individuals driving this on the ground are often middle managers or influential team leaders, who serve as bridges between leadership and frontline employees. They can articulate organisational goals in relatable terms, address resistance and model desired behaviours. A structured change management framework that includes training, incentives and regular communication further strengthens cultural transformation efforts. Over time, the company would observe increased employee satisfaction and improved retention rates, demonstrating the power of integrated governance and cultural initiatives.

ANCHORING SECURITY IN EXECUTIVE ENGAGEMENT

Information and privacy security continues to grapple with the perception that it conflicts with business growth. Overcoming this misconception requires security professionals to align their objectives seamlessly with organisational goals. Each company operates within a unique landscape shaped by historical alliances, unwritten norms and geopolitical influences. Understanding these nuances allows security leaders to tailor their approaches, building alliances and mitigating resistance. Companies operating in multiple regulatory environments must account for the varying levels of risk tolerance across their regions while aligning with corporate objectives.

Mapping out the relationships between key executives and department leaders enables security professionals to align their initiatives with broader corporate priorities. Proposing a strategy that combines cost optimisation with security principles resonates more effectively when presented in terms of shared benefits. Such an approach not only fosters collaboration but also ensures that security measures are embedded within operational processes, while demonstrating how their initiatives contribute to achieving organisational goals. This helps shift perceptions and foster executive buy-in by presenting security as a business enabler rather than a cost centre. One practical approach involves developing detailed case studies that illustrate the return on investment for specific security measures. Another example is showcasing how a robust identity management system can prevent a costly data breach, saving money and ensuring regulatory compliance.

Tailored communication strategies that align security goals with broader business initiatives strengthen executive engagement and foster long-term collaboration. Executive engagement often requires leveraging third-party endorsements. Reports from reputable consulting firms or industry benchmarks can lend credibility to security proposals. Highlighting how competitors have benefited from similar investments can further incentivise executives to prioritise security initiatives.

MAKING SECURITY UNDERSTANDABLE FOR DIVERSE AUDIENCES

Information and privacy security professionals must tailor their messaging to resonate with diverse stakeholders. Leaders across legal, risk, operations, sales, pre-sales, customer experience and supply chain, amongst others, functions interpret risks and investments through the lenses of their respective priorities. Translating technical details into relatable analogies and actionable insights fosters understanding and buy-in. Legal heads prioritise compliance and liability, while supply chain managers focus on third-party assurances and resilience. Security professionals must communicate the implications of security risks in terms of brand trust, operational resilience and market competitiveness. Avoiding technical jargon and emphasising tangible outcomes ensures that security becomes a shared responsibility across the organisation.

To accomplish this, leaders should use storytelling to make their points more relatable. Sharing real-world examples of breaches and their business impacts illustrates the importance of proactive measures. A story about how phishing scams targeted a company's employees, leading to significant operational disruptions, can underscore the importance of awareness training. Relate it (the phishing) to personal's personal lives at home. Visual aids, such as infographics and dashboards, further enhance comprehension by presenting complex information in a digestible format. These tools are particularly effective in bridging communication gaps with non-technical stakeholders.

In addition to storytelling, security leaders should engage in active listening to address stakeholder concerns. Hosting workshops or roundtable discussions allows stakeholders to voice their perspectives, fostering mutual understanding. Professionals can build trust and demonstrate their commitment to shared goals by integrating these insights into security strategies.

Also, expand outreach to include external stakeholders, such as customers and partners, as it broadens the impact of security messaging. Demonstrating how robust security practices enhance customer trust and protect sensitive data can serve as a powerful differentiator in competitive markets.

ADDRESSING COMMUNICATION GAPS IN SECURITY TO DEMONSTRATE VALUE

Communication gaps often arise between technical teams and business leaders. As just mentioned, technical discussions frequently fail to contextualise risks in terms of financial or operational losses. Describing a vulnerability in terms of its technical intricacies may fail to convey the potential revenue impact if the vulnerability is exploited. Many leaders also lack the technical knowledge required to assess the capabilities and limitations of security technologies. Simplify technical concepts and frame them in terms of their impact on business goals to bridge this gap.

Illustrate how robust security measures enable faster product development cycles by mitigating risks early. Use quantitative data to support narratives strengthens the credibility of security initiatives, e.g. historical data demonstrating trends in threat reduction or cost savings from previous investments provides tangible evidence of success. Pairing this data with insights such as employee testimonials creates a compelling case for continued investment in security measures.

Further examples include presenting a case study on how security improvements reduced downtime during a critical product launch, highlighting the tangible benefits of proactive measures. A well-executed case study can include metrics such as downtime reduction, cost savings and enhanced customer satisfaction.

Additionally, involving cross-departmental teams in the development of these narratives ensures that diverse perspectives are incorporated, enhancing their relevance. Expanding the scope of these narratives to include industry benchmarks and competitor comparisons further underscores the value of security initiatives. Showing how an organisation's investment in security surpasses industry averages can enhance its reputation and attract potential clients or partners. Such benchmarking also provides a roadmap for continuous improvement, enabling organisations to stay ahead of evolving threats.

BUILDING A RESILIENT CULTURE

To recap, building a robust security culture extends beyond technical controls to include shared values and behaviours. While awareness programmes educate employees about security risks, a mature culture fosters intrinsic motivation to act securely. Leadership plays a pivotal role in cultivating this culture, ensuring that security priorities permeate every aspect of the organisation. Establishing feedback channels to incorporate employee insights into governance structures enables regular town halls and anonymous surveys that allow employees to voice their concerns and suggestions. Tailoring educational initiatives to diverse roles ensures relevance and comprehension. Training programmes for IT staff can focus on technical skills, while sessions for non-technical employees emphasise behavioural practices. Reinforcing positive behaviours through incentives and holding employees accountable for negligence solidifies a security-first mindset.

This is not to minimise the role technology can play in shaping security culture. Tools that automate routine tasks, such as patch management and access controls, reduce the burden on employees and encourage compliance. Additionally, gamification techniques, such as security-themed challenges and leaderboards, make learning engaging and foster a sense of community.

CONCLUSION

The intersection of governance, risk and culture forms the foundation of resilient and secure organisations. Integrating governance frameworks with cultural practices and aligning security initiatives with business objectives creates cohesive systems that withstand challenges. Leadership's commitment to fostering transparency, accountability and inclusivity ensures that these efforts are not only sustainable but transformative. Security transitions from being a technical function to a strategic enabler, reinforcing the organisation's mission and long-term viability.

Chapter 4

Building an effective business-aligned security programme

As has been iterated in the previous chapters, the role of security in an organisation has evolved far beyond a purely protective function. It is both a risk management and a quality management function; flip sides of the same coin. Security programmes must also enable business services, foster innovation and support the organisation's overall strategic goals. Integrating security into the core of business operations becomes increasingly critical as the pace of digital transformation grows and as countries wracked previously by wars or internal strife look to make up lost time.

It should be clear by now that building an effective business-aligned security programme is not a simple task. It requires a complex interplay of numerous components, ranging from technical controls and policies to organisational structures, behaviours and processes. These elements must be strategically coordinated to ensure the programme not only protects the organisation from cyber threats but also contributes to its business objectives and end-to-end processes. A well-designed security programme enhances business agility, supports innovation and creates a foundation of trust with customers and stakeholders.

Despite the growing importance of aligning security with business goals, many organisations continue to struggle in this area. One of the main reasons is the reliance on traditional security frameworks or standards that emphasise technical controls over business integration. These frameworks often fail to provide the necessary guidance on how security can add value to the business. Consequently, security leaders face challenges in communicating the importance of their programmes to senior management, securing sufficient resources and demonstrating the tangible benefits of security initiatives.

In this chapter, we will explore the fundamental principles of good governance and the structural components that organisations employ to operationalise these principles. We will develop a deeper understanding of how effective governance can drive positive change and contribute to a company's long-term success by examining the core elements of governance. Furthermore, we will discuss the importance of the board of directors, organisational processes,

DOI: 10.1201/9781003543992-5

compliance and ethical standards, financial reporting and the rights of shareholders. We will also consider how governance, risk management and compliance (GRC) come together to form the foundation of a resilient and well-managed organisation.

THE LIMITATIONS OF TRADITIONAL SECURITY FRAMEWORKS

In industries across the board, security frameworks and standards like Center for Internet Security (CIS) and International Organisation for Standardization (ISO) are commonly used to guide security efforts. They offer lists of best practices, technical controls and guidelines that organisations should implement to protect their systems and data.

One of the primary challenges is when an organisation interprets their emphasis to be technical controls at the expense of helping to create a safe space for the business to thrive and operate with internal development, supply chains and partner channels. While they offer valuable guidance on implementing security controls such as firewalls, encryption and access management, the standards often overlook how these measures impact the business as a whole as they are generic by necessity. Security leaders are left with the task of translating technical practices into terms that business stakeholders can understand and appreciate. This communication gap can lead to difficulties in obtaining the necessary executive support and resources to fully implement security programmes.

Another limitation is that most frameworks and standards provide little guidance on how to actually implement their recommendations in a way that is practical for an organisation's specific context. They may list best practices, but they rarely offer detailed instructions on how to integrate these practices into a company's unique processes, culture and risk landscape. This lack of prescriptive guidance can result in inconsistent programme implementation and performance, even among companies operating in the same industry. Without clear implementation steps, security leaders may struggle to create programmes that are both effective and business-aligned, leading to programs that are either too rigid or too reactive.

Moreover, many organisations could make the mistake of treating security programmes as static entities, implementing a set of controls at a particular point in time and assuming that the job is done. However, this approach overlooks the fact that the threat landscape is constantly evolving. New vulnerabilities, technologies and regulations emerge regularly and a security programme that is not continuously updated can quickly become outdated and ineffective. Security programmes must be dynamic, evolving alongside the business to address emerging threats and changing business needs.

ADOPTING A HOLISTIC APPROACH

Given the shortcomings of traditional security standards, a different approach is needed starting with the business itself. Rather than focusing solely on technical controls, security leaders should begin by understanding the organisation's business goals, risk profile and operational context. This business-centric approach ensures that the security programme is not just a set of technical solutions but an integrated part of the company's strategic vision.

The first step in designing an effective security programme is to develop a clear security vision that aligns with the organisation's broader goals. This vision should go beyond protecting data and systems; it should articulate how security will enable the business to achieve its objectives. A company that is focused on innovation and customer trust might craft a security vision that emphasises the protection of customer data while supporting the development of new products and services.

Once the security vision is established, the next step is to develop a security strategy that is tightly aligned with the business strategy. The primary objective of the security strategy should be to reduce the organisation's risk exposure to an acceptable level. However, it should also focus on supporting operational excellence, driving innovation and enhancing customer and stakeholder confidence. The strategy might include initiatives aimed at improving incident response times, increasing the resilience of critical business systems and ensuring compliance with regulatory requirements.

Governance

Corporate governance is the cornerstone of a well-functioning organisation. It serves as the system by which companies are directed and controlled, establishing the framework for responsible decision-making and ethical conduct. Effective governance is vital for ensuring accountability, transparency and integrity within an organisation. It provides the structure through which the company's objectives are set and the means of attaining those objectives are monitored. Governance determines the distribution of roles and responsibilities among different participants in the company, including shareholders, the board of directors, managers and other stakeholders. It also defines the rules and procedures for making decisions on corporate affairs.

The need for effective corporate governance has become increasingly apparent over the past few decades, following numerous high-profile corporate scandals and financial crises that have rocked global markets. These incidents have underscored the potentially catastrophic impact of weak governance, which can lead to unethical behaviour, financial mismanagement and even the collapse of organisations. Effective governance plays a crucial role in fostering innovation, improving operational performance and managing risk.

The success of a business-aligned security programme therefore depends on several critical design factors. These factors help security leaders prioritise their efforts and ensure that the programme is tailored to the organisation's unique needs. Some of the key factors to consider include:

1. Risk profile and threat landscape: Every organisation has a unique risk profile based on its industry, size, geographical footprint and business model. Understanding the key risks the organisation faces is essential for determining where to focus security efforts. A financial institution may be particularly concerned with data breaches and fraud, while a manufacturing company may prioritise securing its supply chain and operational technology. Leaders can allocate resources to address the most critical threats.
2. Business objectives and strategic goals: Security should not be a separate function that operates in isolation from the rest of the business. If a company's goal is to expand into new markets, the security programme should ensure that data privacy regulations in those regions are addressed and that new systems are protected from cyber threats. It is only by aligning security initiatives with business objectives that security leaders can demonstrate the value of their programmes and gain greater executive support.
3. Regulatory and compliance requirements: In many industries, organisations are subject to stringent regulatory requirements regarding data protection, privacy and cybersecurity. These regulations can vary significantly by industry and geography, making it important for security leaders to stay informed about the latest developments. Compliance with regulations is not only a legal requirement but also a key factor in maintaining customer trust and avoiding costly penalties.
4. IT infrastructure and technology adoption: The organisation's IT and OT (Operational Technology) infrastructure and its approach to technology adoption also play a critical role in shaping the security programme. A company that relies heavily on cloud services will need to ensure that cloud security is a top priority, while a company with a large number of legacy systems may need to focus on securing those systems against modern threats. Understanding the company's technology landscape allows security leaders to implement controls that are appropriate for the environment.
5. Organisational culture and governance: The success of a security programme is heavily influenced by the organisation's culture and governance structures. A company that fosters a culture of security awareness and accountability will be more likely to see success in its security efforts than one that treats security as an afterthought. Similarly, clear governance structures that define roles, responsibilities and decision-making processes are essential for ensuring that security initiatives are implemented effectively and that everyone in the organisation understands their role in maintaining security.

Implementation

Once the key design factors have been assessed, the next step is to implement the security programme. This process involves developing a roadmap of initiatives that are aligned with the organisation's business priorities and addressing the most significant risks first. The roadmap should include both short-term and long-term initiatives, allowing the security programme to evolve over time as the business and threat landscape change.

A critical aspect of implementation is defining clear roles and responsibilities for the security programme. It can be difficult to coordinate the various components of the security programme and ensure that everyone is working towards the same goals without well-defined roles. This includes establishing accountability for security at all levels of the organisation, from the executive team down to individual employees. Everyone in the organisation should understand their role in maintaining security, and security should be seen as a shared responsibility.

Another important consideration is the allocation of resources. Security programmes require significant investments of time, money and personnel. However, these resources are often limited, making it essential to prioritise initiatives based on their potential impact on the business. Security leaders must work closely with business stakeholders to ensure that resources are allocated to the areas that will provide the greatest return on investment.

Addressing common challenges

Organisations are likely to encounter several common challenges as they work to implement their security programmes. One of the most significant challenges is the balancing act between enabling business operations and securing the technology infrastructure. Security measures that are too restrictive can hinder innovation, slow down business processes and frustrate employees. On the other hand, weak security measures leave the organisation vulnerable to cyberattacks and data breaches. Finding the right balance requires ongoing collaboration between security and business leaders to ensure that security measures support, rather than hinder, business objectives.

Another challenge is securing executive buy-in and adequate resources for the security programme. Security leaders often struggle to convey the importance of their programmes to executives who may view security as a cost centre rather than a value driver. Additionally, there is the challenge of managing a constantly evolving threat landscape. Cyber threats are becoming increasingly sophisticated, and organisations must be able to respond quickly to new vulnerabilities and attack vectors. This requires a flexible security programme that can adapt to new threats and technologies while maintaining alignment with business objectives.

Finally, establishing meaningful security metrics is a persistent challenge for many organisations. While it is easy to measure technical aspects of security, such as the number of vulnerabilities patched or the time to respond to incidents, these metrics do not always provide a clear picture of how security contributes to business success. You need to develop metrics that tie security performance to business outcomes, such as reducing the financial impact of security incidents or improving customer satisfaction. These metrics can then be used to drive continuous improvement in the security programme.

The benefits

Despite the challenges involved, organisations that successfully align their security programmes with their business objectives can reap significant rewards. Research consistently shows that companies with business-aligned security programmes outperform their peers across a range of metrics, from IT effectiveness to overall business performance.

One of the key benefits of business alignment is improved risk management. By focusing security efforts on the IT assets and data flows that are most critical to the business, organisations can more effectively mitigate the risks that have the greatest potential to disrupt operations. This proactive approach to risk management allows companies to avoid costly security incidents and reduce the overall financial impact of threats.

Business alignment also leads to more efficient use of resources. Organisations can allocate their resources more effectively, ensuring that security investments provide a clear return on investment. This alignment fosters meaningful conversations between security and business leaders about trade-offs and investment decisions, leading to more informed and strategic use of the organisation's budget and personnel.

Finally, a business-aligned security programme enhances trust with customers and stakeholders. In today's data-driven world, customers expect organisations to protect their personal information and ensure the security of the systems they interact with. Organisations can build trust with their customers, differentiate themselves from competitors and enhance their brand reputation by demonstrating a strong commitment to security.

THE CORE PRINCIPLES OF GOOD GOVERNANCE

The foundation of good governance rests upon several guiding principles that create a framework for responsible decision-making, ethical behaviour and long-term value creation. These principles ensure that the organisation operates in a manner that is accountable to shareholders, transparent to stakeholders and responsible in its actions. The most important of these principles are transparency, fairness, accountability and responsibility. They are, for example, famously embedded in the way Toyota is run.

Transparency is critical for building trust between an organisation and its stakeholders. It requires that the company provides clear, accurate and timely information about its operations, financial performance, governance structures and strategic direction. Transparency allows stakeholders to make informed decisions and holds the organisation accountable for its actions. Companies that embrace transparency are more likely to foster investor confidence, reduce the risk of fraud and create a culture of openness and integrity within the organisation.

Fairness refers to the equitable treatment of all stakeholders, including shareholders, employees, customers and the broader community. In the context of governance, fairness means that no individual or group is given preferential treatment at the expense of others. This principle is particularly important in protecting the rights of minority shareholders and ensuring that the interests of all stakeholders are taken into consideration when making corporate decisions. By promoting fairness, companies can build stronger relationships with stakeholders and create an environment where all parties feel valued and respected.

Accountability is another cornerstone of good governance. It ensures that individuals and groups within the organisation are held responsible for their actions and decisions. The board of directors, in particular, has a duty to hold management accountable for the performance and governance of the company. Accountability requires clear roles and responsibilities, along with mechanisms for monitoring, evaluation and enforcement. Without accountability, governance systems can break down, leading to poor decision-making, a lack of oversight and potential ethical breaches. Companies that prioritise accountability are better able to identify and address issues before they escalate into serious problems.

Responsibility refers to the obligation of the board, management and employees to act in the best interests of the company and its stakeholders. This principle encompasses ethical behaviour, compliance with legal and regulatory requirements and a commitment to corporate social responsibility (CSR). Companies that take responsibility for their actions not only protect themselves from legal and reputational risks but also contribute positively to society. In today's business environment, stakeholders increasingly expect companies to demonstrate social responsibility, and organisations that fail to do so may face backlash from consumers, investors and regulators.

These core principles provide the ethical foundation for good governance. However, the effectiveness of governance depends on how these principles are translated into practice through the organisation's structures, processes and systems.

THE ROLE OF THE BOARD OF DIRECTORS

The board of directors plays a central role in corporate governance. It is the body responsible for overseeing the management of the company and ensuring that the organisation's activities align with the interests of shareholders.

The board has a fiduciary duty to act in the best interests of the company and its stakeholders, and it is accountable for the overall direction and performance of the organisation.

One of the key responsibilities of the board of directors is to set the company's strategic objectives and ensure that management has the resources and support needed to achieve those objectives. The board must also monitor the performance of management, assess the company's financial health and ensure compliance with legal and regulatory requirements. Additionally, the board has a critical role in overseeing risk management and ensuring that the company has adequate internal controls in place to mitigate potential risks.

The board must be independent from the company's management to function effectively. This independence allows the board to provide objective oversight and hold management accountable for its actions. Ideally, at least two-thirds of the board members should be independent directors who do not have any direct involvement in the day-to-day operations of the company. Independent directors bring an external perspective to the board's decision-making process and help ensure that the interests of shareholders are protected.

The board of directors is also responsible for appointing and evaluating the performance of the company's CEO and senior management team. This includes setting performance targets, providing guidance on strategic direction and ensuring that management is acting in the best interests of the company. If the board determines that the CEO or other members of the management team are not performing effectively, it has the authority to take corrective action, including replacing key executives if necessary.

In addition to its oversight responsibilities, the board of directors must establish a governance framework that promotes transparency, accountability and ethical behaviour throughout the organisation. This includes creating committees to oversee specific governance functions, such as auditing, compensation and nominations. These committees allow the board to focus on key areas of governance and ensure that the company's operations are being conducted in a manner that aligns with its ethical and legal obligations.

ORGANISATIONAL PROCESSES AND GOVERNANCE STRUCTURES

In addition to the board of directors, effective governance requires a set of well-defined organisational processes and structures that enable the consistent implementation of governance policies. These processes ensure that governance is integrated into the day-to-day operations of the company and that all employees understand their roles and responsibilities.

One of the key components of a strong governance framework is a clear reporting structure that outlines the flow of information and decision-making authority within the organisation. This structure ensures that information is communicated effectively between different levels of the company and that decisions are made in a transparent and accountable manner. Formal organisational charts, role definitions and documented policies help establish clarity around who is responsible for specific tasks and decisions.

Performance monitoring is another critical aspect of governance. Strategic planning, forecasting and performance measurement allow the board and management to track progress towards the company's goals and identify areas where improvement is needed. Key performance indicators (KPIs) provide measurable benchmarks that can be used to evaluate the company's operational and financial performance. Regular reporting on KPIs and other performance metrics helps ensure that the company is on track to meet its objectives and provides transparency to shareholders and other stakeholders.

In addition to monitoring performance, companies must establish processes for managing risk and ensuring compliance with legal and regulatory requirements. This includes creating risk management committees that are responsible for identifying potential risks, assessing their likelihood and impact and developing strategies to mitigate them. Companies should also have compliance programmes in place that ensure adherence to relevant laws, regulations and industry standards. These programmes typically include training for employees, internal audits and mechanisms for reporting and addressing violations of company policies.

Ethics and compliance are central to good governance, and companies must foster a culture that promotes ethical behaviour at all levels of the organisation. Codes of conduct outline the ethical standards that employees are expected to adhere to, and they provide guidance on how to handle ethical dilemmas or report suspected violations. Whistleblower programmes allow employees to report unethical behaviour anonymously, which helps protect the company from fraud, corruption and other forms of misconduct.

Another important element of governance is the company's approach to financial reporting and disclosure. Transparent financial reporting is essential for building trust with investors and ensuring that shareholders have access to accurate and timely information about the company's financial health. Companies must comply with regulatory requirements for financial reporting, but they should also go beyond these requirements by providing clear explanations of their financial performance, disclosing any risks that may impact future results and avoiding the use of non-standard accounting practices that could obscure the company's true financial condition.

SHAREHOLDER RIGHTS AND PARTICIPATION IN GOVERNANCE

Shareholders play a vital role in corporate governance, and it is essential that companies protect their rights and enable their active participation in decision-making. Shareholders are the owners of the company, and they have a vested interest in ensuring that the organisation is managed in a way that maximises shareholder value.

One of the most important rights of shareholders is the ability to vote on significant corporate matters, such as the election of directors, mergers and acquisitions and changes to the company's bylaws. Voting rights allow shareholders to have a say in the governance of the organisation and hold the board of directors accountable for its decisions. Shareholders typically exercise their voting rights at annual general meetings (AGMs), where they can ask questions, voice concerns and propose resolutions.

In addition to voting rights, shareholders have the right to access information about the company's financial performance, governance structures and strategic direction. This includes the ability to review financial statements, meeting minutes and other key documents. In cases where shareholders believe that the board or management has acted negligently or unethically, they have the right to seek legal remedies. This may include filing lawsuits for damages, petitioning for changes to the company's governance structures, or taking other actions to hold the board and management accountable for their actions. Shareholder activism is an important mechanism for ensuring that companies are governed in a manner that aligns with the interests of their owners.

EXAMPLE: THE McKinsey 7-S FRAMEWORK AND GOVERNANCE

The McKinsey 7-S Framework is a well-established organisational tool used to analyse and align key elements within a company to improve performance and effectiveness. Originally developed by McKinsey consultants Robert H. Waterman and Tom Peters in the late 1970s, this framework provides a comprehensive view of the interdependent elements within an organisation that need to work together to achieve success. The framework's seven components – strategy, structure, systems, shared values, skills, style and staff – are grouped into "hard" and "soft" categories and offer a holistic approach to organisational analysis.

When applied to Information Security governance, the McKinsey 7-S Framework becomes a valuable tool for aligning security efforts with broader business objectives. At the heart of the 7-S framework is strategy, which refers to the long-term plan of an organisation to achieve its objectives.

The skills element of the 7-S Framework refers to the capabilities and competencies of an organisation's employees. In the context of Information Security governance, it is essential that staff have the necessary skills to identify risks, implement security measures and respond to security incidents. This requires ongoing investment in training and professional development for security personnel. In addition, other employees throughout the organisation should also be trained in basic security awareness to help identify potential threats, such as phishing attacks or social engineering tactics.

Skills in Information Security governance extend beyond technical expertise. Leadership must also possess the ability to make strategic decisions about risk management, compliance and security investments. The board of directors and executive team need to understand the importance of security in maintaining business continuity and protecting the organisation's reputation. Ensuring that leadership has a knowledge of security threats to the business and risk management strategies allows them to make informed decisions about security policies, investments in technology and the allocation of resources.

Style, in the McKinsey 7-S Framework, refers to the leadership approach and management style of the organisation. In the context of Information Security governance, the leadership style significantly influences the effectiveness of the security programme. Leaders who foster an open and collaborative environment are more likely to encourage cross-departmental cooperation, ensuring that security becomes a shared responsibility rather than a siloed function. This style of leadership promotes transparency, communication and accountability across the organisation, which are all vital to a successful Information Security programme.

An authoritarian or top-down management style, on the other hand, may stifle innovation and discourage employees from engaging in proactive security behaviours. If security policies are seen as rigid and punitive, employees may view them as obstacles rather than essential components of the business strategy. Therefore, effective security governance requires leaders who can balance enforcing security policies with fostering a culture of innovation and openness.

Finally, staff refers to the people within the organisation, including both security professionals and the broader employee base. A successful Information Security governance framework depends on having the right people in the right roles. This means hiring, training and retaining skilled security professionals who can manage the organisation's security infrastructure, respond to incidents and stay ahead of emerging threats. It also means ensuring that all employees understand their role in protecting the organisation's digital assets.

A well-developed security governance framework requires a comprehensive approach to staffing, including succession planning for key security roles, continuous professional development and cross-training employees in multiple aspects of security management.

The McKinsey 7-S Framework provides a valuable lens for evaluating and enhancing Information Security governance within an organisation. The seven interdependent elements – strategy, structure, systems, shared values, skills, style and staff – mean that organisations can ensure that their security governance framework is aligned with their business goals, integrated into their operations and supported by a security-conscious culture. The framework underscores the importance of a holistic approach to security governance, where technical measures are complemented by strong leadership, skilled staff and a culture of responsibility and accountability.

CONCLUSION

Developing a business-aligned security programme is a journey, not a destination. It requires a deep understanding of the organisation's business objectives, a clear vision for how security will enable those objectives and a flexible, dynamic approach to programme design and implementation. While the process may be complex, the benefits of a well-aligned security programme are substantial, ranging from improved risk management and resource efficiency to enhanced business performance and customer trust.

Effective corporate governance is essential for building long-term value, protecting shareholder interests and promoting ethical behaviour within an organisation. The key to success lies in continuous collaboration between security and business leaders. Security leaders can ensure that their programmes remain aligned with the organisation's evolving needs by working together to define priorities, allocate resources and measure progress. This collaboration fosters a culture of security awareness and accountability across the organisation, ensuring that everyone plays a role in protecting the company's assets and enabling its success.

The board of directors plays a central role in governance, providing oversight, setting strategic direction and ensuring that management is acting in the best interests of the company. Organisational processes and structures, such as performance monitoring, risk management and compliance programmes, provide the infrastructure needed to implement governance policies effectively. Shareholders, as the owners of the company, have a vital role in governance, and companies must protect their rights and encourage their active participation.

Governance, risk management and compliance (GRC) are interrelated components that form the foundation of a resilient and well-managed organisation. Companies can build resilience, protect shareholder value and ensure that they are well-positioned to navigate the complex regulatory landscape of today's business environment. Ultimately, effective governance is not a one-time effort, but an ongoing process that requires continuous evaluation, adaptation and improvement. Companies that prioritise good governance are better equipped to manage risks, respond to challenges and capitalise on opportunities. Governance will remain a critical driver of organisational success and long-term sustainability.

Ultimately, a business-aligned security programme is not just about protecting data and systems; it is about enabling the business to thrive in a complex and ever-changing world. By embedding security into the fabric of the organisation, companies can not only protect themselves from threats but also unlock new opportunities for growth, innovation and competitive advantage.

Chapter 5

Introduction to risk management and its role in GRC

Information Security is more than a risk function; risk management and quality management are flip sides of the same coin when done right. It often addresses quality management issues that are sometimes mislabelled as risks. A good example is the Boeing aircraft door failures, which demonstrates the importance of addressing quality management issues in the manufacturing process. While the term "risk" is frequently used, it is essential to acknowledge the underlying quality management aspects of security.

The interconnected digital nature of today's business ecosystem intensifies these matters and the consequences. Threats can quickly propagate across company boundaries and supply chains, impacting multiple organisations simultaneously. Sadly, even today Security is often seen as the "Department of No," shutting down initiatives or raising too many barriers in the name of security. In reality, its mission is to enable businesses to take strategic risks so they can operate with confidence in a digital world. As we will discuss, it does this through risk management (not risk avoidance), digital transformation with secure innovation, resilience (not FUD), building customer trust and regulatory compliance. Properly leveraged, it provides a company with a competitive advantage by making it more attractive to investors, partners and clients, making it easier to take bold steps forward. In a nutshell, it is about making sure the business can quietly but confidently say yes to opportunities.

In 2012, the National Association of Corporate Directors (NACD), the World Economic Forum and PricewaterhouseCoopers issued a critical declaration: "The highly interconnected nature of modern organisations means we run the risk of failures that spread beyond one enterprise to affect entire industries, sectors, and economies. It is no longer sufficient just to ensure the cybersecurity of your own enterprise; rather, cyber resilience demands that organisations work in concert."

So what is risk management? It is the systematic practice of identifying, assessing and mitigating threats to an organisation's resources, reputation, capabilities and objectives. These risks may arise from financial uncertainty, legal liabilities, strategic errors, accidents or natural disasters. Information security and organisational stability hinge on robust governance structures and effective control measures. These include policies, processes, people

DOI: 10.1201/9781003543992-6

and digital initiatives that align with an organisation's business strategy and objectives. As defined by ISO 27002:2022, the primary drivers for information security requirements are the evaluation of risks in alignment with organisational goals, adherence to legal and regulatory obligations, and integration of principles and objectives throughout the lifecycle of organisational information.

Several definitions of risk exist, reflecting the diversity of perspectives across industries and frameworks. According to ISO 31000 and ISO 27005, risk is defined as the "effect of uncertainty on objectives," with the term "effect" encompassing both positive and negative deviations. Uncertainty is characterised as a deficiency in understanding or information about an event, its consequences, or its likelihood. While other frameworks, such as NIST and ISACA, offer variations in their definitions – often emphasising threats and vulnerabilities – the ISO definition is widely regarded for its clarity and applicability. It integrates well with Paul Hopkin's elaboration in his book *Fundamentals of Risk Management*, which views risk as an event that may impact an organisation's efficiency or effectiveness.

A risk scenario describes a sequence of events leading to an undesirable outcome or an outcome which could provide material or financial benefit to the business. A risk owner is the individual or entity responsible for managing a specific risk. Risk sources are elements that have the potential to give rise to risks. Risk appetite defines the level of risk an organisation is willing to accept. Threats are potential causes of harm or disruption, and vulnerabilities represent weaknesses that can be exploited to cause adverse effects. Residual risk refers to the risk that remains after mitigation measures are implemented.

We will explore four prominent standards: ISO 31000, ISO 27005, COSO and the ISACA Risk IT Framework. Each offering unique benefits and best practices for Enterprise Risk Management (ERM). Adopting these frameworks provides organisations with a robust roadmap to enhance governance, reduce operational surprises, improve decision-making and build resilience.

The ISO 31000 framework outlines a structured process for Enterprise Risk Management. This begins with establishing context by defining the internal and external environments, objectives and risk criteria. The next step is risk identification, which involves compiling a comprehensive list of potential risks. This is followed by risk analysis, which assesses the likelihood and impact of each risk using qualitative and quantitative methods. Risk evaluation then determines the significance of each risk and the need for treatment strategies. Risk treatment involves implementing measures such as avoidance, mitigation, or transfer to manage risks. The final step involves continuous monitoring and review to assess risks and adjust strategies as necessary.

Risk management finds applications across various domains. Financial risk management allows organisations to identify vulnerabilities in market conditions, credit exposure and liquidity challenges. Through quantitative tools such as Value at Risk (VaR) models and Monte Carlo simulations, financial institutions can forecast potential losses and implement pre-emptive strategies. A crucial aspect of financial risk management is its impact on decision-making, as it provides organisations with insights into capital allocation and investment strategies to minimise potential losses and enhance profitability.

Operational risk management, on the other hand, emphasises the importance of managing risks inherent in business operations. These include disruptions in supply chains, failures in internal processes, or external events such as natural disasters. Techniques such as business continuity planning, disaster recovery plans and employee training play a pivotal role in minimising the likelihood and impact of operational disruptions. Organisations can ensure a swift response to potential threats and maintain business continuity by fostering transparency in operations and defining clear roles and responsibilities.

Compliance risk management underscores the importance of adhering to a complex landscape of legal and regulatory requirements. Non-compliance can result in severe financial penalties and reputational damage. Organisations integrate compliance risk management into their governance frameworks by conducting regular audits, reviewing policy adherence and implementing corrective actions to address identified gaps. This proactive approach ensures that organisations not only meet legal obligations but also establishes a culture of ethical behaviour and accountability.

Strategic risk management involves addressing uncertainties that may arise from adverse business decisions, shifts in market dynamics, or unforeseen external events. Geopolitical events have highlighted the significance of strategic risk management in anticipating and mitigating long-term risks. Organisations can align their goals with market realities and adapt to changing circumstances by integrating risk assessments into strategic planning processes. Monitoring key performance indicators and trends enables organisations to remain agile and resilient in the face of uncertainty.

Vitally, risk management has to be integrated into governance frameworks to foster a culture of accountability and transparency. Governance mechanisms, such as risk committees and internal audit functions, play a critical role in overseeing risk management practices. The Chief Risk Officer (CRO) serves as a central figure in coordinating risk management efforts across the organisation; you will find examples of companies where the person heading Information Security reports into the CRO.

Despite its importance, risk management faces several challenges. One major challenge is ensuring comprehensive coverage of risks across all levels of the organisation. Managers often struggle to connect enterprise-level risks with local priorities, leading to gaps in risk management practices. Additionally, balancing the need for confidentiality with the demand for transparency poses a significant hurdle. Navigate this tension carefully to build trust while safeguarding sensitive information.

Developing reliable Key Risk Indicators (KRIs) and metrics for measuring risk management effectiveness is another area of difficulty. Without clear metrics, organisations cannot effectively monitor their risk management efforts or make data-driven decisions. Aligning security risk management with broader organisational frameworks is particularly challenging, given the dynamic nature of cyber threats and the complexity of integrating technical controls with strategic objectives.

Technological advancements are rapidly shaping the landscape of risk management. The use of large language models (LLMs) in risk analytics is revolutionising the way organisations identify and address threats. AI-driven tools can process vast amounts of data in real-time, uncovering patterns and anomalies that human analysis might overlook. Predictive analytics can identify potential fraud in financial transactions or detect vulnerabilities in cybersecurity frameworks before they are exploited. Integrating these technologies into risk management strategies is becoming increasingly vital for organisations striving to stay ahead of emerging risks.

Furthermore, the importance of a strong risk culture cannot be overstated. A risk-aware culture ensures that employees at all levels understand the significance of risk management and actively participate in mitigating potential threats. Regular training programmes, open communication channels and leadership commitment are critical components of fostering such a culture.

Globalisation has also added layers of complexity to risk management. As organisations expand their operations across borders, they must contend with diverse regulatory environments, geopolitical uncertainties and cultural differences. Navigating these challenges requires a nuanced understanding of local contexts and a willingness to adapt risk management strategies accordingly. Collaborative efforts with local stakeholders, investments in regional expertise and scenario planning for geopolitical risks are essential for organisations operating in an interconnected world. As we delve deeper into the principles and applications of risk management, it is important to recognise its foundational role in shaping sustainable and adaptive organisations. This governance should integrate privacy concerns, as the lines between privacy and information security continue to blur.

PRIVACY IN THE DIGITAL AGE

Privacy, a fundamental human right, is increasingly difficult to maintain in today's digital world. Traditionally, privacy has been the purview of legal departments or data governance teams. However, as Travis Breaux highlights in *Introduction to IT Privacy: A Handbook for Technologists*, the lack of communication between legal and IT departments often hampers effective privacy protection. Legal teams must articulate privacy goals, while IT teams implement appropriate controls to meet those goals.

The convergence of privacy and information security necessitates that InfoSec professionals understand data privacy laws and regulations beyond the traditional CIA Triad. Significant privacy risks include data collection by companies and governments, which often occurs without sufficient transparency. The increasing amount of personal data stored digitally heightens the risk of cyberattacks, exposing sensitive information like medical and financial records to misuse. Surveillance technologies such as facial recognition and Internet of Things devices also pose serious privacy concerns by enabling mass data collection and tracking. Addressing these risks requires both regulatory efforts and individual vigilance.

One emerging concern is the intersection of privacy with artificial intelligence (AI). Machine learning algorithms often depend on large datasets, some of which include sensitive personal information. Improperly managed AI systems can inadvertently reinforce biases or expose personal data, further complicating privacy issues. Organisations must ensure that AI is used responsibly and that privacy considerations are integrated into the design and deployment of such technologies.

STRATEGIC RESPONSES TO CYBER RISKS

To mitigate these risks, organisations must adopt a proactive and collaborative approach. Implementing basic security best practices across all business units and partners ensures a foundational level of protection. For a foundational, but very much IT-focused, foundational level take a look at the UK's Cyber Essentials and Cyber Essentials Plus list of requirements, which are available online. Real-time visibility into threats, facilitated by advanced monitoring tools, helps organisations stay ahead of emerging challenges. Collaboration among stakeholders, along with diversification of suppliers, enhances resilience. Ensuring vendor compliance with security standards, developing incident response plans and transferring financial risks through cyber insurance are equally critical.

Never underlay employee training, which has a pivotal role in risk management. Educating the workforce on recognising phishing attempts and social engineering tactics empowers employees to act as the first line of defence. Regular training programmes and simulated cyberattack scenarios ensure readiness and minimise vulnerabilities. Beyond this, organisations should foster a culture of continuous learning, adapting training materials to address emerging threats and evolving attack vectors. Research gamification as a tool to engage the Executive to improve their awareness.

GOVERNANCE AND RISK OWNERSHIP

Effective governance structures are essential for managing InfoSec risks. Boards of directors must engage actively in cybersecurity oversight, setting the tone from the top. The National Association of Corporate Directors' 2023 report outlines key considerations, including periodic reviews of regulatory trends, clear oversight responsibilities and regular assessments of information systems and controls. I advise you to download a copy and read it, as it will give you a perspective on what is expected from the other side of the table.

Risk governance is a cornerstone of organisational resilience and success. Robust risk governance enables informed decision-making, safeguards critical assets and fosters a culture of accountability. As the risk landscape evolves, continuous improvement and ethical leadership remain essential for sustaining trust and achieving strategic objectives. Additionally, fostering cross-industry collaborations can help organisations share best practices and stay ahead of evolving challenges.

Senior leadership must establish risk ownership within their organisations. Defining roles and responsibilities, aligning risk management with strategic objectives and establishing robust escalation protocols are vital. Collaboration across departments fosters a culture of shared responsibility, breaking down silos and encouraging cross-functional teamwork.

To strengthen governance further, organisations should implement comprehensive risk dashboards that provide real-time insights into KRIs. These dashboards enable executives and boards to make informed decisions quickly, ensuring that risk management strategies remain effective and relevant. A mature risk management framework, supported by a strong organisational culture, ensures that all employees understand their role in mitigating risks.

ISO 31000 AND 27005

ISO 31000 and ISO 27005 are two internationally recognised standards tailored to specific risk management needs. ISO 31000, first published in 2009 and revised in 2018, is an Enterprise Risk Management standard applicable across industries. ISO 27005, introduced in 2007, focuses specifically on managing risks related to information security.

ISO 31000 emphasises principles such as integration, adaptability, inclusivity and continual improvement. Its framework outlines leadership, commitment and process integration while advocating for a dynamic and tailored approach to risk management. Organisations benefit from enhanced decision-making, better stakeholder confidence and improved identification of opportunities. It addresses both external and internal factors to ensure a comprehensive approach to understanding risk contexts.

ISO 27005 provides detailed guidelines for information security risk management. It aligns closely with ISO 27001 but does not prescribe specific methods, allowing flexibility. Key steps include context establishment, risk identification, analysis, evaluation and treatment. It ensures a systematic approach to safeguarding information by focusing on assets, threats, vulnerabilities and controls. Additionally, it emphasises the importance of stakeholder consultation and communication throughout the risk management lifecycle.

The application of these standards can vary widely depending on organisational needs. ISO 31000 is suitable for holistic risk management across diverse industries, whereas ISO 27005 caters to the specific requirements of information security, enabling organisations to address cyber threats effectively. Together, they create a complementary framework for addressing broad and niche risk domains.

COSO ENTERPRISE RISK MANAGEMENT FRAMEWORK

The COSO ERM framework, established by the Committee of Sponsoring Organisations of the Treadway Commission, offers a comprehensive approach to risk governance. Updated in 2017, it emphasises governance, culture, strategy alignment and performance monitoring.

Key principles of COSO ERM include defining risk appetite, promoting transparency, integrating risk management with strategic objectives and leveraging high-quality data. The framework is adaptable across industries and promotes cross-functional collaboration. COSO's cube model illustrates the relationship between organisational objectives, risk components and operational units, enabling a holistic view of risks. This visual representation aids stakeholders in understanding the multifaceted nature of enterprise risks.

COSO ERM enhances corporate governance through aligning resources with strategic goals. It thereby builds stakeholder confidence. However, challenges such as siloed thinking and resource constraints can hinder its implementation. Organisations can overcome these obstacles through leadership engagement, phased rollouts and robust training programmes.

COBIT: A FRAMEWORK FOR IT GOVERNANCE

COBIT, or Control Objectives for Information and Related Technology, is a comprehensive IT governance framework developed by ISACA. COBIT focuses on aligning IT with business objectives, ensuring value delivery and managing IT risks. Its iterative evolution, culminating in COBIT 2019, reflects changing technological landscapes and business priorities.

The framework is built on principles such as stakeholder needs, end-to-end enterprise coverage and a holistic approach. COBIT's domains are Evaluate, Direct and Monitor (EDM); Align, Plan and Organise (APO); build, acquire and implement (BAI); deliver, service and support (DSS); and monitor, evaluate and assess (MEA). They provide a structured process for managing IT governance effectively.

COBIT integrates seamlessly with other frameworks like ITIL, ISO 27001 and TOGAF, offering a unified approach to IT governance and management. Organisations can improve performance monitoring, regulatory compliance and alignment between IT and business strategies. Additionally, its focus on maturity assessment enables organisations to identify gaps in their governance processes and implement targeted improvements.

ISACA RISK IT FRAMEWORK

The ISACA Risk IT Framework complements COBIT by focusing specifically on IT-related risks. It provides an end-to-end approach, covering risk governance, evaluation and response. Aligned with ISO 31000 principles, it emphasises transparency, accountability and a risk-aware culture.

The framework's lifecycle model includes context establishment, risk assessment, treatment, monitoring and communication. It integrates IT risk management into key areas such as strategy, procurement and business continuity. The Framework positions IT risk as a strategic enabler. Moreover, its emphasis on measurable outcomes ensures that risk management efforts translate into tangible benefits, such as reduced downtime and enhanced operational efficiency.

REALISING THE BENEFITS OF RISK FRAMEWORKS

Implementing these frameworks offers numerous advantages. Organisations gain enhanced resilience, regulatory compliance and optimised resource allocation, while risk management is transformed into a strategic asset. Furthermore, organisations that adopt these frameworks often experience improved stakeholder trust, as transparent risk practices demonstrate a commitment to governance and ethical operations. It does so through enhanced decision-making capabilities and proactive risk treatment, minimising the likelihood of operational disruptions and financial losses.

These standards and frameworks provide robust methodologies to address diverse risk management needs. Their integration fosters a comprehensive approach to governance, enabling organisations to navigate uncertainties and seize opportunities effectively. As risks evolve, these frameworks remain vital tools for building sustainable and adaptive enterprises.

RISK PROFILES

Risk profiles form an integral component of governance. They offer a comprehensive overview of an organisation's key risks and their characteristics. These profiles serve as critical components of risk governance, providing visibility into significant uncertainties that could impact organisational objectives. Developed by risk management teams, risk profiles detail each risk's description, likelihood, potential impact, owner, mitigating controls and overall risk rating.

Risk profiles enable leadership to understand the organisation's risk landscape at a glance. They often categorise risks as strategic, operational, financial, or compliance-related, using tools like visual heat maps to illustrate severity levels through colour coding. Risk rankings further prioritise areas requiring immediate attention or resources. These tools help ensure that decision-makers have a clear understanding of which risks demand immediate mitigation efforts and which can be monitored over time.

As risks evolve, risk profiles must be regularly updated to reflect changes in exposure or the effectiveness of mitigation efforts. These updates can prompt reviews of risk appetite and tolerance levels, ensuring alignment with organisational objectives. Reporting on risk profiles also aids boards in providing oversight and challenging management's assessments. Moreover, these profiles are invaluable for internal audit and second-line oversight functions, as well as for external reporting to regulators and stakeholders. Comprehensive risk profiles strengthen the organisation's ability to forecast potential disruptions and plan strategically for long-term resilience.

RISK APPETITE

Risk appetite defines the amount and type of risk an organisation is willing to accept in pursuit of its objectives. It reflects the boundaries set by senior leadership and the board, shaping the organisation's risk culture and guiding decision-making on risk/reward trade-offs. Expressed through a formal risk appetite statement, this concept often includes key risk indicators (KRIs) with quantitative or qualitative thresholds.

Different levels of risk appetite may be established for specific categories. An organisation might have a high appetite for strategic risks to pursue growth opportunities but maintain a low appetite for compliance risks due to regulatory obligations. Risk appetite should align with the organisation's capacity, strategic priorities, stakeholder expectations and regulatory constraints.

Continuous reassessment is essential to account for internal and external changes. Monitoring helps identify breaches where exposure exceeds acceptable limits. Such breaches trigger escalation mechanisms to refine strategies and bring risks back within permissible boundaries. These are critical aspects of effective risk governance.

A robust risk appetite framework also facilitates alignment across departments. Organisations can prevent siloed decision-making and promote cohesive risk management strategies. Additionally, embedding risk appetite considerations into daily operations empowers employees to make informed choices that align with the organisation's strategic goals.

RISK TOLERANCE

Closely related to risk appetite, risk tolerance defines the acceptable level of variation from achieving objectives. While appetite sets overarching boundaries, tolerance provides more granular guidance on permitted deviations. This concept allows flexibility, recognising that not all risks can be precisely controlled.

Risk tolerance is often defined using quantitative metrics such as target ranges, confidence intervals, or percentage variations. Different tolerances may apply across categories: for instance, tighter thresholds for compliance risks compared to strategic risks. Escalation triggers are typically established to address breaches, ensuring timely reassessment and mitigation.

The board plays a key role in defining risk tolerance when approving the overall risk appetite. Management is responsible for implementing these tolerances, while internal audit focuses on adherence during governance reviews. Organisations can effectively govern risks while maintaining operational agility by combining both appetite and tolerance. This dual approach ensures that strategic goals are met without exposing the organisation to undue risk.

Risk tolerance also serves as a communication tool, clarifying expectations for stakeholders at all levels. Business unit managers can use risk tolerance thresholds to evaluate their performance and make adjustments before deviations become significant. This proactive approach strengthens accountability and enhances decision-making consistency across the organisation.

REGULATORY AND CONTRACTUAL REQUIREMENTS

Regulatory requirements are integral to risk governance, particularly in industries subject to stringent oversight, such as finance, healthcare and technology. Compliance frameworks like PCI-DSS, GDPR and SEC regulations necessitate robust risk management practices to safeguard sensitive information and ensure legal accountability. These regulations also drive organisations to adopt transparent risk reporting practices, enabling stakeholders to evaluate the effectiveness of governance strategies.

Incorporating risk governance clauses into contracts demonstrates a commitment to prudent risk management. These clauses may include requirements for ERM programmes, adherence to governance standards like COSO or ISO 31000 and periodic risk assessments. Additional provisions may address security, privacy, insurance coverage and subcontractor obligations. These enhance accountability and strengthen partnerships.

Beyond regulatory compliance, contractual risk governance clauses provide a framework for managing third-party risks. Organisations can require vendors to undergo regular audits or provide evidence of insurance coverage to mitigate potential liabilities. These measures not only protect the organisation but also build trust (at least in theory) with external partners by demonstrating a shared commitment to risk management excellence.

RISK ASSESSMENTS

A risk assessment is a systematic process for identifying, analysing and evaluating risks. This practice is essential for determining the likelihood and impact of potential events that may negatively affect individuals, assets, or organisations. Risk assessments offer critical insights to prioritise and address the most significant threats by providing a deeper understanding of risks and their potential consequences. They form a cornerstone of effective risk management programmes, enabling organisations to navigate uncertainty with confidence.

Undertaking a risk assessment involves identifying risk sources, describing risks, evaluating their magnitude and prioritising higher risks for mitigation. These assessments may be conducted at various levels, such as specific projects, processes, products, or across the entire enterprise. The scope and methodology depend on the objective and context of the assessment. Risk identification is a foundational step in this process, requiring techniques such as brainstorming, process analysis, loss data reviews, surveys and scenario analysis. The data collected is then analysed using various models to determine risk ratings. Both qualitative methods and quantitative models are applied, and their appropriate usage will be explored below.

The results of a risk assessment are typically documented in a risk register or matrix. This document outlines risk descriptions, causes, probabilities, impacts, controls and assigned risk owners. It also supports the selection of appropriate risk responses (avoidance, transfer, mitigation, or acceptance) and creates visibility into significant risks, guiding strategic decisions and resource allocation. Ongoing monitoring and review of risks are critical, as the conditions surrounding them often change over time.

Conducting a risk assessment involves several methodical steps. First, the scope and objectives of the assessment must be established to define the focus area, resources required, stakeholders involved and desired outcomes. Once the scope is clear, risks can be identified using diverse techniques, such as brainstorming sessions, process mapping, historical incident reviews and stakeholder interviews, to generate a comprehensive list of potential risks. The inclusion of varied perspectives ensures a holistic understanding of risks, covering operational, strategic and external factors.

The next step involves analysing the identified risks to evaluate their likelihood and potential impact using qualitative or quantitative methods. This includes assessing contributing factors to estimate the severity of each threat. Once the analysis is complete, the risks are evaluated against criteria such as risk appetite and tolerance levels to determine which risks require immediate attention. High-priority risks are then ranked and become the focus of treatment plans. Effective prioritisation ensures that resources are allocated where they can have the most significant impact, aligning mitigation efforts with organisational objectives.

Documentation is a crucial component of the process. All details, including risk descriptions, probabilities, impacts, existing controls and assigned owners, should be recorded in a risk register or similar format. These findings are then communicated to stakeholders, highlighting top risks, themes and recommendations, and seeking approval for proposed treatment strategies. A clear and comprehensive risk register serves as a reference point for monitoring progress, tracking changes and ensuring accountability throughout the risk management lifecycle.

You will need to combine multiple techniques for the assessments and engaging diverse stakeholders enriches this process. Common methods include brainstorming workshops to leverage diverse perspectives, process analysis to map workflows and pinpoint vulnerabilities and historical data analysis to review past incidents, audit findings and loss events to identify recurring risks. Surveys and questionnaires can also collect insights from a broad group of stakeholders, while industry benchmarking compares risk profiles with similar organisations to uncover prevalent threats. Risk inventories and checklists help ensure that no significant risks are overlooked. Advanced tools, such as machine learning and data analytics, are increasingly being used to identify emerging risks and detect patterns that may not be apparent through traditional methods.

For analysis, organisations may employ qualitative techniques, such as descriptive scales (e.g., high/medium/low) to prioritise risks based on expert judgment, or quantitative models, such as statistical tools, to estimate probabilities and impacts, offering precise risk metrics. Scenario analysis explores hypothetical situations to assess potential outcomes and impacts, while sensitivity analysis examines how changes in assumptions influence overall risk exposure. Selecting the right combination of methods depends on the nature of risks, available data and organisational priorities. The integration of qualitative insights with quantitative data ensures a balanced and comprehensive analysis.

Risk assessments can face several challenges, including incomplete risk identification, biased analyses and insufficient stakeholder engagement. Addressing these obstacles requires careful planning and execution. Key success factors include clearly defining objectives and scope, engaging diverse stakeholders to capture a broad range of perspectives and combining multiple identification techniques to minimise blind spots. Securing senior leadership sponsorship ensures adequate resources and visibility, while documenting risks comprehensively enables effective tracking and monitoring. Clear communication of findings aligns recommendations with organisational goals and fosters a shared understanding of priorities across all levels of the organisation.

Another critical success factor is the establishment of feedback loops to refine risk assessment processes over time and to continuously improve their methodologies, address recurring challenges, and adapt to changing risk landscapes. The assessments themselves yield actionable insights that drive decision-making across various domains. They inform risk responses by identifying appropriate mitigation strategies and prioritising resource allocation to address the most critical risks. They also shape strategic planning by aligning initiatives with the organisation's risk capacity and enhancing governance through transparent reporting to boards and stakeholders. Supporting compliance by demonstrating adherence to regulatory requirements and cultivating a risk-aware culture by embedding insights into training and development are additional applications. Moreover, risk assessments provide a foundation for scenario planning and stress testing, enabling organisations to evaluate the potential impacts of adverse events under various conditions.

As risk landscapes grow increasingly complex, integrating robust assessment practices into governance frameworks remains a cornerstone of sustainable success. Organisations that prioritise risk assessments as part of their strategic initiatives not only enhance their ability to mitigate threats but also position themselves to seize opportunities arising from a deeper understanding of their operating environments. Through continuous refinement and innovation, these assessments serve as a vital enabler of organisational agility and long-term success.

RISK ANALYSIS METHODS: QUALITATIVE AND QUANTITATIVE

GRC systems rely on effective risk analysis to align organisational strategies with regulatory requirements and operational needs. Overall, risk analysis in information security and GRC is relatively young compared to its application in industries such as insurance, engineering, or finance. This presents an opportunity for innovation, as organisations can adapt methods to suit specific contexts, verticals and cross-sectoral challenges. Let us delve into the characteristics, strengths and limitations of both qualitative and quantitative approaches, and examine how they can be integrated to create a comprehensive risk analysis framework.

Qualitative and quantitative approaches serve distinct purposes within the risk analysis process. While qualitative methods are often quicker and more adaptable for initial screenings, quantitative methods provide precise measurements that support data-driven decisions. A balanced integration of both methods allows organisations to leverage expert judgment alongside objective analysis.

Qualitative risk analysis

Qualitative risk analysis involves descriptive evaluations of the likelihood and impact of risks using non-numerical categories, such as high/medium/low or severe/moderate/minor. Common techniques include risk registers, brainstorming sessions, risk matrices and risk urgency assessments. These methods rely heavily on expert judgment and stakeholder input to identify and evaluate risks.

The key advantages of qualitative risk analysis include its flexibility, simplicity and ability to quickly provide an overview of critical risks. This approach is especially useful when detailed data is unavailable or when organisations need to engage a diverse group of stakeholders. However, qualitative methods are inherently subjective and can lack precision, making it challenging to compare risks across different categories or prioritise them effectively.

For instance, qualitative techniques outlined in ISO 31000 and ISO 27005 include brainstorming, SWOT analysis and risk breakdown structures. These methods help organisations identify potential risks by leveraging the collective knowledge of experts and stakeholders. The results are then documented in a risk register or matrix, offering a visual representation of risk priorities.

Quantitative risk analysis

Quantitative risk analysis assigns numerical values to the likelihood and impact of risks, using statistical models, simulations and probabilistic calculations. Techniques such as Monte Carlo simulations, sensitivity analysis and scenario modelling allow organisations to estimate the probability of risk events and their potential financial or operational consequences.

The primary advantage of quantitative methods lies in their objectivity and precision. These techniques provide measurable insights that support cost-benefit analyses and resource allocation decisions. However, quantitative risk analysis requires accurate and reliable data, and the results can be heavily influenced by the quality of inputs and underlying assumptions.

Frameworks like the Factor Analysis of Information Risk (FAIR) exemplify quantitative approaches in information security. FAIR breaks down risks into components such as asset value, threat frequency, vulnerability and control effectiveness. The FAIR Institute's methodology demonstrates the power of quantitative risk analysis in a real-world context. An organisation concerned about potential data breaches might begin by identifying critical assets and evaluating associated threats and vulnerabilities. They can estimate the probability of loss events and calculate the financial impact of potential breaches.

FAIR also addresses uncertainty by requiring analysts to define confidence levels for their estimates. This has the effect of decision-makers understanding the limitations of the analysis and hopefully factoring them into their strategies. While FAIR's comprehensive nature requires significant effort and expertise, its scalability and adaptability make it a valuable tool for organisations seeking to enhance their risk management capabilities.

Integrating qualitative and quantitative methods

A hybrid approach that combines qualitative and quantitative methods offers a more robust risk analysis framework. Organisations can focus their quantitative efforts on the most critical threats by starting with qualitative techniques to identify and categorise risks. This integration allows for comprehensive evaluations that balance subjective expertise with objective metrics.

For example, a risk matrix developed during the qualitative phase can serve as a foundation for more detailed quantitative analyses. Risks categorised as high-priority can undergo further examination using statistical models or simulations. Additionally, tools like the One-for-One Substitution Model from the book *How to Measure Anything in Cybersecurity Risk* bridge the gap between qualitative and quantitative approaches by calibrating subjective ratings with percentage ranges.

Challenges in qualitative and quantitative risk analysis

Both qualitative and quantitative methods face unique challenges that can impact the accuracy and reliability of risk analysis. Qualitative approaches, while flexible, often rely heavily on subjective input. This can introduce biases, such as overconfidence or anchoring, which skew the results. Additionally, without clear criteria for evaluating risks, stakeholders may interpret likelihood and impact differently, leading to inconsistent assessments.

Quantitative methods, on the other hand, require high-quality data. Incomplete or inaccurate data can compromise the validity of statistical models and probabilistic calculations. Moreover, the complexity of some quantitative techniques, such as Monte Carlo simulations, may deter organisations with limited analytical expertise or resources. Over-reliance on quantitative tools without considering contextual nuances can also result in an incomplete understanding of risks.

RISK RESPONSE AND REPORTING

These are absolutely critical components of an organisation's risk management framework. These elements ensure that identified risks are appropriately managed and communicated to stakeholders, enabling informed decision-making and fostering a proactive risk-aware culture. It is essential to be aware of strategies for developing effective risk responses, best practices for risk reporting and the integration of these processes into organisational workflows.

Developing risk response strategies

Once risks have been identified and analysed, organisations must determine the most appropriate ways to address them. Effective risk response involves selecting strategies that align with the organisation's risk appetite, objectives and resource constraints. Four primary strategies are commonly employed:

Risk avoidance is a strategy that eliminates activities posing unacceptable risks. While it effectively removes the risk, it can also limit potential rewards. An organisation might choose not to enter a high-risk market to avoid regulatory or financial uncertainties. This approach is particularly suited to situations where the risk outweighs the potential benefits or where mitigation measures are either unavailable or impractical.

Risk mitigation, on the other hand, focuses on reducing the likelihood or impact of a risk through proactive measures. Organisations often implement additional controls, enhance training programmes, or upgrade systems to address vulnerabilities. Mitigation requires ongoing monitoring to ensure that the implemented measures remain effective and relevant. A company may upgrade its cybersecurity infrastructure to defend against evolving threats.

In some cases, organisations may accept a risk without making changes, provided it falls within their acceptable risk threshold. This approach, known as risk acceptance, is often used when the cost of mitigation exceeds the potential impact of the risk. Acceptance requires close monitoring to ensure the risk remains within acceptable boundaries. A start-up might accept operational risks associated with rapid growth to capitalise on emerging market opportunities.

Risk transfer involves shifting the impact of a risk to another party, typically through insurance policies, outsourcing, or contractual agreements. Purchasing cyber insurance to manage the financial consequences of a data breach is a common example. This approach allows organisations to focus on their core activities while leveraging external expertise or resources to address specific risks.

The selection of a risk response strategy depends on the nature of the risk, its potential impact and the organisation's objectives. Often, organisations employ a combination of these strategies to address complex risks effectively. Clear accountability, timelines and resource allocation are essential for successful implementation. Additionally, organisations should evaluate the cost-effectiveness of each strategy to ensure optimal use of resources.

Making a risk response effective

To ensure that risk responses are impactful, organisations should adopt collaborative planning processes. Prioritisation of high-priority risks is vital to address the most significant threats to organisational objectives. Resource allocation should reflect these priorities to maximise the effectiveness of mitigation efforts. Additionally, organisations should regularly review and update risk response strategies to adapt to evolving conditions. Involving cross-functional teams in designing and implementing risk responses fosters alignment and ensures that all relevant perspectives are considered. Involving IT, legal and operations teams can provide a holistic view of security risks and mitigation strategies.

Scenario testing is another critical practice for enhancing risk response effectiveness. Organisations can evaluate the potential effectiveness of planned responses. This approach allows them to identify gaps and refine strategies before implementation. Tabletop exercises for disaster recovery plans can highlight weaknesses and help refine response protocols. Continuous improvement processes, informed by past incidents and near-misses, enable organisations to refine their approaches over time.

Risk reporting best practices

Risk reporting ensures that stakeholders are kept informed about key risks and the effectiveness of risk management activities. Effective risk reporting provides the right information to the right audience at the right time, facilitating risk-aware decision-making. Understanding the audience is paramount. Tailoring reports to meet the needs of specific stakeholders enhances their relevance and impact. Senior executives and board members require high-level overviews of critical risks and strategic implications, while project managers need detailed insights into operational risks.

Structuring reports effectively enhances readability and comprehension. Begin with an executive summary highlighting the most significant risks and mitigation strategies. Subsequent sections can provide detailed risk rankings, interdependencies and response progress. Incorporating visual elements, such as charts, graphs and heat maps, makes complex data more accessible. For example, heat maps can visually represent risk likelihood and impact, highlighting critical risks for immediate attention.

Timeliness is another crucial factor in risk reporting. Providing reports at regular intervals, such as quarterly for executive reviews or weekly for dynamic project risks, ensures that stakeholders are equipped to respond effectively to emerging threats. Using existing communication channels, such as board portals, intranet sites, or email, further integrates risk reporting into organisational workflows. Embedding risk discussions in regular meetings ensures that risk management remains a priority across all levels of the organisation.

Integrating risk response activities and reporting into organisational processes enhances their effectiveness and adoption. Key areas for integration include strategic planning, budgeting, project management and performance metrics. Embedding risk management considerations into strategic discussions ensures that potential risks are identified and addressed early in the planning process. Including risks associated with new initiatives in planning sessions can help mitigate potential challenges before they escalate.

Allocating resources for risk responses within annual budgets ensures that adequate funding is available for mitigation measures, insurance premiums, or training programmes. Incorporating risk response steps into project timelines and milestones keeps risk management efforts aligned with organisational goals. Regular project reviews should include updates on identified risks and mitigation progress. Aligning individual and team performance metrics with risk management objectives reinforces the importance of risk management at all levels of the organisation.

MONITORING AND REVIEW

Ongoing monitoring and review are critical to ensuring the continued relevance and effectiveness of risk responses. Tracking KRIs enables organisations to detect changes in risk exposure. Periodically reassessing risk response strategies ensures that they remain aligned with organisational goals and external conditions. Communicating updates to stakeholders on the status of risk responses and any new risks that emerge keeps all parties informed and engaged.

Real-world examples highlight the importance of effective risk response and reporting. During the COVID-19 pandemic, organisations with robust risk management frameworks were better equipped to pivot quickly, addressing disruptions in supply chains and workforce availability. Regular reporting allowed leadership to make informed decisions and communicate transparently with stakeholders. Similarly, organisations that faced cybersecurity incidents leveraged clear risk response strategies, such as incident response teams and predefined escalation protocols, to mitigate the impact of breaches effectively.

CONCLUSION

In today's interconnected business environment, managing information security risks is no longer a standalone function but a collaborative enterprise-wide endeavour. Organisations must integrate security into their governance frameworks, align it with strategic goals, foster transparency and build robust partnerships to navigate the complexities of modern cybersecurity challenges while safeguarding their assets, reputation and stakeholders.

Looking ahead, the importance of adaptability cannot be overstated. As technology and cyber threats continue to evolve, organisations must remain agile, continuously updating their strategies and systems. By doing so, they can not only protect themselves but also contribute to the overall resilience of the global business ecosystem.

Through the balanced use of qualitative and quantitative approaches, organisations can navigate complexities with confidence. Whether addressing security threats, financial risks, or operational uncertainties, robust risk analysis frameworks empower organisations to anticipate challenges, allocate resources efficiently and drive sustainable growth. With the resulting reporting, uncertainties and aligning risk management activities with strategic objectives can be addressed. Integrating these practices into organisational workflows fosters a culture of accountability and resilience, positioning organisations to navigate an increasingly complex risk landscape. A robust framework for risk response and reporting not only safeguards organisational objectives but also strengthens stakeholder confidence and drives sustainable growth.

Chapter 6

GRC automation

Traditionally, Governance, Risk and Compliance (GRC) activities were handled manually through a combination of spreadsheets, reports and human oversight. However, with the increasing complexity of regulatory environments, digital transformation projects and the growing demand for efficiency, businesses are streamlining processes through automation to reduce human error, increase efficiency and improve their overall risk management strategies. In this context, automation is not merely a technological upgrade. It is a critical component of business operations. The ability to monitor compliance in real-time, assess risks with predictive analytics and automate complex audit processes gives businesses a competitive advantage while ensuring that they remain compliant with regulatory frameworks. This chapter will explore the various aspects of GRC automation, from its origins in traditional GRC practices to its role in modern organisations. We will delve into the tools and technologies that make automation possible, examine its benefits and challenges and provide examples of how it is being implemented across industries.

THE TRADITIONAL APPROACH TO GRC

Historically, organisations relied on manual processes involving single spreadsheets, databases and manual workflows to track compliance with internal policies and external regulations. While this approach was adequate in simpler business environments, it became increasingly ineffective as regulatory requirements have grown more complex. Also, if each department within a company managed its own governance and compliance activities independently, siloed approaches led to inefficiencies through duplication and/or failure to share critical information. Additionally, managing compliance manually required significant time and resources, which increased operational costs. Reporting processes were slow with a higher likelihood of human error, which could lead to non-compliance or costly mistakes during audits.

Moreover, manual GRC processes lacked the ability to scale as businesses grew or entered new markets. When organisations expanded internationally,

DOI: 10.1201/9781003543992-7

they were required to comply with a variety of regulations across different jurisdictions, making manual compliance tracking impractical. The limitations of this approach became evident as businesses began to face larger regulatory fines and reputational damage for failing to comply with legal standards.

Risk management, a critical aspect of GRC, also suffered under the traditional model. Without automation, businesses struggled to track emerging risks or predict how different risks could impact the organisation. This reactive approach often left organisations exposed to financial losses, cyberattacks or operational disruptions. The need for a more proactive, integrated and scalable solution to GRC became clear, leading to the development of automated GRC systems.

WHAT IS GRC AUTOMATION?

It refers to the use of software and technology to streamline and integrate governance, risk management and compliance processes. This approach leverages tools that can automatically monitor risk, track compliance and assist in managing governance tasks in real-time to ensure consistent, repeatable and efficient activities. Instead of relying on manual checklists to track compliance with regulations, automated systems can continuously monitor organisational processes and flag potential non-compliance issues in real-time. Automation ensures that policies are consistently applied across departments and that governance decisions are based on up-to-date information. Automated compliance systems can generate audit reports, track regulatory changes and have workflows to help ensure that the organisation remains compliant.

Similarly, risk assessments can be automated using machine learning algorithms that analyse large volumes of data to identify emerging threats that could pose a risk to the business, such as financial volatility, cyber threats or regulatory changes. Predictive analytics is often used to forecast potential risks before they become critical.

Big Data and Artificial Intelligence

The advent of advanced technologies such as Artificial Intelligence (AI), Machine Learning (ML), Robotic Process Automation (RPA) and Big Data Analytics is having a massive impact upon the way GRC automation is implemented. These technologies allow for faster data processing, real-time monitoring and the ability to handle complex datasets that are essential for GRC activities.

- *Artificial Intelligence* (*AI*): AI is used to process large volumes of data and make informed decisions in governance, risk management and compliance. In GRC automation, AI can analyse patterns in data to detect potential risks or non-compliance and offer recommendations for corrective actions.

- *Machine Learning (ML)*: ML algorithms enable systems to learn from past data and improve their predictive capabilities. For example, ML can be used to predict potential risks based on historical trends or to identify compliance issues before they escalate.
- *Robotic Process Automation (RPA)*: RPA automates repetitive tasks, such as generating reports, sending notifications or conducting compliance checks. By automating these routine activities, organisations can free up valuable time for more strategic activities.
- *Big Data Analytics*: It relies on analysing large volumes of data from different sources, including internal business processes, regulatory databases and market data. Big data analytics helps organisations gain insights into their compliance status, risk exposure and governance effectiveness.

These technologies have made it possible for GRC automation to be integrated across all levels of an organisation, from the boardroom to the operational level. They enable businesses to monitor risks and compliance in real-time, which is essential in today's fast-paced regulatory environment.

LEADERSHIP AND ORGANISATIONAL CULTURE

Leadership plays a crucial role. Organisational leaders must set the tone for how automation will be integrated into governance, risk management and compliance processes. Leaders should communicate a clear vision for how it fits into the organisation's broader goals. This vision should emphasise the importance of human oversight, the potential for automation to enhance decision-making and the need for employees to adapt and grow alongside technological advancements. Additionally, creating an organisational culture that encourages continuous learning is essential. This will help align employees' efforts with the organisation's objectives and mitigate concerns about the impact of automation on jobs and responsibilities.

The benefits of automation

One of the most significant drivers is the clear and measurable benefits it offers organisations. These benefits directly address the inefficiencies of manual GRC systems while offering strategic advantages. For instance, compliance monitoring can now be continuously conducted, ensuring that deviations are caught immediately, allowing for rapid responses to regulatory or policy breaches. This allows organisations to allocate resources more strategically to more value-driven activities, such as designing better risk mitigation strategies or ensuring stronger governance frameworks. It has the added benefit of reducing bottlenecks in compliance and risk management processes, increasing overall operational efficiency. Human error is an inevitable part of manual processes. Whether it's forgetting a step in an audit, misreporting a regulatory issue or failing to update compliance documentation, errors can be costly and lead to significant business risks. Automation minimises this risk by ensuring that all processes are executed consistently and precisely. Automated systems follow preset rules and protocols, ensuring that critical tasks are not missed or mismanaged. Furthermore, automated systems can cross-check data against predefined compliance regulations and risk management standards. This reduces the chance that important regulatory changes are overlooked, which can happen in a manual process where large amounts of data need to be processed and monitored. Automated auditing systems can also flag inconsistencies or non-compliance issues that may go unnoticed during a manual review.

You can also bake in enhanced risk visibility. These systems use AI and machine learning algorithms to analyse vast amounts of data, identifying patterns and potential risks before they materialise. For instance, in financial institutions, real-time monitoring of transactional data can flag suspicious activity, alerting risk managers to potential fraud. In manufacturing, continuous monitoring of operational systems can detect early signs of equipment failure, allowing for preventative maintenance before significant disruptions occur. The ability to visualise risks in real time enables organisations to be proactive in their risk management strategies rather than reactive.

Something else you may have or will come across is scalability, whether your organisation is expanding (natural growth or acquisition), or new legislation is on the horizon, or if a compliance programme is being spread across more operational units. Your needs become more complex. Traditional GRC processes often struggle to scale effectively, particularly in multinational corporations where different regions may have their own set of regulatory requirements. Automation enables scalability through permitting easier adaptation of processes to meet the changing business requirements without necessitating a proportional increase in GRC staff or resources.

Therefore, while the initial cost of implementing GRC automation systems can be high, the long-term savings are substantial. Automating GRC processes reduces the need for large compliance teams, costly audits and error-prone manual processes that can lead to fines and penalties. Cost savings also result from the improved accuracy and speed of risk detection and compliance adherence. Automated systems allow for quicker identification of issues through automation, described below, enabling organisations to resolve them before they escalate into expensive legal or regulatory problems. In industries with stringent regulatory requirements, such as finance or healthcare, these cost savings can be especially significant.

KEY AREAS FOR AUTOMATION

Governance

It focuses on improving the processes and decision-making frameworks that define how an organisation is run. Tools can help organisations streamline policy creation, version control and policy distribution. Instead of relying on manual processes to create governance frameworks, automation platforms can generate these policies based on customised, defined templates for review by relevant stakeholders and distribute them in real-time. Additionally, these systems provide automated tracking of policy enforcement, ensuring that procedures are followed consistently across departments.

Board-level decision-making can also benefit from automation. Automated governance tools can generate reports on compliance status, risk exposure and policy adherence. This allows board members to make more informed, data-driven decisions. Workflow automation ensures that governance actions are taken promptly and that follow-ups are tracked automatically.

Risk management

With automation, risk assessments are no longer static, periodic exercises. Instead, they become dynamic, continuous processes that adapt to changing conditions in real-time. Machine learning algorithms can be employed to assess historical data and predict emerging risks. These algorithms can detect patterns that may indicate heightened risk levels, such as unusual financial transactions, security vulnerabilities or regulatory changes in a particular market.

Automated risk management tools also streamline the process of creating risk mitigation strategies by assisting risk managers in implementing mitigation measures quickly and effectively. Automation also improves the reporting of risk factors to leadership, ensuring that decision-makers have the information they need to address risks before they escalate. One of the most powerful features of automated risk management, therefore, is predictive analytics. Predictive models can be developed to forecast potential risks based on historical data and external factors. For example, in supply chain management, automated risk tools can analyse global data related to political instability, environmental factors or market fluctuations to predict potential disruptions in supply chains. Organisations can then proactively take steps to mitigate these risks.

Compliance

Compliance automation is perhaps the most recognised form of GRC automation, as it deals directly with ensuring that the organisation adheres to applicable laws, regulations and internal policies. Compliance failures can result in substantial fines, legal actions and reputational damage, making automation an essential tool for managing these risks.

Compliance automation systems enable continuous monitoring of the organisation's adherence to regulatory frameworks. These systems track regulatory changes and adjust the company's compliance protocols accordingly, reducing the risk of non-compliance due to outdated policies. This is particularly important in industries like finance, healthcare and energy, where regulations are both complex and subject to frequent updates.

Automation simplifies the audit process as well. Instead of manually gathering evidence of compliance, automated systems can generate some of the audit-ready reports. These systems also automate the collection and storage of compliance documentation, ensuring that the organisation is prepared for regulatory inspections at any time.

CHALLENGES AND LIMITATIONS

While automation offers numerous benefits, it also presents a unique set of challenges and limitations. Understanding these issues is crucial for organisations aiming to implement automation solutions successfully. One of the most significant challenges is integrating new automated systems with existing infrastructure. Many organisations have legacy systems in place that were not designed with automation in mind. These older systems may not be compatible with modern GRC automation platforms, requiring costly upgrades or workarounds.

Moreover, organisations often use disparate tools for various business functions, including risk management, compliance tracking and governance. Ensuring seamless integration across these systems is a complicated process that requires careful planning and technical expertise. Without smooth integration, automated tools may not deliver their full potential, leading to inefficiencies and frustration among users.

Organisations must also contend with increasing concerns around data security and privacy. Automation involves the handling of large volumes of sensitive information, including regulatory data, risk assessments, compliance reports and personal information. Ensuring that this data is adequately protected is paramount.

Extra precautions must also be taken to secure automated GRC systems from external cyber threats, internal misuse and data breaches. This includes implementing encryption, multi-factor authentication (MFA) and access control measures. Additionally, automated systems that manage sensitive personal data must comply with privacy regulations such as GDPR, HIPAA and other relevant industry and/or country-specific laws. Failing to address these security and privacy concerns can have severe consequences, both financially and reputationally.

Although automation platforms come with pre-built templates and workflows, they may not always be tailored to the specific needs of every organisation. Customise these systems to align with your unique business processes, industry-specific regulatory requirements and internal governance policies. The initial costs associated with implementing these systems can be high. Setting up automation infrastructure, training staff, customising workflows and ensuring system integration all require substantial investments of time and resources. Small and medium-sized enterprises (SMEs) often struggle to justify these upfront costs, especially if they lack dedicated IT teams or specialised Information Security professionals. The return on investment (ROI) may take time to materialise, which can be a barrier for organisations with limited budgets. It's essential for businesses to perform a thorough cost-benefit analysis before embarking on a GRC automation project.

While automation increases efficiency, there's a risk of becoming overly reliant on it. Automated systems are designed to streamline processes, but they are not infallible. GRC automation tools can identify risks, generate reports and monitor compliance, but they still require human oversight and intervention. Otherwise, overreliance can lead to complacency, where employees assume that the system will handle all aspects of governance, risk and compliance without human review. This can result in critical issues being missed or mishandled. Automation is most effective when used to complement human expertise, not replace it. Consequently, businesses need skilled professionals who can manage and maintain these automated systems. Many businesses face a skills gap, as employees may lack the technical expertise needed to operate these platforms. This gap becomes more pronounced when implementing complex technologies like AI and machine learning into GRC systems. Without proper training and upskilling, employees may struggle to fully leverage the capabilities of automated GRC tools, resulting in suboptimal outcomes.

BEST PRACTICES FOR IMPLEMENTING GRC AUTOMATION

Successfully implementing automation requires careful planning, strategic execution and continuous evaluation to maximise the benefits of automation while minimising disruptions to existing processes. Below are certain key best practices to guide implementation.

Assess organisational needs

You must conduct a thorough assessment of existing GRC processes. This involves identifying areas where manual processes are inefficient or prone to errors, as well as evaluating the current regulatory landscape and risk profile.

This is the only way you can choose the right automation tools and tailor them to address the most pressing challenges. This assessment phase is also critical for identifying which processes are suitable for automation and which may still require manual oversight.

Choose the right automation tools

There are many software platforms available, each offering different features and capabilities. Organisations should evaluate these tools based on their specific requirements, such as industry regulations, the size of the business and integration with existing systems. Consider factors such as ease of use, scalability, vendor support and customisation options. The platforms must also offer robust security features to ensure that sensitive data is protected.

Implement in phases

Implementation should be done in phases to minimise disruption to daily operations. A phased approach allows organisations to test and fine-tune automation tools before rolling them out across the entire organisation. Start with automating high-impact, low-risk processes, such as policy management or compliance reporting, before moving on to more complex areas like risk management or security. Phased implementation also enables teams to identify any integration issues or customisation needs early in the process, ensuring that these are addressed before full deployment.

Ensure employee training

Even the most advanced systems require skilled professionals to operate them effectively. Training employees on how to use new automation tools is crucial to the success of the implementation. This includes not only GRC professionals but also IT staff, compliance officers and risk managers. Training programmes should cover both the technical aspects of the automation tools and their practical applications in daily operations. Ongoing training and development ensure that employees stay updated on system upgrades, new features and best practices.

Monitor and evaluate success

Once automation is in place, organisations must continuously monitor and evaluate its performance. Regularly assess whether the automation tools are delivering the expected benefits, such as increased efficiency, reduced risk and improved compliance. Gather feedback from employees using the system to identify any pain points or areas for improvement. Automation tools should also be regularly updated to ensure they remain aligned with evolving regulatory requirements and business needs. Monitoring system performance and making adjustments as needed will help maintain the effectiveness of GRC automation over time.

Compliance with laws

It is essential to ensure that automated systems comply with laws and regulations. This is especially critical when handling sensitive personal data or customer information. Automated systems must be designed with privacy protections in mind, such as data encryption, access controls and compliance with regulations. You should work closely with legal and compliance teams to ensure that their GRC automation systems meet all regulatory requirements for data privacy and security.

In industries such as finance, where compliance with anti-money laundering (AML) and Know Your Customer (KYC) regulations is critical, AI-driven compliance monitoring has become essential. Automated systems can continuously scan transactions, customer profiles and financial activities, flagging suspicious behaviour or non-compliance with financial regulations.

CONSIDERATIONS FOR TECHNICAL IMPLEMENTATION

As organisations adopt automation solutions, security becomes a critical concern. Automated systems often handle sensitive data, including compliance reports, risk assessments and internal governance policies. The systems typically integrate with various parts of the business, from finance to operations to IT. This interconnectedness makes them attractive targets for cybercriminals, who may seek to exploit vulnerabilities in the system to gain access to sensitive data or disrupt business operations.

Accordingly, robust security measures are necessary. These include encrypting sensitive data, using MFA to control access to the system and regularly updating the software to patch security vulnerabilities. It's also important to conduct regular security audits of the system to identify potential weaknesses. In addition to these technical measures, strong governance policies are needed around the use of automated systems. This includes defining who has access to the system, what data they can view or modify and how the system is monitored for suspicious activity.

To protect sensitive data, incorporate data anonymisation and encryption techniques and maintain transparency in how data is used within the system. The systems should provide detailed audit logs that track who accessed the data, what actions they took and whether any unauthorised attempts were made to modify or view the information. These audit logs can help ensure accountability and compliance with data privacy regulations.

In addition to securing the GRC system itself, organisations must also protect against broader cyber threats that could impact their GRC processes.

Cyberattacks, such as ransomware, data breaches or denial-of-service (DoS) attacks, can disrupt the functioning of automated GRC systems and compromise sensitive data. Tools such as intrusion detection systems (IDS) and intrusion prevention systems (IPS) can help detect and mitigate these threats before they cause significant damage. The systems can also be integrated with cybersecurity monitoring tools to provide real-time visibility into potential threats.

Another important consideration is the security posture of third-party vendors. Organisations must ensure that these vendors have strong cybersecurity measures in place. Conducting due diligence on vendors' security practices and ensuring that they comply with relevant data protection regulations is critical to protecting the organisation from third-party risks.

WHAT DOES IT ALL MEAN FOR SMALL AND MEDIUM-SIZED ENTERPRISES

While automation is often associated with large enterprises, SMEs can also benefit significantly from automating their GRC processes. In fact, automation can be especially valuable for SMEs that lack the resources or personnel to manage governance, risk and compliance manually. SMEs typically have smaller compliance teams and fewer risk management resources compared to large organisations, making it difficult to keep up with regulatory requirements and manage risks effectively.

Manual GRC processes also increase the risk of errors, as compliance officers may struggle to keep track of evolving regulations or miss important deadlines for audits or compliance reporting. Additionally, without automation, SMEs may not have the real-time visibility they need to identify and mitigate emerging risks. Fortunately, there are many affordable solutions designed specifically for SMEs. These platforms offer scalable, easy-to-use tools that streamline compliance tracking, risk assessments and governance processes. Cloud-based GRC automation tools, in particular, are cost-effective for SMEs, as they do not require significant upfront investments in infrastructure. Such platforms often come with pre-built templates for industry-specific regulations, such as GDPR for European companies. These templates allow SMEs to quickly set up compliance workflows and ensure that they meet regulatory requirements.

One of the key benefits of automation for SMEs is scalability. As an SME grows, its GRC needs become more complex. What might begin as a simple compliance tracking system can evolve into a full-fledged risk management platform that integrates with the organisation's financial, operational and IT systems. As new regulations are introduced or as the company enters new markets, the system can be easily adjusted to accommodate these changes. This scalability allows SMEs to grow without being held back by the limitations of manual processes.

ETHICAL CONSIDERATIONS IN AI-DRIVEN AUTOMATION

While AI and ML offer powerful advantages in GRC automation, their use also raises ethical considerations. AI algorithms, by nature, are only as good as the data they are trained on. If biased or incomplete data is used to train AI systems, it can result in skewed outcomes or reinforce existing biases in governance and risk management. AI models need to be transparent, explainable and regularly audited for fairness. It's also important to maintain human oversight over AI-driven decisions. AI should be viewed as a tool to enhance decision-making, not a replacement for human judgment. Furthermore, consider the ethical implications of automating tasks that involve personal data. AI systems that handle sensitive information, such as personal financial or health records, must be designed with robust data privacy protections.

While automated systems can perform tasks more efficiently and consistently than humans, they lack the intuition, judgment and contextual understanding that human professionals bring. It cannot fully account for the complexities and nuances of real-world decision-making. Human oversight is therefore essential for interpreting the results of automated processes. A compliance officer might receive an automated alert about a potential regulatory violation. While the system can provide data on the violation, the compliance officer must determine the appropriate course of action, taking into account the broader business context and potential legal implications. Regular audits of systems by human professionals will also help identify errors, biases or malfunctions in the system. Otherwise, you may find that you have ended up with flawed systems that could lead to non-compliance, financial losses or reputational damage.

TRANSPARENCY, ACCOUNTABILITY AND LEGAL CONSIDERATIONS

Regulators are increasingly focused on improving transparency and accountability in industries such as finance, healthcare and energy. Audit trails show who accessed the system. Regulators can use these logs to trace the organisation's decision-making processes and ensure that appropriate risk management and compliance measures are in place. This transparency reduces the risk of regulatory violations and builds trust between organisations and regulatory bodies.

Regulators are also paying close attention to the ethical and legal implications of automated decision-making. Regulators are particularly concerned about the potential for biased AI algorithms in industries like finance and healthcare, where automated systems may disproportionately impact certain demographic groups. One potential area of focus for regulators is ensuring that data privacy laws keep pace with the increasing use of automated systems. To address these concerns, regulatory bodies are working to establish guidelines for the ethical use of AI. These guidelines focus on issues such as data privacy, accountability, fairness and transparency in automated decision-making. Several international organisations and governments have begun developing standards and guidelines that promote ethical AI use in GRC and other applications. These guidelines are designed to provide a framework for the development and deployment of AI technologies in ways that protect individual rights, ensure accountability and mitigate risks associated with automation. However, the pace of innovation and pushback from powerful players on the market currently means that regulators are on the backfoot.

One of the leading international efforts in this area is the OECD AI Principles, established by the Organisation for Economic Co-operation and Development (OECD). These principles serve as a foundational set of guidelines for responsible AI use, emphasising fairness, transparency, accountability and human rights. While not specific to GRC, the OECD's guidelines offer a blueprint for organisations looking to ensure that their AI-driven GRC systems align with international best practices.

Additionally, the ISO/IEC Joint Technical Committee on AI has developed global technical standards for AI, which will cover a wide range of issues, including ethics, trust, safety and security. These standards are expected to guide the development of AI technologies in compliance with international regulatory frameworks, helping organisations that use AI for GRC automation to meet global expectations for ethical and secure AI use.

In the European Union (EU), data privacy and protection laws are at the forefront of regulatory efforts to govern the use of AI. The GDPR, which went into effect in 2018, sets stringent requirements for how organisations collect, store and process personal data. These requirements have significant implications for AI-driven GRC systems, particularly when it comes to automated decision-making and data processing. One of the most relevant aspects of GDPR for AI is Article 22, which addresses automated decision-making. Under this article, individuals have the right not to be subject to decisions made solely by automated processes, particularly when these decisions have legal or similarly significant effects. This means that organisations must ensure that AI-driven decisions in areas like compliance and risk management are subject to human oversight, especially when they impact individuals. Moreover, GDPR's strict requirements for data minimisation, consent and data protection impact assessments (DPIAs) also apply to AI systems. Organisations using AI-driven GRC systems must ensure that they collect and process only the data necessary for the task at hand and that they obtain explicit consent from individuals when processing personal data.

In addition to GDPR, the European Union has a regulatory framework specifically for AI, known as the AI Act. The AI Act creates a unified legal framework for AI across the EU, with a focus on ensuring that AI systems are safe, trustworthy and respectful of fundamental rights. It uses a risk-based approach to AI regulation, categorising AI systems into four risk levels: Unacceptable risk, high risk, limited risk and minimal risk. GRC automation systems, particularly those used in highly regulated industries like finance or healthcare, are likely to be classified as high-risk AI applications due to their potential impact.

High-risk AI systems under the AI Act are subject to strict requirements, including:

- *Transparency and Disclosure*: Organisations must clearly disclose when AI is being used in decision-making processes and provide explanations for how the system reaches its conclusions.
- *Human Oversight*: High-risk AI systems must have mechanisms in place to ensure human involvement in key decisions, preventing fully autonomous decision-making.
- *Risk Management*: Organisations using high-risk AI systems must implement rigorous risk management processes, including continuous monitoring, auditing and risk assessments to ensure that the AI system operates safely and ethically.

The AI Act requires organisations to implement robust governance frameworks to ensure that their AI-driven GRC systems comply with these requirements. Companies that fail to meet the standards set out in the AI Act could face significant fines and reputational damage.

In the United States, AI regulation is still in its early stages, but several regulatory agencies and government bodies establishing guidelines for the ethical and responsible use of AI. These efforts, while not yet fully developed, are likely to have a significant impact on how organisations implement AI-driven GRC systems. One of the key regulatory bodies involved in AI governance is the Federal Trade Commission (FTC). In 2020, the FTC released guidance on AI and algorithmic decision-making, emphasising the importance of transparency, fairness and accountability in automated systems. The FTC's guidelines encourage organisations to ensure that their AI systems are free from bias, provide explanations for how decisions are made and maintain human oversight of automated processes. In addition to the FTC, other U.S. regulatory bodies, such as the Securities and Exchange Commission (SEC) and the Office of the Comptroller of the Currency (OCC), are attempting to address the use of AI in industries like finance.

At the federal level, the National Institute of Standards and Technology (NIST) is also playing a critical role in shaping AI governance in the US NIST's AI Risk Management Framework is designed to provide organisations with guidance on managing the risks associated with AI technologies. This framework will likely serve as a reference point for organisations using AI in GRC automation, helping them ensure that their systems are secure, fair and accountable.

THE FUTURE OF AUTOMATION IN THIRD-PARTY RISK MANAGEMENT

As organisations increasingly rely on external vendors, suppliers, contractors and service providers to support their operations, third-party risk management (TPRM) is an integral of the broader GRC landscape. Third-party risks can expose businesses to a wide range of threats, including regulatory non-compliance, financial losses, operational disruptions and reputational damage. Automation is also transforming how organisations approach these challenges, offering real-time insights, increased efficiency and enhanced risk mitigation capabilities.

Automated TPRM systems solve this problem by providing real-time monitoring of third-party activities, performance and compliance. These systems can analyse vast amounts of data from multiple sources (e.g., financial reports, regulatory filings, news articles, social media and industry databases) to detect early warning signs of risk. This allows businesses to respond quickly to potential issues, such as a vendor facing financial instability or regulatory violations, before they become critical. It might flag a supplier for experiencing sudden financial losses or negative media coverage, prompting the organisation to take proactive steps, such as renegotiating contracts or sourcing from alternative suppliers. This capability to monitor and respond in real time ensures that third-party risks are managed dynamically and continuously, rather than relying on static, outdated assessments.

The process of onboarding new third parties and conducting due diligence is one of the most resource-intensive aspects. Traditional due diligence often involves reviewing financial statements, regulatory filings, certifications, compliance history and other documents, which can be time-consuming and prone to human error. Automation streamlines the due diligence process by using data aggregation tools and AI-powered analytics to automatically gather and assess relevant information about potential third-party partners from a wide variety of sources, both structured and unstructured, such as legal databases, regulatory filings, credit reports and industry benchmarks.

At the same time, organisations must remember that not all third parties represent the same level of risk. A small vendor providing non-critical services may pose minimal risk, while a large supplier involved in essential operations could present significant financial, operational or compliance risks. Automated risk scoring allows organisations to categorise their third parties based on the level of risk they pose, using sophisticated algorithms that evaluate factors such as the vendor's financial stability, regulatory compliance, geographical location, industry and historical performance. Each third party is assigned a risk score based on real-time data analysis and preset risk criteria. These scores are updated dynamically as new information becomes available, providing an accurate, up-to-date view of each vendor's risk profile. If a vendor's risk score increases due to a recent cybersecurity breach or regulatory fine, the system can trigger an alert, prompting further investigation or remediation efforts. Automated categorisation also allows organisations to prioritise their risk management efforts, focusing their resources on managing high-risk relationships while applying lighter oversight to low-risk partners.

Proactive remediation efforts can be initiated in the event that a third-party risk materialises. These systems can trigger workflows that guide risk professionals through the necessary steps to mitigate the risk, whether it's renegotiating contracts, terminating the vendor relationship or implementing corrective measures. If a supplier experiences a security breach, the automated system might flag the vendor as high-risk, send an alert to the compliance teams and initiate a remediation plan. This might include conducting an audit of the vendor's security protocols, requesting updated certifications or transitioning critical operations to alternative suppliers.

The other advantage is that such automated systems are highly scalable, making them an ideal solution for organisations that are experiencing rapid growth or operating in global markets. They can manage thousands of vendor relationships simultaneously, ensuring that each third party is continuously monitored, assessed and managed according to its risk profile. This scalability is particularly valuable for large multinational corporations or businesses in highly regulated industries like finance, healthcare and manufacturing, where third-party risks can have a significant impact on operations and compliance.

MANAGING THE TRANSITION TO GRC AUTOMATION

The transition to automation requires significant organisational change, especially for businesses that have traditionally relied on manual processes. For many employees, the shift to automation can be disruptive, leading to concerns about job displacement, changes in responsibilities and the need for new skills. Employees must be equipped with the skills and knowledge needed to operate and oversee automated systems. This includes understanding how the system works, how to interpret its output and how to troubleshoot potential issues. This will also foster a sense of ownership and collaboration. Employees who feel that they have a stake in the success of the automation process are more likely to embrace the change and use the new tools effectively.

Chapter 7

Data privacy and protection

Data privacy refers to the responsible handling of personal data, ensuring compliance with legal requirements and respect for individual rights. This involves collecting only necessary data, obtaining informed consent, allowing individuals access to their information, securely storing data, sharing it for legitimate purposes only, retaining it for appropriate durations and disposing of it securely. Strong data privacy measures are essential for several reasons. Organisations collect, store and process vast amounts of personal and sensitive data, whether digital or otherwise, often for legitimate business purposes. However, high-profile data breaches and the misuse of consumer data have heightened public awareness and driven demands for stricter data privacy regulations. Ensuring robust data privacy is not only a regulatory necessity but also a critical factor for maintaining customer trust and safeguarding brand reputation. Compliance with regulations in areas that your company operates such as the General Data Protection Regulation (GDPR) and the California Consumer Privacy Act (CCPA) is non-negotiable. Non-compliance carries substantial financial and legal consequences. Moreover, customers expect their personal data to be handled responsibly, and breaches of this trust can cause irreparable damage to an organisation's reputation.

In addition to compliance and trust, data privacy measures aid the mitigation of mitigates security risks, including data breaches, fraud and identity theft. From an ethical perspective, individuals have a fundamental right to privacy and mishandling their data undermines personal autonomy. Several principles and regulations underpin effective practices. Data minimisation requires organisations to collect and retain only the data necessary for specified purposes, while purpose limitation ensures that personal data is used solely for the purposes communicated at the time of collection. Transparency and consent are equally critical; individuals must provide clear, affirmative consent for the collection and use of their data and organisations must offer mechanisms to revoke this consent. Other principles include ensuring data accuracy, implementing robust security measures, maintaining detailed records of processing activities and conducting privacy impact assessments for new projects involving personal data. In cases of data breaches, organisations

DOI: 10.1201/9781003543992-8

must have procedures in place to notify regulators and affected individuals promptly, as required by law.

Despite the criticality of data privacy, organisations face numerous challenges in implementing and maintaining effective privacy programmes. The regulatory landscape is complex, with laws imposing stringent requirements that vary across jurisdictions. Customers increasingly demand transparency and control over their data, making it essential for organisations to meet these expectations to maintain trust. Additionally, organisations face growing threats from data breaches, insider misuse and cybercrime, particularly as volumes of personal data commands high value on the black market.

Complex data ecosystems add further complications, as organisations rely on networks of third-party vendors and service providers, increasing the risk of uncontrolled data use or leakage. Technologies such as artificial intelligence, biometrics and the Internet of Things create new privacy challenges, while legacy systems often lack the security mechanisms required to protect sensitive data. Resource constraints, unclear accountability and difficulties in tracking data flows across large organisations further exacerbate these challenges. Addressing these issues requires a proactive and sustained commitment to privacy.

Therefore, a structured privacy management programme is essential for effective data governance. This programme should include comprehensive policies outlining permitted data uses, retention schedules, access controls and breach response protocols. Standards must be defined for handling data in compliance with regulations, covering encryption, consent mechanisms and data retention. Governance structures should involve cross-functional teams, with designated roles such as Chief Privacy Officers and Data Protection Officers to ensure accountability. Risk assessments are crucial for identifying vulnerabilities, while legal reviews validate compliance with applicable laws. Secure data infrastructures, robust access controls and continuous monitoring help safeguard sensitive data.

Underpinning these programmes, processes and tools are people. Regular training ensures employees understand their responsibilities and comply with privacy policies, reducing the risk of negligence or misconduct. Audit controls and incident response plans further strengthen the programme by enabling organisations to detect and respond to breaches swiftly. Additionally, privacy reviews should be conducted periodically to identify and implement improvements in data collection, consent mechanisms and other privacy practices.

DATA GOVERNANCE AND DATA LIFECYCLES

Data governance and data lifecycles are fundamental to effective data management. Data governance refers to the comprehensive strategy, policies, processes, standards and technologies that organisations use to manage their data assets. It establishes authority and control over data, determining how data is used and managed to meet organisational objectives. Effective data governance aligns diverse stakeholders, ensures data quality, reduces costs and drives business value through analytics and intelligence. Additionally, it manages risks, ensures regulatory compliance and defines clear data ownership. Successful governance requires the participation of executive sponsors, data owners, data stewards, compliance officers and analysts, often coordinated through a cross-functional governance council.

These programmes are multi-faceted and rely on foundational components such as policies, standards and quality practices. Policies set expectations for data handling, covering acquisition, storage, lifecycle management, security and usage. Standards define consistent data specifications, such as format and metadata, while quality practices ensure data accuracy and timeliness. Security controls safeguard data against breaches and risk management strategies prepare organisations to address data-related challenges. Data literacy training fosters stakeholder engagement, while performance monitoring ensures governance processes remain effective. Together, these components enable organisations to harness the full value of their data.

Several frameworks guide organisations in designing and implementing such programmes. The DAMA-DMBOK framework defines areas such as data principles, policies, standards and metrics. Similarly, the Data Governance Institute (DGI) framework focuses on structured approaches to governance. While IBM's Data Governance Council Maturity Model provides progressive paths for organisations to enhance their governance capabilities.

Governance is complemented by the concept of a data lifecycle through mapping the phases data undergoes from creation to disposal. Typical lifecycle stages include planning, creation, management, use, sharing, archiving and destruction. Each stage demands tailored governance processes. The creation phase emphasises data quality and proper acquisition methods, while the management phase focuses on ongoing maintenance and security. Archiving data reduces governance obligations while preserving information for future use and the destruction phase has to be in compliance with retention policies.

The benefits of robust data governance and lifecycle management are significant. Improved data quality enhances analytics and reporting, while stricter controls reduce risks such as non-compliance and data breaches. Reliable data enables better decision-making, driving operational efficiency and uncovering new revenue opportunities. However, implementing data governance is not without challenges. Securing participation from leaders and stakeholders can be difficult, especially in organisations with siloed data practices. Incrementally or haphazardly introducing governance processes may add complexity, slowing down workflows. Ensuring sufficient resources, managing evolving technologies and maintaining momentum after initial compliance efforts also pose obstacles.

Best practices have emerged to guide organisations in their governance efforts. Starting with high-priority data and aligning governance objectives with business goals ensures relevance and impact. Securing executive sponsorship fosters organisational commitment. Involving data owners in policy development ensures policies meet operational needs, while promoting data literacy empowers employees to act as stewards.

Successful governance also relies on well-defined roles and responsibilities. The Chief Data Officer (CDO) oversees governance strategies, while cross-functional governance councils establish policies and resolve issues. Data owners and stewards ensure compliance and enforce standards within their domains, supported by data architects and custodians responsible for infrastructure and security. Compliance officers monitor regulatory adherence, and business analysts use governed data to deliver insights. This collaborative approach ensures accountability throughout the data lifecycle.

Automation and artificial intelligence are reducing manual oversight by streamlining tasks such as data classification and quality checks. The rise of self-service analytics and real-time data pipelines presents new challenges for governance, as does the growing use of cloud platforms and external data sharing. As data landscapes continue to evolve, agile and adaptive governance programmes will be critical to maintaining compliance, fostering innovation and achieving long-term success. Accordingly, let us take a look at the regulations and laws in the USA and Europe, in general.

OVERVIEW OF UNITED STATES DATA PROTECTION LAWS AND REGULATIONS

Unlike the European Union and the UK, the United States lacks a comprehensive federal data privacy law. Instead, it relies on a complex patchwork of federal and state laws to address data privacy and information security. These regulations target specific industries or types of data and address diverse issues such as data privacy, breach notification, cybercrime, critical infrastructure protection, government information security and sector-specific regulations for financial and healthcare industries. This fragmented approach reflects the diversity and decentralisation of the US legal system, providing sector-specific frameworks while leaving gaps that continue to spark calls for comprehensive federal legislation.

The Family Educational Rights and Privacy Act (FERPA) protects the privacy of student education records and requires schools receiving federal funding to obtain written consent before disclosing such records. Similarly, the Health Insurance Portability and Accountability Act (HIPAA) safeguards patient health information and outlines strict rules for its use and disclosure. The Fair Credit Reporting Act (FCRA) governs the collection and use of consumer report data, ensuring accuracy and giving consumers the right to access and correct their information. The Children's Online Privacy Protection Act (COPPA) regulates the collection of personal data from children under 13, mandating verifiable parental consent. At the state level, to use one example, the California Consumer Privacy Act (CCPA) stands out for granting

California residents the right to know what data is collected about them and the ability to request its deletion. Together, these laws provide varying degrees of protection across specific domains, though they leave room for improvement in unifying privacy standards.

Data breach notification laws are another critical aspect of US data protection legislation. Federal laws, such as the HIPAA Breach Notification Rule and the HITECH Act, require healthcare organisations and their business associates to notify individuals and the Department of Health and Human Services within 60 days of a breach involving protected health information. At the state level, all 50 states, along with territories such as Guam and Puerto Rico, have enacted data breach notification laws, though timeframes for notification vary. These laws aim to protect individuals by ensuring they are informed promptly of breaches so they can mitigate potential harm, such as identity theft.

Federal cybercrime laws address the growing threat of malicious activities in the digital realm. The Computer Fraud and Abuse Act (CFAA) serves as the primary federal anti-hacking statute, prohibiting unauthorised access to computers and systems. Additional laws like the Wiretap Act and the Stored Communications Act extend protections to electronic communications, making it illegal to intercept or access such data without authorisation. Specific legislation, such as the Identity Theft and Assumption Deterrence Act, criminalises identity theft, while the CAN-SPAM Act sets rules for commercial email, requiring transparency and the inclusion of opt-out mechanisms.

There are also applicable laws covering critical infrastructure, given the reliance of the economy and public safety on systems like power grids, water supplies and communication networks. Federal laws such as the Critical Infrastructures Protection Act and the Patriot Act establish the legal foundation for safeguarding these assets. Presidential directives define responsibilities for infrastructure protection, while specific regulations like the Chemical Facility Anti-Terrorism Standards (CFATS) require high-risk facilities to implement security measures. Despite these efforts, the interconnected nature of modern infrastructure continues to pose significant security challenges.

The US government also emphasises the security of its information systems. The Federal Information Security Management Act (FISMA) and its successor, the Federal Information Security Modernization Act, set out requirements for federal agencies to protect sensitive data. These laws mandate annual security audits, continuous monitoring and adherence to standards developed by the National Institute of Standards and Technology (NIST). However, high-profile breaches, such as the SolarWinds incident, underscore the ongoing vulnerabilities in government systems.

In the financial sector, stringent regulations aim to protect sensitive customer data and ensure the integrity of financial systems. The Gramm-Leach-Bliley Act (GLBA) requires financial institutions to implement safeguards to protect customer information, while the Sarbanes-Oxley Act (SOX) mandates robust internal controls and annual security audits for public companies.

Regulatory bodies such as the Securities and Exchange Commission (SEC) provide guidance on managing cybersecurity risks and reporting incidents, while initiatives like the Federal Financial Institutions Examination Council's (FFIEC) security assessments help evaluate the resilience of financial institutions. State-level laws, such as New York's Department of Financial Services Cybersecurity Regulations, add further requirements, reflecting an increasing focus on cyber resilience in the financial sector.

Healthcare regulations build on HIPAA's foundational principles, addressing emerging cybersecurity threats to patient safety. The HIPAA Security Rule mandates administrative, physical and technical safeguards to protect electronic protected health information (ePHI), while the Food and Drug Administration (FDA) provides guidance for securing medical devices and hospital networks. Agencies like the Department of Health and Human Services (HHS) issue additional recommendations to help healthcare organisations prepare for and respond to cyber threats.

Finally, internet privacy laws, though somewhat fragmented, aim to address privacy concerns specific to online activities. The Electronic Communications Privacy Act (ECPA) extends government restrictions on electronic surveillance to online communications, while the Telephone Consumer Protection Act (TCPA) regulates telemarketing practices. The Cable Communications Policy Act (CCPA) prohibits cable providers from disclosing subscriber information without consent. While these laws provide some protections, the rapid evolution of digital technology raises ongoing questions about their adequacy in addressing modern privacy concerns.

The United States' legal framework for data protection is therefore complex, reflecting its federal structure and the varying priorities of different sectors. While this patchwork of laws addresses many aspects of information security, gaps remain, particularly in establishing comprehensive privacy protections at the federal level. The regulatory landscape will need to adapt as technology continues to evolve and new threats emerge, balancing innovation with the need to protect individual privacy and national security. This dynamic environment highlights the importance of ongoing education, vigilance and collaboration among lawmakers, businesses and consumers.

UK: THE DATA PROTECTION ACT AND GDPR

The Data Protection Act 2018 (DPA 2018) replaced its predecessor, the Data Protection Act 1998, and supplements the UK GDPR by tailoring its application to the UK context. Enacted on 23 May 2018, the DPA 2018 modernised data protection practices to address the complexities of the digital age. While the DPA works alongside GDPR, it is not a direct implementation of the regulation. GDPR is a regulation that came into force automatically without requiring national legislation. However, following Brexit, GDPR was incorporated into UK law through the Brexit Withdrawal Act, becoming known as the UK GDPR. Minor adjustments were made to reflect UK-based institutions, and the EU recognises the UK's data protection framework as equivalent to its own.

The DPA 2018 serves multiple purposes. It provides national legislation to bridge gaps in GDPR where flexibility is permitted at the member state level, such as exemptions and derogations tailored to specific national requirements. It also extends data protection into areas not directly addressed by GDPR, such as national security, defence, immigration and judicial activities. Furthermore, the DPA grants the Information Commissioner's Office (ICO) powers to oversee and enforce compliance and outlines offences, such as unlawfully obtaining or disclosing personal data and tampering with information requests.

The relationship between the DPA and GDPR means organisations processing personal data in the UK must comply with both frameworks. However, there are key distinctions between them. For instance, the DPA sets the age of consent for online services at 13, lower than GDPR's recommended 16 years. It also specifies additional conditions for processing special category data, such as criminal offence information, and exempts courts and tribunals from appointing Data Protection Officers (DPOs). While the administrative fines under the DPA align with GDPR's framework, the DPA ensures the amounts account for currency fluctuations, capping fines at £17 million or 4% of global turnover, whichever is higher.

The DPA upholds the core principles of data protection established by GDPR, including lawfulness, fairness, transparency, purpose limitation, data minimisation, accuracy, storage limitation, integrity, confidentiality and accountability. These principles form the foundation for lawful processing, ensuring organisations handle personal data responsibly and transparently. At least one lawful basis must apply to data processing, such as the data subject's consent, contractual necessity, legal obligations or public interest. For special category data like health, genetic or biometric information, an additional lawful condition is required.

Data subjects retain the same rights under the DPA as under GDPR. These include the right to be informed about data processing activities, the right of access to their personal data and the right to rectify inaccuracies. They also have the right to request data erasure (the "right to be forgotten"), restrict processing and object to certain activities. Furthermore, data subjects can request data portability, allowing them to receive and reuse their data across different organisations. The DPA also addresses rights related to automated decision-making and profiling.

The DPA outlines specific obligations for data controllers and processors, ensuring alignment with GDPR requirements for accountability, data protection by design and data security. Organisations must maintain records of processing activities, cooperate with the ICO and implement technical and organisational measures to safeguard personal data. Additionally, controllers are required to conduct Data Protection Impact Assessments (DPIAs) for high-risk processing activities and consult with the ICO when necessary.

The DPA introduces exemptions and derogations tailored to the UK's needs. For instance, exemptions apply to national security, defence and immigration processes, as well as activities related to journalism, academia and artistic or literary purposes. Special provisions exist for processing data for research and statistical purposes, while health data processing by coroners and related professionals is also addressed. Legal professional privilege and disclosures required by law are safeguarded within the Act, ensuring sensitive and regulated activities comply with the broader data protection framework.

The supervision and enforcement of the DPA is managed by the ICO, the UK's independent supervisory authority. The ICO has powers similar to those outlined in GDPR, including conducting audits, issuing warnings and imposing temporary or permanent bans on data processing. Non-compliance can lead to fines, suspensions of data flows or even criminal prosecutions for offences such as unlawfully obtaining personal data or obstructing ICO investigations.

The implementation of the DPA 2018 and UK GDPR marked a transformative period for UK organisations, requiring significant changes to data policies and practices. While some viewed the requirements as burdensome, the strengthened framework provided individuals with greater control over their personal information. It modernised legal standards for the digital economy, promoted responsible innovation and aimed to foster consumer trust.

The DPA has reshaped how organisations approach data privacy, embedding accountability and transparency into business operations. It has elevated privacy and ethics as core considerations, ensuring data protection is not just a compliance issue but a strategic priority. It has also positioned UK organisations to compete globally based on responsible data practices. Its influence extends beyond the UK, as other countries align their data protection laws with these modernised standards. The DPA exemplifies how effective regulation can transform societal norms and organisational behaviour, making privacy and data protection integral to the digital age.

OVERVIEW OF GDPR IMPLEMENTATION IN THE EU

Enforced on May 25, 2018, the EU's GDPR replaced the 1995 EU Data Protection Directive, marking a significant shift in how organisations worldwide manage personal data. Its primary objectives are to harmonise data privacy laws across the EU, safeguard EU citizens' personal information and establish global standards for responsible data handling. Unlike previous legislation, GDPR applies extraterritorially, meaning any organisation processing the personal data of EU residents, regardless of where it is located, must comply. This far-reaching applicability, combined with penalties of up to €20 million or

4% of global annual turnover, underscores the regulation's global impact and strict enforcement.

Central to GDPR is the principle of transparency and accountability in handling personally identifiable information (PII). Organisations are required to implement robust measures to ensure data is collected, processed and stored responsibly. The regulation expands the definition of PII to include a wide array of identifiers, such as names, email addresses, IP addresses and biometric data. It also mandates that data processing must be based on clear, affirmative consent from individuals. Companies must explain why data is being collected, how it will be used and obtain explicit agreement from the data subject.

A critical aspect of GDPR is its emphasis on individual rights. EU citizens are granted extensive control over their personal information. They have the right to access their data, rectify inaccuracies and request deletion of information that is no longer needed, also known as the "right to be forgotten." Additionally, they can transfer their data between organisations using standardised formats, a provision called data portability. Citizens can also object to data processing for specific purposes, such as marketing, and withdraw consent at any time. These rights aim to empower individuals and ensure their personal information is handled ethically and transparently.

To enforce these principles, GDPR requires organisations to integrate data protection into every aspect of their operations. This concept, known as "privacy by design," mandates that safeguards like encryption and pseudonymisation be embedded into systems and processes from the outset. Organisations must also ensure data minimisation, collecting only what is necessary for a specific purpose. Security protocols such as strong passwords, multi-factor authentication and role-based access controls are crucial to preventing unauthorised access. Data controllers (entities that determine the purpose and means of data processing) must maintain detailed records of their activities to demonstrate compliance. For high-risk processing activities, such as using new technologies or handling vulnerable populations' data, data protection impact assessments are mandatory.

The regulation also stipulates that organisations appoint a Data Protection Officer (DPO) in certain cases. This is particularly required for entities processing large-scale or sensitive data, such as health information or racial and political profiles. The DPO is responsible for overseeing compliance, advising on data protection practices and serving as a point of contact for supervisory authorities and data subjects. In cases of data breaches, organisations must notify supervisory authorities within 72 hours and, in some instances, inform affected individuals.

Supervisory authorities in each EU member state are empowered to investigate complaints, audit organisations and impose penalties. Violations of GDPR can result in severe fines, tiered according to the gravity of the infringement. High-profile cases have already illustrated the consequences of non-compliance. Google was fined €50 million for transparency and consent violations, while British Airways and Marriott faced substantial penalties for data breaches affecting millions of customers. These cases highlight the regulation's intent to hold even the largest multinational corporations accountable.

The introduction of GDPR has had profound global implications. It has inspired similar data privacy laws in jurisdictions outside the EU, such as the CCPA in the United States. Multinational corporations have adopted GDPR principles universally to streamline compliance and build trust with their customers. The regulation has also raised awareness among consumers about their privacy rights, compelling organisations to prioritise data protection as a core business objective.

While critics argue that GDPR has introduced bureaucratic burdens and led to "consent fatigue" among users, its benefits are undeniable. The regulation has set a high standard for privacy, fostering safer data handling practices and strengthening individual rights. It has also prompted organisations to re-evaluate their data policies, though the extent to which many do place privacy at the forefront of their operations is questionable. GDPR's legacy is one of empowerment for individuals and accountability for organisations, ensuring that data protection remains a critical priority in the digital age.

CONCLUSION

Data privacy and protection are dynamic and evolving disciplines that require a proactive approach. Organisations must embed privacy into their core values and operational practices to ensure compliance, maintain customer trust and safeguard sensitive information. Organisations can navigate the complexities of modern data ecosystems, mitigate security risks and uphold ethical standards by adopting a proactive and comprehensive approach to data governance.

Effective data privacy measures not only fulfil regulatory requirements but also provide a competitive advantage through demonstrating a commitment to responsible data handling. Continuous improvement and adaptation are essential as technologies advance and new challenges emerge. Organisations should invest in robust privacy management programmes, foster a culture of data protection and stay informed about evolving best practices and regulations. Ultimately, a steadfast commitment to data privacy and protection will enable organisations to thrive in the digital age, fostering innovation, building customer loyalty and ensuring long-term success and resilience.

Chapter 8

The strategic role of enterprise security architecture in governance, risk and compliance[1]

Robert Campbell

Enterprise Security Architecture (ESA) has evolved far beyond its original role as a technical or compliance framework.

Today, it is a critical strategic capability that helps organisations build resilience, manage risk proactively and ensure continuous governance and regulatory alignment, all while enabling business agility and transformation.

Effective ESA creates a vital bridge between security measures, business objectives and operational resilience.

Rather than focusing narrowly on technical controls or checklists, ESA ensures that:

- Security initiatives are directly linked to protecting and enabling business priorities.
- Risk management practices are embedded across the service lifecycle, not bolted on as afterthoughts.
- Compliance outcomes are the natural result of sound architectural and operational practices, not reactive exercises.
- Governance structures evolve dynamically alongside changing business models, regulatory landscapes and threat environments.

By designing architectures that anticipate threats, align to business risk appetites and adapt to ongoing change, organisations can move away from static compliance models and embrace continuous governance, dynamic risk management and sustainable business protection.

At its heart, modern ESA operationalises the core intent behind leading security, risk and governance frameworks:

- To integrate security decision-making into enterprise strategy.
- To manage risk proportionally to business value and impact.

DOI: 10.1201/9781003543992-9

- To deliver operational resilience as a built-in service outcome.
- To enable regulatory confidence without slowing innovation or growth.

Achieving this level of integration demands more than technical frameworks; it requires a fundamental shift in how organisations view security architecture itself, transitioning from a defensive cost centre to a proactive business enabler.

PERSISTENT CHALLENGES

Despite decades of investment in security practices, organisations consistently face structural challenges when attempting to integrate ESA into Governance, Risk and Compliance (GRC) frameworks. These persistent issues create enduring barriers to achieving security by design, proactive risk management and continuous compliance (Figure 8.1).

- *Siloed Functions*: Security, risk and compliance activities are often fragmented across different teams, business units and service lifecycles. This lack of integration leads to duplicated efforts, conflicting priorities and missed opportunities for proactive governance.

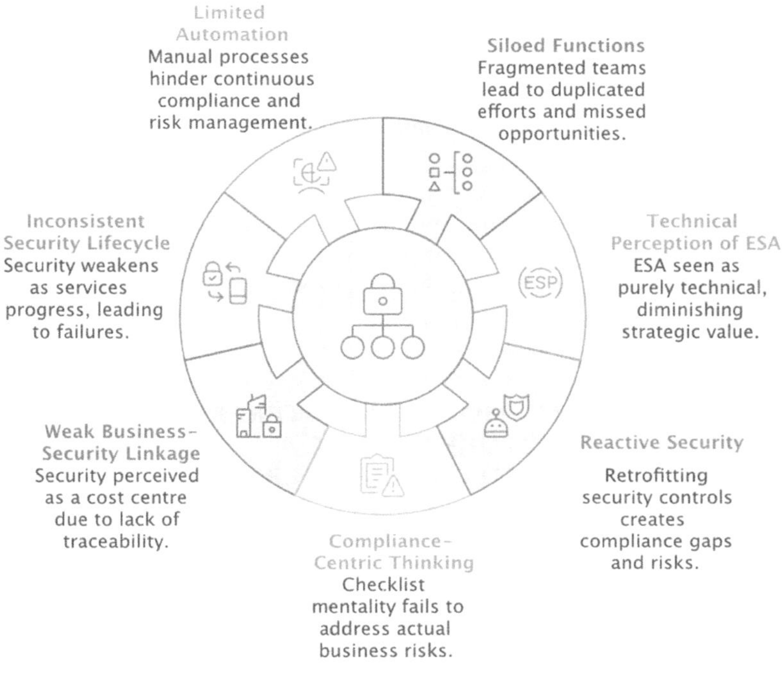

Figure 8.1 Challenges.

- *Perception of ESA as Purely Technical*: ESA is frequently seen as a deeply technical discipline disconnected from business strategy and risk management. As a result, its outputs are sometimes overlooked by GRC professionals and executive leadership, diminishing its strategic value.
- *Reactive Rather than Proactive Security*: Security controls are often retrofitted into services after design and development are complete, creating compliance gaps, expensive remediation and heightened operational risk. Proactive, lifecycle-driven security architecture remains the exception rather than the rule.
- *Compliance-Centric Rather than Risk-Centric Thinking*: Many organisations adopt a checklist mentality towards regulatory compliance rather than embedding risk-based security architecture that evolves with the threat landscape. This approach often results in superficial control implementations that fail to address actual business risks.
- *Weak Linkage between Business Goals and Security Controls*: Security architectures often struggle to clearly distinguish between business objectives, risk appetite and technical controls. Without this traceability, security is perceived as a cost centre rather than a business enabler.
- *Inconsistent Security across the Service Lifecycle*: Security requirements frequently weaken or fragment as services move from planning through to operation and retirement. Lack of lifecycle integration leads to security "drop-offs," creating audit failures, compliance gaps and unmanaged risk exposure.
- *Limited Use of Automation and Analytics*: Manual processes dominate risk management, compliance reporting and control validation. Organisations struggle to implement automated, intelligence-driven approaches that enable continuous compliance and dynamic risk management at scale.

These challenges are enduring and highlight the need for a structured, business-aligned and lifecycle-driven approach to ESA that fully embeds security into GRC frameworks and service management practices, enabling resilience, agility and demonstrable business value.

THE KEY QUESTION – HOW CAN ENTERPRISE SECURITY ARCHITECTURE BECOME A BUSINESS-INTEGRATED GRC ENABLER?

Faced with these persistent challenges, organisations need to rethink the role of ESA.

The central question we are trying to address is:

How can ESA be systematically integrated with Governance, Risk Management and Compliance (GRC) frameworks while aligning with the full Through Life Service Lifecycle to create proactive, resilient and continuously compliant security outcomes that deliver measurable business value?

Answering this question requires a shift in perspective:

- ESA must be seen not merely as a technical activity but as a strategic business function.
- Security architecture must be mapped directly to business goals, risk tolerances and compliance obligations.
- Controls must be embedded proactively into every phase of service planning, development, operation and retirement.
- Governance mechanisms must ensure that security outcomes are measurable, verifiable and continuously improved.

Solving this challenge requires a strategic shift: moving ESA beyond static control sets towards a dynamic model that continuously enables business resilience, operational adaptability and regulatory integrity. This evolution is essential but demands a deliberate, sustained transformation, not a tactical quick fix.

Why is solving this so difficult

Even with strong intent and growing awareness, several persistent barriers complicate the effective integration of ESA into GRC frameworks across the service lifecycle.

1. *Perception Gap between Business and Security*: If ESA is considered at all, it is often viewed through a technical lens, making it difficult for non-technical stakeholders, such as governance, risk and compliance leaders, to see its strategic value. This perception isolates security architecture from critical business decisions, weakening its ability to influence risk management and compliance outcomes effectively.
2. *Misalignment with Business Strategy and Risk Appetite*: Many security architectures are developed without a clear linkage to organisational goals, risk tolerance levels or regulatory priorities. Without this alignment, security initiatives risk becoming tactical, expensive and disconnected from measurable business value.
3. *Fragmentation across the Service Lifecycle*: Security activities frequently "drop off" or degrade as services move through different lifecycle phases. Controls defined during planning and design often lose fidelity during build, transition or operation, resulting in compliance gaps, unmanaged risks and weakened resilience.
4. *Manual, Siloed and Reactive Approaches*: Despite automation tools' growing availability, many organisations manage risk and compliance

manually. Siloed practices across security, operations and risk teams create bottlenecks, slow down assurance activities and limit visibility into emerging threats and control weaknesses.

5. *Lack of Continuous Risk and Compliance Integration*: Traditional GRC models rely on point-in-time assessments rather than embedding dynamic, continuous risk management into everyday service operations. As services and threats evolve rapidly, these static models become outdated, exposing organisations.
6. *Resource and Skill Constraints*: Security architects are often stretched too thin across projects, with insufficient capacity to embed security properly at every lifecycle stage. Compounded by a shortage of professionals skilled in technical security architecture and business risk management, organisations struggle to scale ESA practices effectively.

These complications highlight why integrating ESA with GRC is not merely a matter of adding new controls or updating checklists.

It requires a fundamental rethinking of how security architecture is positioned, governed, implemented and evolved across the business and operational environment.

GOVERNING THOUGHT – ESA AS A STRATEGIC ENABLER, NOT A TECHNICAL LAYER

ESA must be understood not merely as a collection of technical safeguards but as a strategic enabler of GRC across the organisation (Figure 8.2).

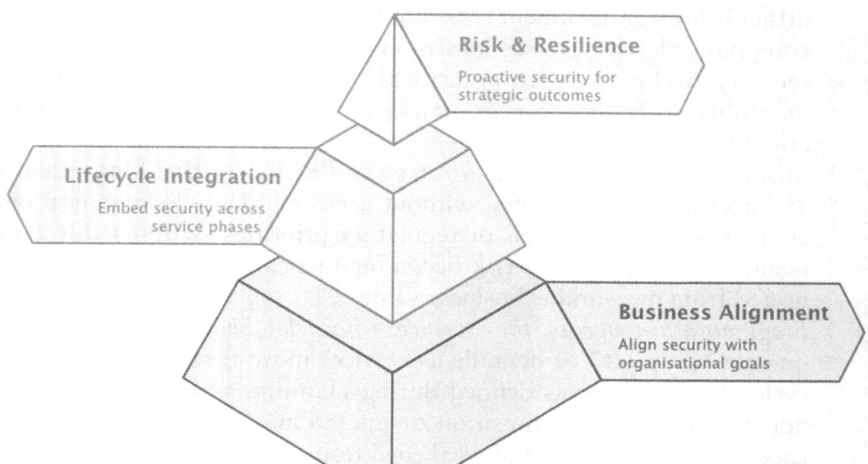

Figure 8.2 Success criteria.

To succeed, ESA must be:

- Business-driven, aligning security controls to organisational goals, risk appetite and regulatory requirements.
- Lifecycle-integrated, ensuring that security principles are embedded and continuously reinforced across every phase of service development, operation and retirement.
- Risk-centric and resilience-focused, enabling organisations to move beyond checkbox compliance towards proactive, adaptable security postures that strengthen operational and strategic outcomes.

ESA cannot remain isolated within technical teams. It should function as a vital component of business planning, risk management and service delivery by translating intricate security requirements into understandable business value, quantifiable risk reductions and clear regulatory assurance.

This strategic repositioning of ESA establishes the foundation for embedding security governance "by design" rather than "by audit," leading to stronger, more sustainable GRC outcomes across the enterprise.

Throughout this chapter, references to the 'Through Life Service Lifecycle' describe a broad, end-to-end service and capability management model – from planning and design through to operation and secure retirement – that integrates security, risk and compliance activities at every stage. A full description is provided later.

ESA can be visualised as a dynamic bridge connecting business drivers, risk appetite, GRC frameworks and operational service delivery. The following illustrates this integration across the Through Life Service Lifecycle (Figure 8.3).

Organisations can adopt structured, business-aligned security methodologies and frameworks that connect technical controls with governance and risk management to achieve this strategic integration. Methodologies and frameworks such as SABSA, the NIST Cybersecurity Framework and others form the foundation for doing so effectively.

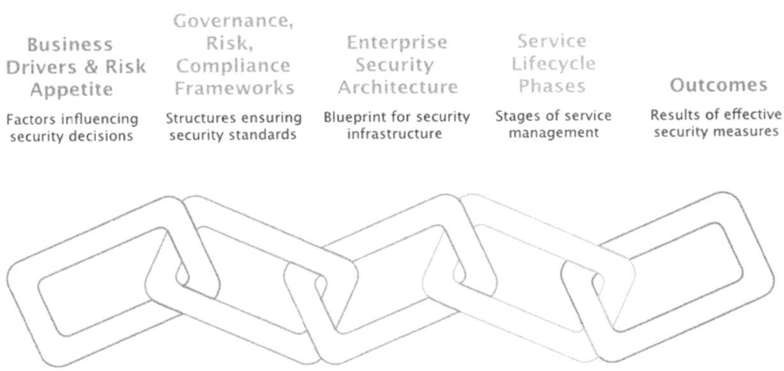

Figure 8.3 ESA as a bridge.

Throughout this chapter, reference will be made to structured security architecture models that translate business needs into operational security outcomes. One of the most prominent of these models, SABSA, will be introduced shortly.

Effective ESA requires continuous measurement of performance and risk posture. Later in this chapter, we introduce how Key Performance Indicators (KPIs), Key Control Indicators (KCIs) and Key Risk Indicators (KRIs) are used to measure success.

A FRAMEWORK-BASED PERSPECTIVE

Security hasn't been "just an IT issue" for a long time now; it's a business driver. The SABSA methodology is currently the only horse in the race when it comes to ESA. It takes a business-driven approach to ESA, ensuring security architecture aligns with organisational objectives (Figure 8.4).

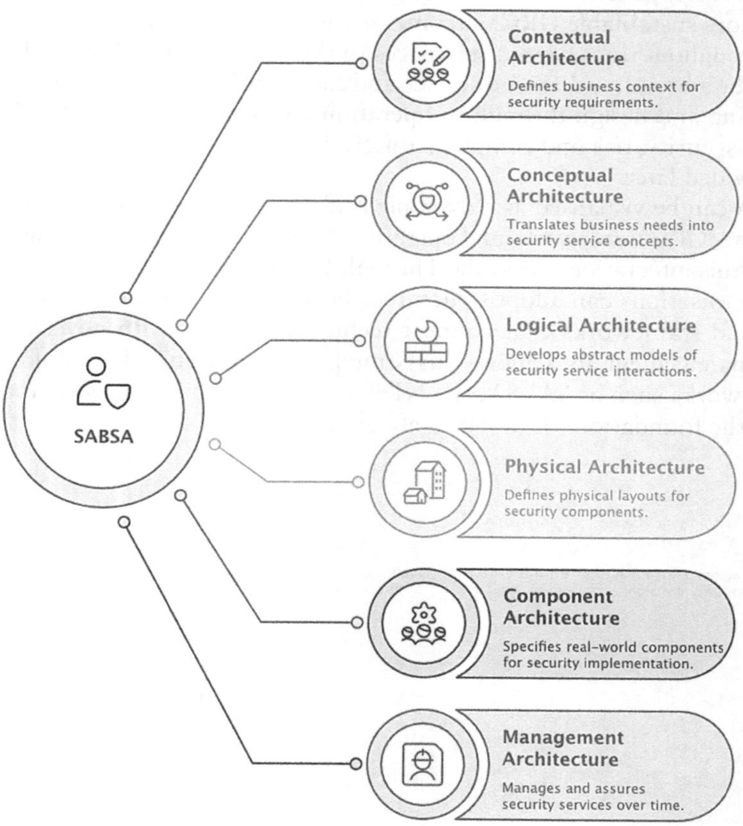

Figure 8.4 SABSA layers.

SABSA's® architecture model breaks security down into six perspectives.

SABSA layer	*Focus*	*Key purpose*	*Questions answered*
Contextual architecture (business view)	Business goals, drivers and risk appetite.	Define the *business context* for security – what needs to be protected, why and for whom.	What does the business need? Who are the stakeholders? What risks matter? What business attributes define success?
Conceptual architecture (architect's view)	Security strategy, policy and control objectives.	Translate business requirements into *conceptual security services* without diving into technical specifics.	What types of security services are needed? What policies must be enforced? What threats and risks must be addressed?
Logical architecture (designer's view)	Logical models of security services and relationships.	Develop *abstract security models* – logical designs of how security services interact without committing to specific technologies.	How should security services be logically structured and related? What workflows and processes should exist?
Physical architecture (builder's view)	Technology-agnostic system designs.	Define *physical layouts* of security components, systems and infrastructures – preparing for technology-specific decisions.	Where will systems be located? How will components be arranged? What flows and boundaries must be maintained?
Component architecture (tradesman's view)	Specific products, technologies and implementations.	Select and specify *real-world components* – products, platforms, configurations – that fulfil logical and physical designs.	Which tools, platforms and services will deliver the architecture? What configurations are required?
Management architecture (manager's view)	Day-to-day operation, monitoring and maintenance.	Define *how security services are managed and assured* over time, including monitoring, reporting, metrics and continuous improvement.	How is security performance measured and improved? Who is responsible? How is assurance demonstrated?

The SABSA framework is useful because it helps describe how security controls directly support business goals while considering stakeholder risk tolerance.

This aligns with NIST CSF 2.0's Governance (GV) category, which incorporates cybersecurity risk management into essential governance processes such as policy development, oversight and supply chain risk management. Similarly, CISM's information security governance domain mandates that companies establish a security strategy that prioritises risks with the highest business impact.

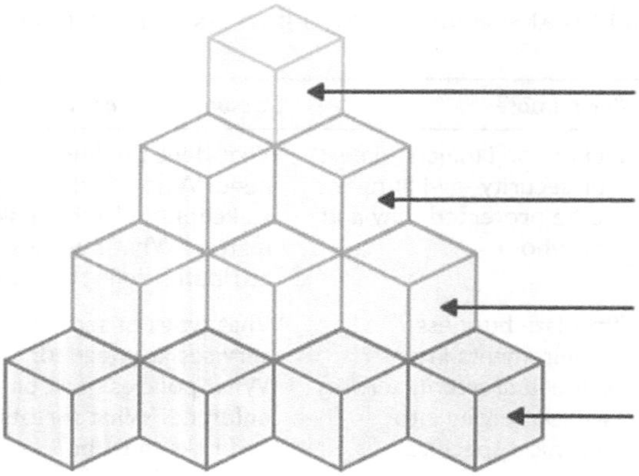

Figure 8.5 Connecting controls to decisions.

By utilising the SABSA framework, organisations move away from outdated "checklist compliance" and adopt proactive risk governance, where ESA plays a key role in connecting technical controls to executive decision-making (Figure 8.5).

ACHIEVING COMPLIANCE THROUGH SECURITY ARCHITECTURE

Regulatory compliance is more than a mere checkbox exercise; it embodies the demonstration of due diligence and the alignment of security practices with business objectives. ESA, especially when structured using the SABSA methodology, provides a strategic approach to achieving and evidencing compliance.

SABSA advocates for a business-driven, risk-based methodology that ensures security measures are not only technically sound but also aligned with the organisation's goals and regulatory obligations. By initiating the security architecture process with a thorough analysis of business requirements, the SABSA methodology facilitates the development of security controls that are directly traceable to these needs, thereby ensuring that compliance efforts are both relevant and effective.

ESA, under the SABSA methodology, employs a layered architecture that maps business objectives to security strategies, policies and controls. This structured approach enables organisations to:

- *Align Security with Business Goals*: By identifying and prioritising business attributes, organisations can ensure that security measures support and enhance their business operations.
- *Establish Traceability*: Each security control is connected to business requirements, offering clear justification for its implementation and aiding in audits and assessments.

- *Integrate Risk Management*: Organisations can proactively address potential threats and vulnerabilities by embedding risk assessment into every layer of the architecture.
- *Promote Continuous Improvement*: The lifecycle approach of SABSA ensures that security architectures are regularly reviewed and updated in response to evolving business and regulatory landscapes.

SABSA is a comprehensive and flexible methodology that enables organisations to not only meet regulatory requirements but also to show a proactive and integrated approach to security and compliance.

STRENGTHENING RISK MANAGEMENT THROUGH ENTERPRISE SECURITY ARCHITECTURE

While governance and compliance are critical drivers for ESA, risk management lies at the heart of achieving real-world security effectiveness and business resilience.

Too often, risk is treated as an afterthought to compliance: organisations focus on satisfying auditors rather than managing the real threats and vulnerabilities that endanger business operations.

ESA presents a chance to realign by positioning risk identification, evaluation and mitigation at the core of service and security design decisions.

To do so, we need to consider how risk management is embedded into the lifecycle of a system or service.

Effective risk management activity should be embedded throughout the service lifecycle:

- During planning risk assessments identify key business impacts, regulatory drivers and threat actors.
- During the design phase, threat modelling informs security architecture decisions, ensuring that controls are aligned with risk.
- During development and testing, vulnerabilities are identified and addressed before going live, which reduces residual risk.
- Continuous monitoring ensures that risks remain within acceptable thresholds as environments evolve in operation and maintenance.
- During retirement, secure decommissioning ensures that residual risks are eliminated and no legacy exposures remain.

By mapping risk activities to service phases, ESA transforms risk management from a one-time project activity into a continuous, embedded discipline.

LINKING SECURITY CONTROLS TO BUSINESS RISK APPETITE

SABSA and other methodologies enable security architects to trace each control back to a business attribute and associated risk tolerance.

This traceability ensures that security controls are:

- Proportionate to the business impact
- Justifiable in cost and complexity
- Aligned with regulatory and contractual obligations
- Responsive to dynamic threat environments

Without this linkage, organisations risk over-investing in low-value controls or under-protecting critical assets.

ESA should also align with broader Enterprise Risk Management (ERM) frameworks, not exist in isolation.

This requires:

- Shared language between Risk and Security teams
- Common risk scoring methodologies
- Integration of security risk metrics into enterprise risk dashboards and reports
- Regular reviews of emerging threats, regulatory shifts and business model changes

By embedding ESA into the ERM ecosystem, organisations achieve a single, coherent view of operational, financial, regulatory and security risks.

Static risk registers and annual reviews are no longer sufficient.

Modern ESA practices support:

- Real-time threat intelligence integration
- Dynamic risk re-evaluation based on changes in assets, threats or vulnerabilities
- Automated control validation (e.g., using SIEM, SOAR and GRC platforms)
- Continuous feedback loops between operations, architecture and risk governance

This dynamic, data-driven risk model ensures that security remains effective even as the business and threat landscape evolve (Figure 8.6).

A strong ESA:

- Positions risk, not just compliance, as the primary driver for security decisions

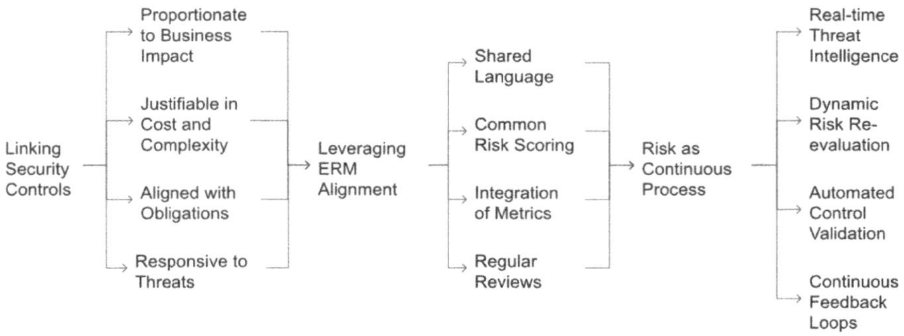

Figure 8.6 Linking controls.

- Integrates risk management activities seamlessly across the service lifecycle
- Aligns controls with business risk appetite and critical assets
- Embeds security into Enterprise Risk Management processes and reporting
- Enables dynamic, adaptive risk mitigation in a rapidly changing world

ESA not only safeguards the organisation but also boosts business agility, operational resilience and regulatory assurance.

DEVELOPING APPROPRIATE METRICS

Effective governance of ESA demands more than good intentions and robust designs. It requires systematic measurement of performance, control effectiveness and emerging risk trends.

To achieve this, organisations should establish a balanced measurement system that combines (Figure 8.7):

- *KPIs*: How well are security and risk objectives being achieved?
- *KCIs*: Are critical security controls present, operational and effective?
- *KRIs*: Are there early signs that risk exposures are increasing?

Together, KPIs, KCIs and KRIs provide a full-spectrum view of ESA's impact, health and resilience across the business and service lifecycle.

Key performance indicators

KPIs measure the outcomes of security and risk management efforts in supporting business objectives.

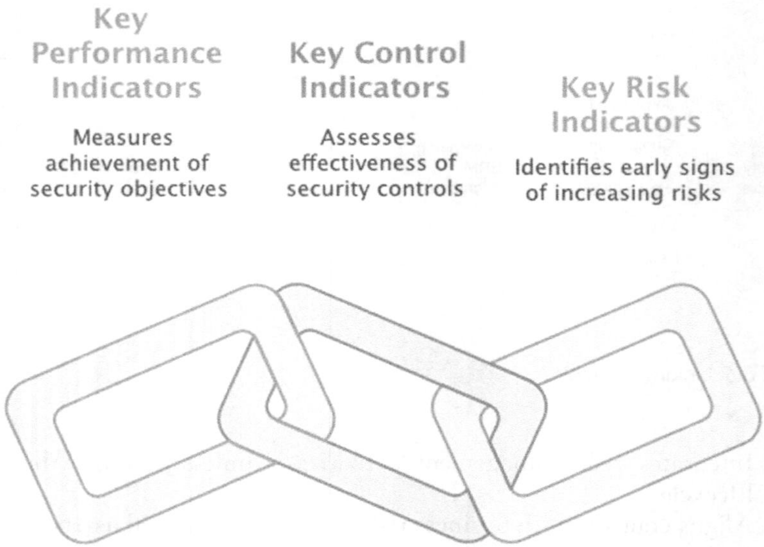

Figure 8.7 Indicators.

KPI	*Purpose*	*Example target*
Business-aligned security coverage	Percentage of critical services with risk-aligned security architectures.	95%
Compliance audit pass rate	Percentage of audits passed without significant security findings.	100% critical services pass
Security by design adoption	Percentage of projects integrating ESA principles from Planning phase onward.	90%
Risk-to-control traceability	Percentage of controls explicitly linked to business risks and regulatory obligations.	100% in high-risk areas
Reduction in reactive security work	Decrease in urgent or unplanned security interventions.	30% YoY reduction

Key Control Indicators (KCIs)

KCIs assess the presence and health of critical security controls ensuring that protective measures are operational and effective over time.

KCI	*Purpose*	*Example target*
Control validation frequency	Percentage of controls validated through technical testing (e.g., pen tests, audits).	90% validated every 6 months

(Continued)

KCI	*Purpose*	*Example target*
Vulnerability remediation SLA compliance	Percentage of critical vulnerabilities remediated within defined SLA.	95% within 48 hours
Change risk assessment completion	Percentage of change requests with completed security risk assessments.	95% of changes assessed
Control drift detection rate	Percentage of configuration changes triggering control revalidation.	100% drift events reviewed within 24 hours
Secure decommissioning compliance	Percentage of retired systems meeting secure disposal standards (e.g., NIST SP 800-88).	100%

Key Risk Indicators (KRIs)

KRIs provide early warning signals that underlying risk exposures may be increasing even before incidents or control failures occur.

KRI	*Purpose*	*Example threshold*
increase in unaddressed vulnerabilities	Growing backlog of unremediated critical vulnerabilities.	>10% rise over 30 days triggers escalation
third-party risk score changes	Decrease in security posture of key suppliers or partners.	>1 supplier downgraded to "high risk" status triggers review
policy exception requests	Spike in the number of policy waivers requested.	>20% increase QoQ prompts policy or training review
security incident frequency	Rising trend in minor security incidents (precursors to major breaches).	15% increase in minor incidents triggers readiness check
soc alert volume	Significant increase in critical SOC alerts not linked to known changes.	>20% spike over baseline requires threat hunting activity

WHY DO THESE MATTER?

All three of these metrics matter because:

Type	*Focus*	*Benefit*
KPIs	Outcome success	Demonstrate business value and achievement of security objectives
KCIs	Control assurance	Prove that critical safeguards are effective and sustainable
KRIs	Risk foresight	Enable proactive intervention before risks materialise into incidents

Together, KPIs, KCIs and KRIs allow the organisation to:

- Monitor performance
- Validate operational control effectiveness
- Detect risk escalation early
- Link security activities directly to business and regulatory expectations
- Support informed, data-driven governance decisions

Metrics and Through Life Management

Strong metrics alone are not enough; they must be tied to actionable activities across the service lifecycle. Embedding ESA principles across the Through Life Service Lifecycle ensures that security is proactively built into every phase, from planning to retirement.

Sourcing metrics from across the Through Life Service Management phases enables ESA to continuously validate control effectiveness, align security outcomes with business objectives and drive adaptive risk management throughout the full-service lifecycle. Some example metrics are below:

Through Life Phase	*KPI (performance)*	*KCI (control effectiveness)*	*KRI (emerging risk)*
Planning	% of initiatives with early security architecture involvement	% of business cases including preliminary threat models	% increase in unassessed high-impact initiatives
Design	% of designs meeting security architecture standards and business risk appetite	% of architecture reviews identifying no critical control gaps	% of designs requiring significant rework due to missed security requirements
Development	% of codebases passing secure coding and vulnerability scans before release	% of CI/CD pipelines enforcing automated security testing gates	% rise in critical vulnerabilities detected in late-stage development
Testing	% of test plans covering security and compliance validation	% of security controls validated during testing phase	% of failed critical security test cases compared to baseline
Deployment	% of deployments completing security hardening and access control validation	% of deployment checklists with security sign-off	% increase in configuration deviations at go-live compared to standards
Transition	% of transition plans including operational security monitoring and incident readiness	% of SOC onboarding activities completed before service handover	% increase in incident response gaps detected during post-transition reviews

(Continued)

Through Life Phase	*KPI (performance)*	*KCI (control effectiveness)*	*KRI (emerging risk)*
Operation	% of operational services with continuous security monitoring coverage	% of security incidents detected within SLA thresholds	% upward trend in high-severity incident frequency over baseline
Maintenance	% of maintenance activities assessed for security impact	% of patching windows meeting SLA for critical vulnerabilities	% of configuration drift alerts unresolved within 72 hours
Retirement	% of services retired following secure decommissioning procedures	% of data assets securely wiped or archived to standard	% of retirement projects missing secure data destruction validation

METRICS AND SABSA ALIGNMENT

In alignment with the SABSA methodology, measurement indicators (KPIs, KCIs and KRIs) are mapped across the architecture layers to ensure comprehensive oversight from business drivers down to operational controls.

SABSA layer	*Focus*	*Example KPI*	*Example KCI*	*Example KRI*
Contextual (business view)	Align security with business goals and objectives.	Percentage of business initiatives with defined security objectives.	Existence of security governance frameworks aligned with business strategy.	Frequency of changes in business risk appetite or regulatory landscape.
Conceptual (architect's view)	Define high-level security concepts and strategies.	Percentage of security policies derived from business objectives.	Implementation rate of security strategies across business units.	Number of identified gaps between business objectives and security strategies.
Logical (designer's view)	Design logical security components and their interactions.	Coverage percentage of systems with defined logical security models.	Rate of adherence to logical access control models.	Increase in exceptions to logical security designs.

(Continued)

SABSA layer	*Focus*	*Example KPI*	*Example KCI*	*Example KRI*
Physical (builder's view)	Translate logical designs into physical implementations.	Percentage of systems built according to physical security specifications.	Compliance rate of physical security controls with design specifications.	Number of deviations from physical security standards during implementation.
Component (tradesman's view)	Implement actual components (systems, software, vendors).	Deployment rate of components meeting security requirements.	Frequency of security configuration audits on components.	Number of security incidents linked to specific components.
Operational (manager's view)	Manage day-to-day operations, monitoring and maintenance.	Mean Time to Detect (MTTD) and Mean Time to Respond (MTTR) to security incidents.	Percentage of operational controls tested and validated regularly.	Trends in security incident volumes and types over time.

THE CHALLENGE OF PRODUCING EFFECTIVE SECURITY METRICS

Developing meaningful security metrics is inherently challenging. It requires not only identifying appropriate indicators but also ensuring the availability of high-quality, reliable data. Without accurate and timely data, metrics can lead to misguided decisions, potentially exacerbating security risks instead of mitigating them.

A mature and effective ESA is fundamental to this process. ESA provides the structured framework necessary for integrating security measures across the organisation, ensuring that data collection aligns with business objectives and risk management strategies.

Given these complexities, metrics should not be static. They must be designed, implemented and evolved to reflect the current state of the ESA and the broader security function. This iterative approach enables organisations to adapt to emerging threats, changing business landscapes and evolving regulatory requirements, ensuring that security metrics remain relevant and effective in guiding decision-making processes.

Doing metrics well is hard and is a subject deserving of a book in its own right!

A mature, business-aligned ESA programme should design and embed controls, measure performance, validate control effectiveness and anticipate emerging risks.

Using KPIs, KCIs and KRIs together ensures that ESA becomes:

- A living, measurable enabler of GRC
- A trusted source of security assurance for business leaders, risk owners and regulators
- A dynamic feedback loop supporting continuous improvement and operational resilience

This will shift the conversation from "Is security in place?" to "Is security delivering measurable risk reduction, business value and resilience?" Many CISOS consider this the Holy Grail!

INTEGRATING ESA WITH THE THROUGH LIFE LIFECYCLE – NIST, IT SERVICE LIFECYCLE AND SECURE BY DESIGN ALIGNMENT

What is the Through-Life Lifecycle?

The Through Life Lifecycle has been mentioned a few times and deserves a more comprehensive description because it is an essential component of ESA. The lifecycle below may resemble the IT Service Lifecycle, but this Through Life representation is deliberately broader and more generic. It is designed to apply across a wide range of service, solution and capability lifecycles, not just within IT service management. It reflects a complete end-to-end view, from initial strategic planning through to retirement, incorporating elements such as architecture, development, transition and ongoing operations in a way that aligns security, risk and compliance throughout (Figure 8.8).

Unlike IT Service Lifecycles, which primarily focuses on IT service management processes, this model offers a framework for integrating security and GRC practices across the enterprise's multidisciplinary delivery and operational environments. This makes it suitable for business services, digital platforms, infrastructure projects and more. It provides a flexible structure for embedding security from inception to decommission, regardless of

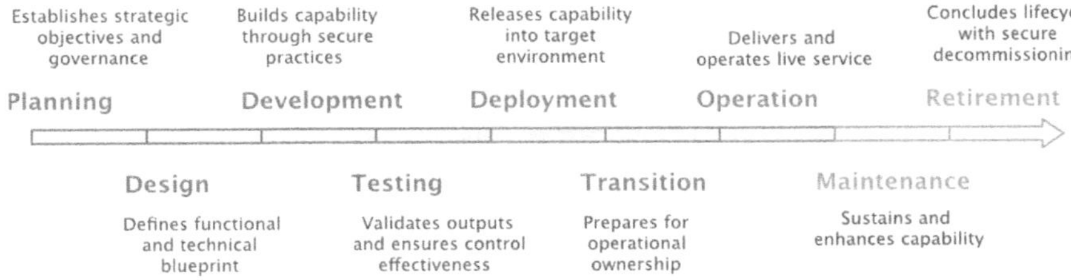

Figure 8.8 Through-Life Lifecycle.

whether the organisation follows agile, DevOps, waterfall or hybrid delivery models.

Through life phase	*General description*	*Security & GRC focused description*
Planning	Establishes strategic objectives, governance frameworks and foundational planning for services, capabilities or initiatives.	Integrates security, compliance and risk considerations into strategic planning and governance structures from the outset.
Design	Defines the functional and technical blueprint, aligning business, service and solution requirements with organisational goals.	Defines security architecture, control requirements and compliance mappings across business, technical and service layers.
Development	Builds the capability through secure development, configuration and integration of systems, processes and people.	Implements secure development practices, embeds compliance requirements and mitigates identified risks in real-time.
Testing	Validates that outputs meet defined requirements through structured testing of function, performance and resilience.	Ensures controls are effective through targeted validation of security, compliance and risk mitigations.
Deployment	Releases the capability into its target environment, ensuring it is technically sound, operationally ready and well supported.	Implements security hardening, access controls and resilience measures prior to go-live, ensuring policy conformance.
Transition	Prepares the organisation for operational ownership through knowledge transfer, validation and handover activities.	Validates post-deployment security, ensures monitoring is in place and prepares for operational incident management.
Operation	Delivers and operates the live service or capability, maintaining performance, availability and value delivery to users.	Maintains operational security controls, enforces policies and manages risk events and compliance obligations.
Maintenance	Sustains and enhances the capability through issue resolution, updates and optimisation aligned to user and business feedback.	Monitors control effectiveness, addresses vulnerabilities and adapts to evolving threats and regulatory changes.
Retirement	Concludes the lifecycle through controlled shutdown, archiving and decommissioning of systems, services and related data.	Executes secure and compliant decommissioning, including data sanitisation, access revocation and risk closure.

Security must be built into services from the start, not bolted on later. The NIST Cybersecurity Framework (CSF) 2.0's *Identify (ID)* function emphasises asset management, risk assessment and alignment with business context – all of which should be embedded throughout the lifecycle.

Too often, architects are stuck in "firefighting" mode, reviewing incomplete documentation after the design is finished or even at transition. By that point, it's too late to influence outcomes meaningfully. This reactive approach usually stems from too many projects and too few resources.

Clearly defining security activities at each stage of the lifecycle helps allocate responsibility, enhances the quality of available information and lessens the workload on architects performing assurance.

WHAT IS AN ARCHITECT?

A common challenge when building an effective ESA capability is the lack of clarity around what security architects actually do. As a result, individuals with the title often take on too much. A more effective model is to split the architectural responsibilities into three distinct roles (Figure 8.9):

- *Enterprise Security Architect*: Sets strategic direction, defines security standards and ensures consistent governance across services and initiatives.
- *Security Solutions Architect*: Works with delivery teams to embed enterprise security requirements from concept through to go-live.
- *Operational Security Architect*: Maintains and evolves the security of live services, ensuring controls remain effective until service retirement.

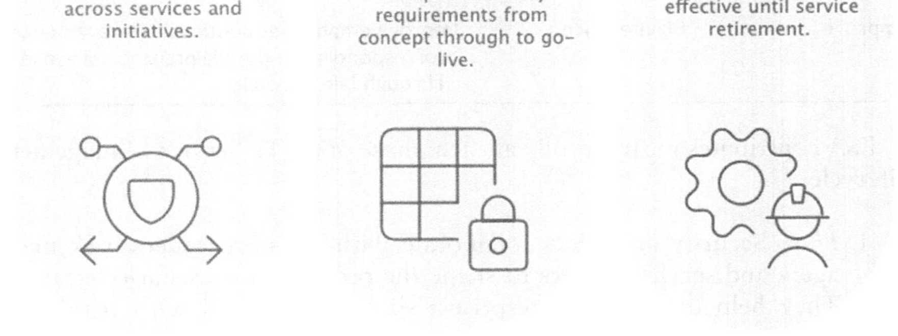

Figure 8.9 Architect roles.

This role separation also supports clearer budgeting. For instance, project teams can directly fund Security Solutions Architects and receive high-quality, delivery-focused security artefacts in return. The high-quality artefacts facilitate the assurance process and set the operational security architect up for success.

ESA ACROSS THE IT SERVICE MANAGEMENT LIFECYCLE

By integrating ESA with an IT Service Lifecycle, a unified approach to delivering secure, reliable services is created, familiar to a large proportion of organisations, as most of them use IT Service Management practices in some capacity. Rather than treating security as a compliance hurdle, it becomes a value-enabler, supporting business outcomes, improving service quality and reducing operational risk.

The IT Service Management Lifecycle maps to the Through Life lifecycle well.

Typical service management value chain activity	*Through Life Lifecycle Phase(s)*	*Notes*
Plan	Planning	Both involve establishing strategic objectives and governance frameworks.
Engage	Planning, Design	Engage encompasses stakeholder interactions, aligning with Planning and Design phases in Through Life Lifecycle.
Design & Transition	Design, development, transition	Design & transition covers the creation and deployment of services, aligning with these through life lifecycle phases.
Obtain/Build	Development	Obtain/Build focuses on acquiring and building service components, corresponding to Development in Through Life Lifecycle.
Deliver & Support	Deployment, operation	Deliver & support ensures services are delivered and supported, aligning with deployment and operation phases.
Improve	Maintenance	Improve emphasises continual improvement, corresponding to the Maintenance phase in Through Life Lifecycle.

ESA contributes meaningfully at each phase of the IT Service Management lifecycle:

1. *Plan*: Security architects collaborate with business leaders, risk managers and service owners to shape the organisation's security strategy. They help define the enterprise risk appetite, align with regulatory expectations and embed security into portfolio planning.

This stage ensures new initiatives are secure by intent, treating risk and compliance as design inputs alongside cost and value. Security architecture contributes foundational design principles that enable secure, compliant and forward-looking service planning.

2. *Engage*: Security architecture supports stakeholder engagement by aligning requirements, constraints and obligations from regulators, customers and internal governance bodies.

   Early engagement ensures that GRC obligations and risk awareness are integrated into expectations and service designs, rather than retrofitted later. Security architects often assist in vendor evaluation, contract input and third-party risk assessments, enabling trusted and transparent service relationships.
3. *Design and Transition*: This is where secure-by-design becomes real. Security architects embed controls, threat models and assurance requirements into service and solution architectures.

   They also verify implementation through risk assessments and control validation, contributing to readiness reviews and formal transition checkpoints. Their role ensures service handovers include appropriate security governance, documentation and monitoring hooks, reducing go-live friction and operational risk.
4. *Obtain and Build*: Security Solutions Architects influence the secure development lifecycle, collaborating with delivery teams to ensure that controls are built in, not bolted on.

   They align development activities with enterprise standards, automate secure coding checks and facilitate vulnerability management across environments. GRC-aligned practices are reinforced from prototype to production, minimising rework and supporting audit readiness.
5. *Deliver and Support*: Once services go live, Operational Security Architects maintain the security posture through monitoring, incident response and control validation.

   Security becomes an embedded, continuous service supporting change management, performance optimisation and event detection. This stage ensures that security contributes to availability, user trust and regulatory compliance across the live estate.
6. *Improve*: Improvement is data-driven and continuous. Security architects analyse incidents, control effectiveness and audit results to guide future-state architecture, automation and policy updates.

   This ensures security evolves with the threat landscape and keeps pace with business and technology change. By participating directly in service improvement initiatives, ESA helps maintain resilience, enable adaptive change and support smarter security investments.

The Joint Benefits of ESA-IT Service Management Integration include:

Benefit	*For ESA*	*For Service Management*
Improved alignment with business risk	Easier to prioritise security investments	Helps prioritise service enhancements based on real risk
Reduced firefighting	Fewer last-minute design changes or escalations	Smoother transitions and better go-live readiness
Reusable artefacts and processes	Standardised templates for security reviews and threat models	Consistent quality and easier audits across services
Better cost control	Architects' time is focused where it matters most	Project teams can plan and budget for security earlier
Operational resilience	Controls are monitored and improved over time	Fewer incidents and faster recovery when issues occur

By embedding ESA into the lifecycle, Service Management becomes more proactive, risk-informed and resilient while ESA becomes more integrated, effective and business-aligned.

ALIGNMENT WITH NCSC SECURE BY DESIGN

The NCSC's Secure by Design principles strengthen this model by encouraging early, continuous security decisions. Its focus on operational resilience, threat-informed architecture and automation directly supports ESA.

Key principles include:

1. *Establish the Context before Designing a System*: Understand the system's purpose, environment and potential threats to inform a secure design.
2. *Make Compromise Difficult*: Implement measures to prevent unauthorised access and reduce vulnerabilities.
3. *Make Disruption Difficult*: Design systems to resist denial-of-service attacks and maintain availability.
4. *Make Detection Easy*: Ensure that security breaches can be quickly identified through effective monitoring and logging.
5. *Reduce the Impact of Compromise*: Limit the potential damage from security incidents through compartmentalisation and least privilege.
6. *Design for Usability, Manageability and Verifiability*: Create systems that are user-friendly, easy to manage and whose security can be verified.
7. *Design for Operational Resilience*: Ensure systems can continue to operate under adverse conditions and recover quickly from disruptions.

8. *Automate where Possible*: Use automation tools like Infrastructure as Code (IaC) validation, Software Bill of Materials (SBOM) checks and CI/CD-integrated scanning to enforce secure defaults and reduce human error.

These principles support ESA and GRC by embedding security considerations throughout the Through Life Lifecycle, from strategy and design to operation and continual improvement.

Here are some examples of how aligning ESA with the lifecycle meets the Secure by Design requirements.

Lifecycle phase	*Enterprise security architecture considerations*	*NCSC secure by design alignment*
Planning	Define enterprise security objectives, governance and risk appetite. ESA, SSA and OSA define current and target states.	Embed security and privacy by default. Threat modelling and resilience planning are foundational activities.
Design	Architect services with embedded controls (encryption, zoning, identity). SSA leads detailed design. ESA assures alignment.	Design for operational security, monitoring, logging and secure management are considered essential design elements.
Development	Embed secure coding, privacy engineering, policy-driven development. CI/CD security is integrated. OSA ensures ops viability.	Use automated code scanning, SBOM generation and dependency management to reduce attack surface early.
Build	Implement hardened infrastructure with automated validation. SSA and OSA guide secure builds.	Enforce secure configurations via Infrastructure as Code. Validate baseline images for known vulnerabilities.
Testing	Perform threat modelling, SAST/DAST, compliance testing and risk validation. All roles ensure fidelity to enterprise needs.	Security verification is continuous. Build pipelines must include automated test gates and config drift detection.
Deployment	Apply secure release protocols, access enforcement and live config validation. SSA leads security go-live.	Default-deny principles and identity-aware deployment are embedded. Secrets management and logging are configured before go-live.
Transition	Transfer operational readiness, enable SIEM/SOC onboarding and incident response alignment. ESA ensures traceability.	Secure handover includes playbooks, alert mappings and documented security architecture context.
Operation	Monitor threats, respond to incidents, manage vulnerabilities. OSA ensures real-time readiness.	Logging, detection and response capabilities are active and routinely exercised. Ops staff are trained on secure operations.

(Continued)

Lifecycle phase	*Enterprise security architecture considerations*	*NCSC secure by design alignment*
Maintenance	Patch and review controls. ESA/OSA support secure change governance.	Patching windows and config drift are tracked. Security decisions and assumptions are periodically revalidated.
Retirement	Securely decommission services and data. Plan for revocation and auditability.	Decommissioning is designed to preserve confidentiality and integrity. Secure deletion, offboarding and verification are automated.

The NCSC Secure by Design requirements are fulfilled by integrating ESA into the Service Lifecycle. It meets the compliance requirement and enables better through-life management of risks.

ENSURING AUDIT READINESS WITH LIFECYCLE INTEGRATION

In a truly operationalised security architecture, audit readiness is not an event but a continuous state.

Rather than treating audits as stressful, last-minute exercises in documentation gathering and firefighting, organisations should build assurance activities naturally into the service lifecycle.

Each phase of the Through Life Service Lifecycle presents an opportunity to create verifiable evidence that security controls are planned, implemented, operated and maintained effectively:

- Planning and Design phases should produce traceable security requirements and risk assessments that demonstrate intent and coverage.
- Development and Testing activities should generate validation artefacts such as threat models, test results and control verification as normal outputs of delivery, not special one-off exercises.
- Deployment and Transition processes should include formal security handover artefacts, operational procedures, monitoring integrations and escalation paths that prove control readiness for operations.
- Operation and Maintenance phases should produce continuous monitoring logs, evidence of vulnerability management and incident management records as a natural part of service delivery.
- Retirement activities should include secure decommissioning documentation that validates data protection, access revocation and risk closure.

Audit readiness becomes much easier when operational teams understand that their daily activities, such as patching, monitoring, access reviews and configuration management, are not only good security practices but also critical assurance activities.

Service Level Agreements (SLAs) for security services, such as incident response times or patching windows, and Protection Level Agreements (PLAs) for data confidentiality or system resilience, should be designed to naturally align operational commitments with regulatory and risk-based obligations.

By doing this:

- Compliance reporting can be largely automated based on real operational data.
- Assurance evidence can be pulled dynamically from operational platforms rather than manually recreated during audits.
- The effort and disruption caused by audits can be dramatically reduced, freeing resources for proactive improvement.

Building audit readiness into the lifecycle means moving away from static, point-in-time control reviews.

Instead, it requires:

- Continuous control validation includes regular vulnerability scanning, configuration drift detection and access rights reviews.
- Real-time reporting dashboards that demonstrate control status, incidents and risk mitigation activities on demand.
- Feedback loops that ensure lessons learned from incidents, changes and audits continuously refine security architecture and operational practices.

This approach ensures that compliance is not only achieved but also sustained, demonstrating a culture of accountability, resilience and continuous improvement to regulators, auditors and stakeholders.

To ensure audit readiness through lifecycle integration:

- Treat assurance as a continuous operational activity, not a periodic scramble.
- Design services and security architectures to produce audit evidence as natural outputs.
- Align operational security activities directly to regulatory and risk-based obligations.
- Automate control validation and reporting wherever possible.
- Use audits as opportunities to strengthen resilience, not just to satisfy checklists.

Audit readiness becomes a by-product of delivering well-governed, secure and resilient services, not an additional burden.

MAKING GRC OPERATIONAL

Turning Governance, Risk and Compliance (GRC) strategy into day-to-day operational reality is one of the most important and often the most challenging aspects of security architecture. It requires embedding risk awareness, enforcing controls and integrating assurance activities directly into the operational fabric of the business, rather than treating them as external add-ons.

Operationalising Risk in Change Management

Change is a significant vector for introducing new risks.

Operational GRC requires security architects and risk managers to integrate security risk assessments directly into change processes not as afterthoughts, but as standard steps that evaluate how each proposed change could impact confidentiality, integrity, availability, privacy or regulatory obligations.

Risk-based decision-making must become a natural part of change governance. It should help teams prioritise changes that align with their business risk appetite while identifying those that require extra scrutiny, mitigation or delay.

Embedding Risk and Assurance into Incident Management

Security incidents are inevitable, but reactive firefighting should not be.

An operational GRC model requires incident response processes tightly linked to risk prioritisation. Response actions should be guided by business impact, ensuring that resources focus first on incidents that threaten critical services, compliance obligations or organisational reputation.

Assurance activities such as forensic readiness, evidence collection and post-incident reviews should be embedded within operational practices to create learning loops and improve resilience over time.

Streamlining Compliance through Operational Asset Intelligence

Maintaining compliance is difficult without clear, dynamic visibility into assets, configurations and responsibilities.

Operational GRC demands that asset management is not a static inventory exercise, but a live, continuously updated system of record that identifies:

- Business ownership
- Security classification
- Compliance obligations
- Risk relevance

By tagging and tracking assets according to their criticality and regulatory exposure, organisations can automate compliance reporting, accelerate audit readiness and focus assurance activities on what matters most.

Creating Self-Reinforcing Security Capabilities

The end goal of operational GRC is to create self-reinforcing security behaviours:

- Risk thinking becomes intuitive for engineers, service owners and operations teams.
- Control monitoring becomes continuous through automation and intelligent analytics.
- Compliance becomes a by-product of good architecture and sound operational hygiene, not a separate audit-driven activity.

Achieving this goal means that security is no longer perceived as a blocker or an external policing function but instead becomes part of how high-quality, resilient services are delivered daily.

To make GRC operational:

- Risk assessment must be embedded into every change, decision and delivery.
- Incident response must be risk-driven and assurance-focused.
- Compliance must be automated wherever possible, driven by accurate asset intelligence.
- Security must be integrated into service and business operations' culture, behaviours and daily workflows.

Only then can GRC become a proactive enabler of business value rather than a reactive burden.

ADAPTIVE SECURITY ARCHITECTURES

Modern enterprise environments are dynamic, complex and constantly under threat.

Static security architectures built once and left unchanged are no longer fit for purpose. To maintain resilience and compliance over time, security architectures must be adaptive by design, evolving with changing risk landscapes, business needs and technological advancements.

The goal of adaptive security architecture is not simply to prevent breaches, but to anticipate, withstand, respond to and recover from threats with minimal human intervention.

This requires embedding capabilities that:

- Continuously monitor system health and security posture.
- Detect anomalous behaviours that indicate potential compromise.
- Trigger automated defensive responses such as access revocation, segmentation or reconfiguration.
- Prioritise recovery actions based on critical business impacts.

For example, adaptive security can be applied to cloud-native environments by deploying self-healing container clusters that automatically isolate compromised nodes and initiate auto-scaling clean replacements without human intervention, maintaining service resilience under attack.

By building "self-healing" capabilities into infrastructure, applications and services, organisations can move from reactive incident response to proactive resilience.

Risk decisions cannot wait for manual reviews in an adaptive security model.

Organisations should empower systems to:

- Re-evaluate access rights based on real-time contextual signals (e.g., device trust, geolocation, behavioural anomalies).
- Adjust protection levels dynamically based on threat intelligence feeds and emerging risk indicators.
- Implement micro segmentation, policy adjustments or workload isolation automatically in response to shifting conditions.

Adaptive architectures align protection efforts with real-time business risk, maintaining security at the pace of change.

Adaptive security depends on more than static controls; it requires integrating intelligence, analytics and automation into day-to-day operations.

Examples include:

- Automated vulnerability scanning tied directly to patching workflows.
- Continuous compliance validation integrated into DevOps pipelines.
- Machine learning models predicting likely attack paths or insider threat behaviours.
- Risk scoring of third-party suppliers based on dynamic assessments, not annual checklists.

These capabilities allow security operations to be faster and smarter, improving decision-making without overwhelming human teams.

Adaptive security is not just a technical enhancement; it is a business resilience strategy.

By embedding dynamic security into services and platforms:

- Digital transformation initiatives can move faster without unacceptable risk exposure.
- Regulatory obligations around privacy, data protection and operational resilience can be met more reliably.
- Customer trust and brand reputation can be better protected against fast-moving threats.

Adaptive security turns architecture into a strategic differentiator, enabling the organisation to move confidently through complex, evolving environments.

Adaptive security architecture is built on three pillars:

- Proactive defence and autonomous recovery systems anticipate, resist and heal without waiting for manual interventions.
- Risk-driven, dynamic decision-making protection measures align with current threats and business priorities in real time.
- Intelligence-led automation, analytics and machine learning drive smarter, faster operational responses.

This ensures that ESA remains effective at the point of design and throughout the lifecycle of services, technologies and business models.

STRATEGIC IMPLEMENTATION ROADMAP

Transforming ESA from a conceptual strategy into a dynamic, operational reality requires a structured but adaptable approach.

The goal is not to pursue compliance for its own sake, but to embed security governance, risk management and continuous assurance into the fabric of business and service operations.

Step 1: Assess maturity and identify gaps

Start by understanding where you are today.

Assess the maturity of your current security architecture practices in terms of:

- Business alignment
- Risk integration
- Lifecycle coverage
- Operational control validation
- Continuous improvement capability

Gap analysis should be attribute-driven, focus on what the business needs to protect and enable, and compare those needs against existing architectural, control, and operational practices.

Prioritise gaps that expose the organisation to the most significant risk or undermine key business objectives.

Step 2: Design for integration and adaptability

Security architecture must be designed not just for compliance, but for resilience, scalability and business adaptability.

Design principles should ensure that ESA:

- Embeds security into service lifecycles from inception to retirement.
- Aligns with operational workflows, not stands apart from them.
- Can flex and scale in response to business change and emerging threats.

Integration is key. ESA must plug seamlessly into service management, risk governance, development and digital transformation initiatives.

Step 3: Embed risk and compliance as dynamic, continuous activities

Risk and compliance management must move from point-in-time activities to continuous, embedded processes.

This requires:

- Integrating risk evaluation into project governance, change management and service operations.
- Automating compliance evidence generation through operational tooling wherever possible.
- Establishing real-time risk visibility, not just after-the-fact reporting.

By doing so, organisations create a living, breathing GRC capability that adapts with the business rather than lagging behind it.

Step 4: Accelerate with automation and intelligence

Manual security operations cannot keep pace with complex, evolving environments.

Adaptive ESA must leverage:

- Automation of repetitive assurance activities (e.g., requirements development, configuration checks, access reviews, compliance reporting).

- Intelligence-driven insights (e.g., threat intelligence integration, predictive vulnerability management, real-time risk scoring).
- Orchestration of security responses based on dynamic business impact assessments.

The goal is to increase both speed and quality – detecting issues faster, resolving them sooner and continuously improving control effectiveness.

Step 5: Build deep, sustainable expertise

Security architecture must be supported by teams who understand both technical depth and business value. Investment in skills development is essential:

- Train architects not just in technology, but in risk management, governance and operational resilience.
- Develop multidisciplinary expertise that spans security, service management, compliance and enterprise risk.
- Create clear career paths and organisational structures that support ESA as a business-critical function, not just a technical discipline.

Security architects must be equipped to speak the language of business, risk and value, not just the language of controls and threats.

Step 6: Evolve through continuous learning and improvement

Finally, ESA must not be a "set and forget" initiative.

Establish mechanisms for continuous learning:

- Use incidents, audit findings, regulatory changes and business feedback as catalysts for architectural refinement.
- Regularly revisit risk assumptions, threat models and protection priorities.
- Benchmark progress against meaningful KPIs, KCIs and KRIs – not just compliance checklists.

In an adaptive organisation, ESA evolves alongside the business, becoming stronger, smarter and more valuable.

MANAGING THE COST OF ENTERPRISE SECURITY ARCHITECTURE RESOURCES

Enterprise Security Architects are among the most in-demand and costly resources in the security profession today.

Their skills, combining technical depth, business acumen and risk management expertise, are both rare and critical for enabling effective Governance, Risk and Compliance (GRC) outcomes.

However, architects can easily become overburdened with administrative tasks, operational reporting, service management coordination and non-architectural activities without careful workload management. This dilutes their effectiveness, delays strategic work and increases the number of architects required to meet demand, driving up costs without delivering proportional value.

To maximise the benefit of ESA resources while controlling costs, organisations should:

- Delegate non-architectural tasks to lower-cost roles such as service coordinators, security administrators, GRC analysts or operational support staff.
- Centralise workload management by having a dedicated function track project allocations, deliverable deadlines and stakeholder interactions, freeing architects to focus on higher-value activities.
- Outsource or automate operational reporting and metrics collection where possible, allowing architects to contribute insights rather than compile data manually.
- Integrate ESA support into service management teams, ensuring that operational roles handle routine escalations, meeting scheduling and change management tracking.

By systematically offloading administrative and coordination activities to non-architectural roles, organisations can:

- Increase the effective output per architect.
- Improve the quality and consistency of architectural deliverables.
- Reduce architectural bottlenecks in projects and service management.
- Minimise the total number of architects needed to deliver high-quality security architecture outcomes across the enterprise.

Architects, in general, are inherently inquisitive and enjoy solving problems; consequently, they can easily become distracted by the next challenge. Implementing task management oversight ensures that work is completed on time and meets the desired quality.

When freed from administrative burden, Security Architects can:

- Focus on strategic security planning, risk-driven design and GRC integration.
- Provide deeper engagement with critical initiatives and executive stakeholders.
- Deliver higher-value artefacts that strengthen assurance, resilience and business alignment.

This not only optimises operational costs but also ensures that ESA is seen as a high-impact, high-value enabler of business and risk objectives, not simply a technical overhead.

Strategic implementation of ESA is not a linear project; it is an ongoing organisational capability development journey.

It requires:

- Clear vision aligned to business resilience and risk appetite.
- Practical integration into operations and service delivery.
- Dynamic risk and compliance management embedded into workflows.
- Smart use of automation and intelligence to scale security effectiveness.
- Continuous investment in expertise, learning and improvement.

When executed thoughtfully, ESA becomes a core enabler of GRC, delivering security by design, resilience by default and business value by intent.

TRANSFORMING ESA INTO A STRATEGIC ASSET

For too long, ESA, when recognised at all, has been seen as a technical discipline operating at the margins of business strategy.

In a modern, digitally driven, risk-aware organisation, ESA must be positioned and treated as a core strategic asset that directly enables business resilience, operational agility and sustained regulatory confidence.

True transformation occurs when ESA moves beyond static frameworks and compliance-driven controls and becomes:

- A living architecture that evolves dynamically with business needs and risk environments.
- A trusted advisor to executive leadership, translating complex technical risks into clear, actionable business insights.
- A risk management engine, embedding proactive threat anticipation and continuous control validation into every service lifecycle.
- A resilience catalyst, ensuring that critical services and digital platforms can withstand and recover from disruption without loss of trust or value.

A mature, strategically aligned ESA:

- Protects business-critical assets without slowing innovation or customer experience.
- Reduces operational risk exposure by embedding risk-aware decision-making into service planning, change management and operations.
- Accelerates compliance readiness by automating assurance activities and linking them naturally to service operations.

- Enables faster, smarter recovery from incidents and disruptions through embedded resilience and architectural foresight.
- Optimises security investment by focusing protection where it delivers the greatest business impact, avoiding overengineering and waste.

A strategic ESA serves not merely as a cost centre, but as a catalyst for enhancing business performance, trust and competitive edge.

The journey to strategic ESA is not quick and does not end with initial implementation.

Ongoing success demands:

- Continuous alignment with evolving business goals, regulatory landscapes and threat models.
- Investment in architectural excellence, automation and intelligence-driven operations.
- A governance model that treats security architecture as an enterprise-wide capability, not a project-by-project consulting service.
- Cultural integration, where business leaders, risk owners and service managers view security architecture as an essential partner in achieving business success.

Organisations that embrace ESA as a strategic asset will:

- Move faster and more securely into new markets and digital opportunities.
- Manage risk proactively, with fewer surprises and lower costs.
- Build stronger relationships with regulators, partners and customers based on demonstrable trust and resilience.
- Turn security architecture from a defensive obligation into a proactive source of strategic advantage.

Organisations that succeed in the changing landscape of digital risk and resilience will view security architecture as necessary for confident and sustainable business growth, rather than a limitation.

SUMMARY

ESA has evolved into a critical strategic capability that aligns security controls with business objectives, proactively manages risk and ensures continuous compliance and operational resilience.

This chapter demonstrates how ESA must move beyond technical compliance frameworks to become a living, business-driven function that embeds security governance into every phase of the service lifecycle.

Key takeaways include:

- *Positioning ESA as a Strategic Business Function*: ESA must directly support governance, risk management, compliance and resilience objectives, not operate as a siloed technical discipline.
- *Embedding Security across the Through Life Service Lifecycle*: Security and risk management must be integrated from planning and design through to operation, maintenance and secure retirement.
- *Risk-Centric, Lifecycle-Driven Security*: ESA must prioritise business-aligned risk management activities across service phases, moving beyond point-in-time compliance to continuous assurance and adaptive resilience.
- *Metrics-Driven Governance*: Using KPIs, KCIs and KRIs aligned to SABSA architectural layers enables organisations to continuously validate security effectiveness and proactively manage risk exposure.
- *Operationalising GRC*: Governance, risk and compliance must become embedded in everyday operations, with assurance activities integrated into change management, incident response and service maintenance practices.
- *Building Adaptive Security Architectures*: Future-ready ESA must incorporate intelligence-led, automated and self-healing capabilities to align protection dynamically with evolving threats and business priorities.
- *Maximising Architectural Impact and Efficiency*: By managing costs and freeing architects from administrative overheads, organisations can optimise ESA output, strengthen architectural quality and reduce resourcing needs.
- *Transforming ESA into a Core Strategic Asset*: Organisations that view ESA as a business enabler – not just a security requirement – will move faster, manage risk more effectively, strengthen regulatory trust and sustain competitive advantage.

When implemented thoughtfully and continually enhanced, ESA acts as a driver for assured, sustainable business growth, providing quantifiable resilience, trust and value throughout the entire service lifecycle.

NOTE

1. This publication contains material subject to third-party intellectual property rights:
   SABSA methodology references used with permission of The SABSA Institute C.I.C. SABSA® is a registered trademark of The SABSA Institute.
   Contains public sector information licensed under the Open Government Licence v3.0.

Chapter 9

Developing assurance programmes and controls

Compliance and assurance are no longer supplementary functions within organisations; they are a cornerstone of sustainable and ethical business practices. Compliance in this chapter is used as shorthand for both terms. Developing robust compliance programmes and controls has become essential for managing risks, safeguarding reputations and ensuring long-term success with increasing regulatory scrutiny and complex legal frameworks. Periodic updates to risk assessments ensure that compliance efforts remain aligned with evolving operational and regulatory landscapes.

Effective compliance programmes require clear, actionable policies and procedures tailored to an organisation's unique needs. Policies should target identified risks and designate ownership for their implementation and monitoring. Aligning these policies with relevant regulations ensures comprehensive coverage of legal obligations. Defining acceptable practices and using accessible language helps employees understand their responsibilities, while mechanisms for regular updates ensure policies remain relevant and effective.

Core compliance policy areas typically include anti-bribery measures, data privacy regulations, conflict of interest management, whistleblowing protections and acceptable use of technology. Making these policies readily accessible fosters an environment of transparency and accountability, empowering employees to adhere to organisational standards. Furthermore, integrating policy compliance into performance metrics can incentivise adherence and embed compliance into the organisational culture.

This short chapter explores the essential components of compliance programmes, from conducting risk assessments to managing third-party relationships.

TRAINING EMPLOYEES

Employee training is essential for embedding compliance into organisational culture. Regular training ensures employees understand policies, recognise risks and act ethically. Annual training programmes should be updated as regulations evolve, and role-specific content can address risks unique to

 DOI: 10.1201/9781003543992-10

different positions. Using diverse formats, such as online courses, in-person workshops and quizzes, keeps training engaging and effective.

Introducing compliance principles during new hire orientations establishes a baseline understanding for all employees. Providing accessible resources and involving senior management in training sessions underscores the importance of compliance. Evaluating training effectiveness through feedback and behavioural changes helps refine future programmes, ensuring continuous improvement. Incorporating real-world scenarios and case studies into training can further enhance employee understanding of complex compliance issues.

MONITORING AND AUDITING COMPLIANCE PROGRAMMES

Ongoing monitoring and auditing are crucial for maintaining effective compliance programmes. Activities such as policy attestation, employee surveys, transaction testing and communication reviews help identify gaps and assess the effectiveness of policies. Key Risk Indicators (KRIs) provide valuable insights into trends and anomalies, while internal and external audits offer objective evaluations of compliance processes. Empowering departments to conduct control self-assessments encourages ownership of compliance responsibilities and fosters a proactive approach to risk management.

Findings from monitoring and auditing activities should inform management reports, highlighting areas for improvement and ensuring transparency. Addressing identified gaps promptly reinforces organisational commitment to ethical practices and regulatory adherence. Additionally, integrating automated compliance tools into monitoring processes can streamline reporting and improve the accuracy of compliance metrics.

RESPONDING TO INCIDENTS

Even the most robust compliance programmes cannot eliminate all risks. Clear procedures must be established for addressing compliance incidents. Reporting mechanisms, such as confidential hotlines or online platforms, enable employees to report concerns without fear of reprisal. Incidents should be triaged based on severity, with protocols in place for thorough investigations.

Root cause analysis identifies underlying issues, guiding corrective actions to prevent recurrence. Implementing new controls, enhancing training and applying consistent disciplinary measures demonstrate accountability. Where necessary, organisations must fulfil legal and regulatory obligations for disclosure, maintaining transparency with stakeholders. Using lessons learned from incidents to strengthen the compliance programme ensures continual improvement and resilience. Regular post-incident reviews and stakeholder feedback loops further enhance the organisation's ability to prevent future occurrences.

MANAGING THIRD-PARTY COMPLIANCE RISK

As organisations increasingly rely on third parties, managing vendor compliance has become a critical component of compliance programmes. Due diligence processes should evaluate vendors' ownership, financial stability, compliance history and industry risks. Contractual provisions can specify regulatory requirements, allow audits and define penalties for noncompliance.

Ongoing oversight ensures that vendors maintain compliance over time. Regular performance reviews, periodic attestations and audits help organisations monitor third-party adherence to contractual obligations. Additionally, leveraging technology such as vendor management platforms can provide real-time visibility into third-party compliance status and streamline oversight activities.

BEST PRACTICES

To ensure success, compliance programmes must receive ongoing support from senior leadership and be integrated across organisational functions. Visible support from the CEO and board demonstrates commitment, while allocating sufficient financial and human resources ensures programme effectiveness. Centralised oversight under a Chief Compliance Officer facilitates coordination and consistency.

Leveraging technology, such as compliance software and data analytics, streamlines processes and enhances efficiency. Regular evaluations of the compliance programme, informed by stakeholder feedback and regulatory changes, enable continuous optimisation. Integrating compliance into the organisational fabric fosters a culture of ethical behaviour and regulatory adherence, ensuring sustainable growth. Additionally, promoting cross-departmental collaboration in compliance initiatives can improve alignment and foster a shared sense of accountability across the organisation.

CONCLUSION

Developing and managing compliance programmes and controls is a multifaceted endeavour that requires commitment, adaptability and collaboration. By conducting thorough risk assessments, establishing clear policies, investing in training and maintaining vigilant oversight, organisations can build robust compliance frameworks. These efforts not only safeguard against regulatory risks but also foster trust among stakeholders, paving the way for sustainable growth in an increasingly complex world.

Expanding compliance beyond traditional boundaries requires continuous innovation and proactive adaptation to emerging risks. Leveraging advanced technologies, fostering a culture of transparency and engaging in cross-industry collaborations will position organisations to excel in a dynamic regulatory environment. Ultimately, effective compliance programmes serve as a foundation for ethical business practices and long-term organisational success.

Chapter 10

Standards and frameworks

I want to take a break and start off this chapter differently with a short story. In too many companies still these days the security function gets handed to IT. Or to someone in IT. Let's follow that thread and begin. A young systems administrator finds themself immersed in the complex realm of information security standards. Tasked with developing a comprehensive security framework for their organisation, she recruits a colleague from her team and they delve into the intricacies of ISO 27001 and ISO 27002.

As they begin their research, our protagonists quickly discovers that ISO 27001 is a renowned international standard that outlines the requirements for establishing, implementing, maintaining and continually improving an Information Security Management System (ISMS). It focuses on managing risks to ensure the confidentiality, integrity and availability of sensitive information within an organisation. Excited by this newfound knowledge, they embrace the challenge of creating a robust ISMS based on ISO 27001. However, as they dig deeper into their research, they stumble upon ISO 27002.

ISO 27002 catches their attention as it complements and expands upon the implementation guidance provided in ISO 27001. Our protagonists realise that while ISO 27001 provides the framework for an effective ISMS, ISO 27002 offers a comprehensive set of best practices and controls to help mitigate specific security risks.

They become engrossed in understanding the differences between these two standards. They carefully examine each control outlined in ISO 27002 to determine how it aligns with the risk management approach defined in ISO 27001. They start mapping out how these controls can be implemented within their organisation to enhance its overall security posture.

Throughout this journey, they encounter various challenges and dilemmas. They grapple with striking a balance between adhering strictly to the requirements of ISO 27001 while leveraging the additional insights provided by ISO 27002. They also face resistance from certain stakeholders who find implementing these standards burdensome or unnecessary.

However, armed with their newfound knowledge and unwavering determination, they manage to overcome these obstacles. Through careful persuasion

DOI: 10.1201/9781003543992-11

and collaboration with key stakeholders, they successfully integrate both ISO 27001 and ISO 27002 into their organisation's security framework.

In the end, they emerge as knowledgeable and respected cybersecurity professionals, admired for their ability to navigate the complexities of information security standards. Their organisation thrives under the robust ISMS they established, safeguarding valuable information against potential threats.

As the story concludes, our initial person reflects on her journey and the lessons learned. She realises that while ISO 27001 provides a solid foundation for information security management, it is the combination of both ISO 27001 and ISO 27002 that truly enables organisations to build a resilient and secure environment in today's ever-evolving digital landscape.

KEY FACTS

ISO 27001 is an international standard published by the International Organisation for Standardization (ISO) for implementing and certifying an effective ISMS in an organisation. It provides a model to proactively manage information security risks. It helps organisations manage and protect their information assets through a systematic approach to identifying, assessing and addressing information security risks. Some of the information security areas covered by ISO 27001 include physical, technical and organisational controls for access control, cryptography, operations security, communications security, system acquisition and more.

To achieve certification, an organisation's ISMS is audited by an accredited third-party certification body against the ISO 27001 standard requirements. Certifications are valid for 3 years and require annual surveillance audits and re-certification at the end of the third year.

The key components of an ISO 27001 ISMS are:

- Information security policies and procedures
- Organisation of information security (roles and responsibilities)
- Human resources security
- Asset management
- Access control
- Cryptography
- Physical and environmental security
- Operations security
- Communications security
- System acquisition, development and maintenance
- Supplier relationships
- Information security incident management
- Business continuity management
- Compliance with legal requirements

The benefits of ISO 27001 certification include:

- Independent validation of information security controls
- Increased credibility and trust with customers and partners
- Competitive advantage in bids and tenders
- Baseline, and I stress baselines, alignment to industry best practices

What does this mean for companies?

Forward-thinking organisations are evolving their view of the ISO 27001 information security standard from a check-box compliance and risk management burden to a mechanism that enables business initiatives, uplifts governance and provides competitive differentiation. This shift requires a holistic mindset across processes, intrinsically embedding security along with quantifying the customer trust, revenue enablement and cost optimisation benefits.

Remember, security moves from being perceived as only driving cost and limiting agility into a value-add by taking an expansive approach beyond a traditional risk lens. Several key opportunities exist to leverage an ISMS as a business positive spanning leadership vision, product development, partnership models and corporate governance.

First, executive leadership plays a vital role in embedding security intrinsically from the initial stages by setting the vision and budget priorities. An ISMS can shift left into product lifecycles from secure design practices to privacy-preserving features which market demands. Building security in from concept including layered controls for sensitive data avoids extensive delays from rework downstream once products get customer traction. It also reduces technical debt accumulation from corner-cutting projects to meet accelerated launch timelines. Showcasing adherence to codes of practice further engenders client confidence and trust in the brand promise.

Second, mature security controls and cyber hygiene foster a wide array of third-party business partnerships given extensive global digital ecosystems. Especially where suppliers handle sensitive client data, integrating technologies into core delivery platforms or provide crucial business process outsourcing, robust assessments and contractual protections are paramount. Validating vendor security posture eases expansion into new geographies and collaboration scenarios without heightening risk exposure. Promoting ISO 27001 compliance also creates preference in regulated sectors like finance, healthcare and energy where baseline standards from Request for Proposal (RFP) criteria.

Third, an integrated information security model provides enriched visibility into operational risks allowing leadership to make judicious technology investments. The CISO can guide resilience upgrades by right-sizing controls across various scenarios and business units by weighing application vulnerabilities, infrastructure weaknesses, skill gaps and process lapses. Threat modelling allows balance between security and unrestrained innovation through sustainable frameworks mapped to risk appetite. Furthermore, a systemic approach facilitates expansion into global markets by allowing rigorous compliance mapping against complex and evolving regional regulations. From EU's GDPR to Hong Kong's Privacy Commissioner rules around customer data, each has nuances on breach notification, coding practices and data sovereignty. Likewise, scalable security smooths rapid merger and acquisition cycles by quickly onboarding products, systems and teams through baseline control integration.

On governance, embedding ISO 27001 into strategic plans, budget processes and leadership incentives sustains focus beyond periodic audit checklists. Regular security health reporting into board meetings and executive dashboards provides visibility enabling risk-aware decisions. Ultimately, the commercial benefits manifest through accelerated speed to market, reduced liability buffers, optimised audit costs and preference in prospect selection processes.

Forward thinking leadership therefore has a tremendous opportunity to shift dialogues through messaging and embedding security into processes transforming its positioning as a business driver rather than ancillary function. The outcomes span engendering customer trust, enhanced governance through metrics-based performance dialogues, streamlined innovation cycles and responsible risk balancing.

TERMINOLOGY

Before we continue, we need to take a few minutes to understand the terminology used with regards to establishing leadership commitment not just in ISO but also other Standards. For this, let's turn to another ISO Standard, namely 27014 whose guidelines establish leading practices for instituting information security governance supporting business strategy protection across organisations. It articulates models for senior leadership steering security policies, resource prioritisation plus performance monitoring upholding mission resilience.

- *Business Alignment*: Embed security protection into core strategic documents like vision statements, operating plans and technology architectures validating necessity supporting corporate goals.
- *Metrics Integration*: Incorporate security key performance indicators (KPIs) into enterprise dashboards for financial risk status, operations resilience metrics and leaderships scorecards expanding visibility.
- *Security Charter*: Publish an official security charter document endorsed visibly by top management codifying programme mission, roles and ongoing commitment.
- *Standards Mandates*: Issue executive support on formal regulations like data protection laws as well as voluntary frameworks validating leadership buy in enforcing adequate resourcing for compliance needs.
- *Public Commitment*: Leverage avenues like annual report narratives, leadership page profiles on company websites highlighting security and data stewardship given reputational exposure.

- *Third Party Security*: Issue procurement guidelines and vendor management policies stressing security requirements in external partnerships protecting critical assets by design upfront.
- *Chief Information Security Officer*: Appoint dedicated senior leadership through a Chief Information Security Officer role empowered by board commitment steers strategies balancing innovation and protection.
- *Security Forum*: Establishes a cross functional security forum with executive membership providing oversight, standards ratification, budget approval and risk acceptance decisions upholding policies guardrails.
- *Distributed Data/System Owners*: Embed data owners and system administrators formally into architecture owning asset classification plus technical control implementation upholding corporate security policy locally.

Having set these understanding, let us delve into more detail about ISO 27001, building upon what was established previously.

ISO 27001 ANNEX A AND 27002

27001 has an Annex of controls and there is also 27002. So, what is the relationship?

ISO 27001 is the formal specification for an ISMS. It defines requirements for implementing, monitoring, maintaining and continually improving an ISMS. Annex A is a specific part of the ISO 27001 standard that outlines the security control objectives and provides guidelines for the recommended security controls. However, Annex A does not contain the actual details or implementation guidance for the security controls themselves. It only lists the control objectives.

This is where ISO 27002 comes in. It serves as a companion guide to ISO 27001 by providing code of practice for information security controls. ISO 27002 takes the control objectives outlined in Annex A and expands each one with implementation guidance. For example, Annex A can state an objective like "Information access control policy." ISO 27002 provides guidance and procedures to meet that objective.

So in summary, 27001 Annex A defines WHAT should be achieved – the information security control objectives. 27002 defines HOW to achieve it – the detailed control implementation guidance

BEST PRACTICES FOR STARTING AN ISO 27001 IMPLEMENTATION PROJECT

A previous company of mine followed a five step process, which comes from a UK-based company called Inavate. I highly recommend getting in touch with

Inavate if you require consultancy at any stage of your ISO 27001 journey. Without revealing the inner workings of their approach, think through the following:

Understand the company and its context. You determine the Scope, define the Security Policy (inclusive of the Risk Appetite statement) and business objectives which feed into the top-level security objectives, and undertake an Inventory of Assets to establish the baselines upon which you will proceed.

Once you have understood the needs and expectations of interested parties and have secured the commitment of the Leadership, you now should define roles and responsibilities. You develop a plan to achieve the information security objectives and undertake the risk assessment. You also structure the communications and define competencies and resources. You compile this information together into an ISMS handbook, however you wish to present it.

Afterwards, this is where the engine revs up: How you turn all the planning into actions. These are actions to address risks and opportunities; Operation, Planning and Control; information security risk assessment and information security risk treatment.

Next, you start demonstrating competence, awareness, documented information, internal audit, nonconformity and corrective action plan.

Finally, you need to monitor, measure, analyse, evaluate and undertake management and internal audit reviews before proceeding to the external certification audit.

Therefore, to reiterate, the steps involve planning, risk assessment, implementing controls, formalising system, internal testing, official audit and maintenance. This staged approach ensures ISO 27001 success. To put it another way, you need to:

1. *Obtain Leadership Commitment*: Executive support is vital for success. Ensure management is onboard and will allocate required resources.
2. *Appoint Project Team*: Assemble a cross-functional team with representation from areas like IT, security, legal, HR, finance. Appoint a project manager.
3. *Define Scope*: Determine which parts of the organisation will be included in the ISMS's scope. This could be company-wide or limited based on risk.
4. *Perform Gap Analysis*: Assess current security practices vs. ISO 27001 requirements to identify gaps. Focus initial efforts on priority gaps.
5. *Develop Project Plan*: Outline all activities, responsibilities, milestones and timelines needed for implementation.

6. *Review Information Risks*: Conduct an information risk assessment to identify key risks to confidentiality, integrity and availability of information assets.
7. *Define ISMS Policies and Procedures*: Document the policies, processes, controls to manage the identified information security risks.
8. *Implement Controls and Processes*: Develop and deploy new controls and processes per the policies and procedures.
9. *Train Employees*: Educate all employees within the ISMS scope on new policies, controls and their responsibilities.
10. *Conduct Internal Audit*: Audit the ISMS against ISO 27001 requirements to validate functionality before certification audit.
11. *Select Certification Body*: Choose an accredited company to perform the formal ISO 27001 certification audit.
12. *Take Corrective Actions*: Remediate any nonconformities identified during audit to pass certification.
13. *Achieve Certification*: Receive official certification once the audit is passed. Maintain through periodic surveillance audits.

ISO RISK ASSESSMENTS

There are key things to know about risk assessments in ISO 27001. A risk assessment is crucial. It systematically identifies, analyses and evaluates information security risks to the organisation. They help determine which information security controls are necessary to adequately protect important assets and data.

There are two risk assessment methodologies defined in ISO 27001:

1. *Asset-based Risk Assessment*: Evaluates risks associated with specific information assets like systems, databases, servers, etc.
2. *Context-based Risk Assessment*: Considers risks derived from the overall business environment, stakeholders, processes and objectives.

Typical steps in an ISO 27001 risk assessment include:

1. Identifying assets, threats, existing controls and vulnerabilities
2. Determining likelihood and impact levels for potential security events
3. Calculating risk levels (typically based on likelihood x impact)
4. Prioritising risks from highest to lowest
5. Making recommendations for implementing new controls to mitigate unacceptable risks

Quantitative and qualitative data are used, including threat intelligence, incident data, system logs, expert judgment and historical information. The assessments should be performed at least annually, or whenever there are major changes that impact the information security landscape. The methodologies should be documented, repeatable and generate results to input into the overall ISMS.

Key characteristics of an ISO 27001 risk register

The risk register is a pivotal ISO 27001 tool for documenting assessed information security risks and managing risk treatment plans to guide improvements. It contains details on identified risks such as risk description, risk category, root causes, existing controls, likelihood, impact, risk rating, risk owner and treatment plans. The register lists risks in order of priority based on risk ratings, typically from high to low. This enables focusing on the most critical risks.

For each risk, it outlines specific actions to further mitigate the risk to an acceptable level per the organisation's risk appetite. These are documented in the treatment plan. It assigns clear risk owners who are responsible for managing and reporting on risk treatment.

The risk register should also document residual risk levels after considering existing controls. This highlights areas of greater exposure. It should outline specific risk acceptance decisions according to the organisation's risk assessment criteria.

The register serves as a central inventory for tracking and reporting on information security risks across the organisation. It is a living document that should be regularly reviewed and updated as part of continual improvement processes. It helps provide key inputs into ISMS documents like security policies, statement of applicability and training programmes.

ISO 27001 language

Because of the ISO drafting rules none of the Annex A controls are worded in a way people would understand controls to be written. It is my firm view that they should not use the word "shall" as it implies some future intent, but must instead written as a statement of true fact. For example:

> Information security shall be integrated into project management.

Needs to be understood as "Information security is integrated into project management."

And

> Rules to control physical and logical access to information and other associated assets shall be established and implemented based on business and information security requirements.

Needs to be understood as "Rules to control physical and logical access to information and other associated assets are implemented based on business and information security requirements."

CATEGORISING THIRD PARTY VENDORS BASED ON RISK LEVELS

This is a fairly common concern and issue. Let's explore the details before reaching a conclusion. The main factors that affect information risk levels in the supply chain from a customer's perspective include:

- Nature of products procured – information, IP or technology content
- Volume and value of products procured annually
- Significance of products to the customer's business and information security needs
- Importance of specific suppliers to the customer
- Importance of the customer to the supplier
- Potential for security issues in products to impact the customer
- Potential for incidents affecting suppliers' ability to deliver
- Formality of business relationships and contracts
- Closeness of relationships and trust levels
- History of past incidents and issues
- Forward projection of risks with suppliers
- Comparative risk levels across suppliers
- Risk controls like contracts, policies, audits, metrics, etc.
- Visibility into supplier activities and information sharing
- Broader external factors like politics, markets, technology
- Strategic opportunities relating to suppliers

Key challenges include:

- Subjective, difficult to substantiate factors
- Complex, large supply chains
- Immature or changing organisations face more difficulty
- Residual risk acceptability is a management judgment
- Need for management decisions on strategies, policies, assurance measures
- Theft of IP
- Theft of product
- Delivery of inauthentic product (deviates from design/requirements)
- Lack of visibility into third-party employees accessing your data or IP

In practice, focus is often on the top riskiest supplies, with "riskiest" determined through assessments and management judgment. The depth of assessments depends on resources applied as per management's risk perception and opportunity costs.

So, what are the processes involved in the management and operation of information risk and security from the perspective of ISO 27001? Well, there are a variety of them. In no particular order, a non-exhaustive list includes:

1. Information asset management
2. Audit management, both internal and external
3. Business continuity management
4. Change management plus configuration management and version control
5. Continuous improvement and maturity management
6. Database security management
7. Exemption management (management-approved nonconformity with policies)
8. Facilities management including power and other services for the server room
9. Identity, access rights and user account management
10. Incident management including incident investigation and forensics
11. Information management in general
12. Information security risk management
13. Information Security Management System
14. IT
15. Internal audits and certification audits
16. Key management, plus the rest of cryptography
17. Log management, plus alarms and alerts
18. Metrics, measurement and the management of management information
19. Monitoring and oversight of the risk management and security arrangements
20. Patching, including emergency arrangements for urgent fixes
21. Performance and capacity management
22. Personnel/HR management including contracting, onboarding and off-boarding, awareness, training and support, plus resourcing for the security function
23. Preventive and corrective actions
24. Quality management, especially quality assurance
25. Information service management
26. Supplier/vendor relationship management, including telecoms, Internet and cloud services, outsourced development, contract security guards, maintenance/servicing, professional services + consulting/contracting etc.
27. System and network security management
28. System/software development and testing, particularly for the security aspects

LET'S BRING ALL THIS TOGETHER

The current version is ISO 27001:2022, published in September 2022. This latest edition replaces the previous 2013 version. It provides updates to reflect changes in information security threats, technology and best practices over recent years. The purpose of ISO 27001 is to help organisations manage the security of organisational assets such as financial information, intellectual property, employee details or any information that has value to the organisation. The standard outlines a risk-based approach to information security management.

ISO 27001 does not prescribe specific information security controls. Rather, it provides a framework and model for setting up an ISMS that is tailored to the organisation's unique needs and risk environment. The standard is designed to cover all types of organisations, regardless of type, size or nature of business. Any organisation that requires management of information security risks can benefit from ISO 27001.

A key emphasis in ISO 27001 is the need for a structured information security risk management process. Organisations must regularly identify, analyse and evaluate information security risks. Factors to consider include internal and external threats, vulnerabilities, likelihood and potential impacts. The standard provides guidelines to assess risks to the confidentiality, integrity and availability of information. Organisations should define criteria for determining risk levels, based on estimated business impacts and probabilities of security failures.

Top management must ensure the risk assessment process is comprehensive and covers the entire organisation. Identified risks are then addressed by applying appropriate controls to either reduce, transfer or avoid risks. For residual risks, management must make decisions on risk acceptance. The risk assessment methodology should be regularly reviewed and improved as needed. If business circumstances change, additional risk assessments may be required to account for new threats that arise.

The standard does not prescribe any specific technical controls or solutions for mitigating risks. Organisations must review the options and select a set of security controls that align with their business needs and risk tolerance. However, Annex A of ISO 27001:2022 does provide a comprehensive catalogue of control objectives and controls for consideration. Typical categories of controls include:

- Policies covering security requirements, change management, device usage, access control etc.
- Organisational/HR controls like security roles, background checks, training, personnel changes, etc.
- Asset management tools and procedures to inventory, classify and properly handle information assets.
- Physical and environmental controls like access cards, alarm systems, video surveillance, etc.
- Network/infrastructure controls, e.g., firewalls, network segmentation, remote access, etc.
- System acquisition, development and maintenance controls during the system lifecycle.
- Encryption, logging, backups and other technical controls.

The controls selected should cover all relevant asset types and address the various requirements needed to achieve the organisation's security objectives.

A key factor for successful ISO 27001 implementation is genuine commitment from leadership. Management must actively participate and provide strategic direction for the ISMS. Responsibilities of top management include:

- Defining the information security policy and setting security objectives.
- Ensuring sufficient resources are allocated to establish and operate the ISMS.
- Appointing competent staff to manage the ISMS.
- Ensuring risk assessments are done and appropriate controls implemented.
- Reviewing the effectiveness of the ISMS and initiating improvements where needed.
- Supporting other managers to demonstrate leadership in their areas of responsibility.
- Communicating the importance of information security compliance internally and externally.

Top management has a responsibility to integrate security governance deeply into the organisation's culture and business processes. They need to establish information security as an organisation-wide responsibility, not just the domain of the IT department.

The standard mandates documenting several key components of the ISMS. Organisations must develop and maintain documented information on:

- The information security policy and objectives
- Risk assessment methodology and risk treatment plans
- Scope of the ISMS (e.g., sites, assets and technologies covered)
- Procedures, processes and controls related to each ISMS requirement
- Evidence of monitoring, measurement, analysis, evaluation and improvements

Internal audits check for conformity to the requirements set out in ISO 27001 and the organisation's own policies and procedures. Audits must be conducted at planned intervals by members who are independent from the area being evaluated.

The audit findings are documented and presented to management for review. Corrective actions are taken promptly to remedy any nonconformities or system weaknesses identified. The audit programme should cover all elements of the ISMS and every site included in the scope over the 3-year certification period.

Let's move on to 27002:2022. It was published in September 2022. As just stated, 27002 serves as a companion standard to ISO 27001. While ISO 27001 specifies the requirements for an ISMS, ISO 27002 provides guidance to help select, implement and manage information security controls for mitigating risks. Using ISO 27002 guidance allows organisations to customise their information security controls according to their risk environment and objectives.

Some key features of ISO 27002:2022 include:

- Applicable to all organisation types and adaptable to unique risk environments
- Agnostic of specific technologies or solutions
- Risk-based approach to guide appropriate control selection
- Focus on people, processes and technology, not just technical controls
- Managerial rather than purely technical perspective
- Significant overlap with ISO 27701 on privacy management

The standard provides guidance on defining an overarching information security policy and more specific policies, procedures and guidelines to cover all relevant areas of concern. Clear documentation of security expectations and responsibilities is essential.

ISO 27002 outlines 14 sections of information security controls and objectives to potentially implement:

1. Information security policies
2. Organisation of information security
3. Human resources security
4. Asset management
5. Access control
6. Cryptography
7. Physical and environmental security
8. Operations security
9. Communications security
10. System acquisition, development and maintenance
11. Supplier relationships
12. Information security incident management
13. Information security aspects of business continuity

For each control area, ISO 27002 provides a statement of the control objective, suggested list of controls and implementation guidance. Organisations should start from this extensive catalogue of controls and select those most suitable to their context.

While organisations cannot get certified against ISO 27002, they can get certified against ISO 27001, which requires implementing suitable sets of information security controls. During ISO 27001 certification audits, ISO 27002 serves as a guideline for auditors to assess the appropriateness of implemented controls. Companies that adhere to ISO 27002 recommendations demonstrate the application of best practices. Organisations should cross-check their controls against ISO 27002 and evaluate if they have covered the baseline expectations. Any gaps can be addressed prior to undergoing formal certification.

What does this mean though for companies wanting to know if meeting ISO 27001 also fulfils their obligations to be aligned with other information security regulations and laws? Let us take the DORA ACT as an example.

UNDERSTANDING THE DIGITAL OPERATIONAL RESILIENCE ACT

A contemporary example of compliance in practice is the Digital Operational Resilience Act (DORA), a European Union regulation aimed at standardising cybersecurity requirements across sectors. DORA embodies a comprehensive approach to resilience by enforcing harmonised standards through several mechanisms. These include minimum harmonisation to establish a common baseline of security obligations, clear criteria to define essential services and implementation acts issued by the European Commission to tailor requirements to specific sectors. Reporting obligations ensure cross-sector information sharing, while supervisory coordination among national authorities guarantees unified application of DORA regulations. Furthermore, greater visibility into supplier risks is mandated, requiring organisations to conduct regular audits and establish contractual obligations for cybersecurity compliance. DORA also emphasises information sharing, requiring entities to participate in coordinated threat intelligence sharing to enhance situational awareness and incident response capabilities.

DORA exemplifies how harmonised regulations enhance resilience by integrating governance, supply chain oversight and standardised mechanisms into a unified framework. Organisations can use such regulatory benchmarks to design their compliance programmes, ensuring both adherence to requirements and operational efficiency. In addition, DORA highlights the importance of cybersecurity as a pillar of organisational resilience, setting a precedent for similar regulations globally.

Therefore, using ISO 27001 as a baseline will satisfy the compliance requirements with DORA, with appropriate tweaking. This is ever more important given what else has been launched and what is in the pipeline. Let's cover some of those.

LATEST DEVELOPMENTS IN AI REGULATION AND GOVERNANCE

Artificial Intelligence (AI) has rapidly evolved, becoming integral to various industries and societal functions. This rapid advancement brings immense opportunities but also significant risks and challenges. To navigate this complex landscape, regulatory bodies and international organisations formulated standards and frameworks to ensure AI is developed and deployed responsibly.

UK Information Commissioner's Office guidance on AI

The UK Information Commissioner's Office (ICO) has issued new guidance to balance innovation with privacy rights in AI applications. This approach highlights the importance of embedding data protection principles into AI systems, focusing on a nuanced, risk-based approach.

The guidance underscores the principle of data minimisation, ensuring that AI systems process only the personal data necessary for their purposes. Furthermore, the ICO stresses the preservation of human agency in AI decision-making. High-risk decisions impacting individuals should not rely entirely on AI, requiring meaningful human oversight.

The guidance also promotes privacy by design, integrating data protection considerations into AI systems from their inception. Tools like data protection impact assessments are recommended to identify and mitigate risks pre-emptively. Transparency and accountability remain critical, empowering individuals to understand how AI systems use their data while ensuring governance processes uphold ethical development.

European Union AI Act

The EU AI Act represents one of the most comprehensive regulatory efforts to govern AI. It classifies AI systems based on risk levels: unacceptable, high, limited and minimal risk. It prescribes tailored requirements for each category. Unacceptable-risk AI systems, such as those violating fundamental rights, are prohibited outright. High-risk systems, often used in critical sectors like healthcare, education and law enforcement, face stringent requirements.

These requirements include high data quality standards, rigorous bias and error testing, human oversight and robust privacy protections. Transparency obligations mandate clear explanations of how high-risk AI systems make decisions, ensuring accountability.

The Act establishes an EU-wide governance framework, binding all AI providers and users in the single market. Non-compliance can lead to substantial penalties, including fines of up to 6% of global revenue. While fostering trustworthy AI, the Act aims to sustain innovation, potentially setting global benchmarks for AI regulation. The Act also includes a risk management framework for organisations to identify and mitigate risks, supported by comprehensive documentation requirements that enhance traceability and accountability.

ISO/IEC Standards for AI and Cybersecurity

ISO/IEC has developed pivotal standards to address AI's privacy risks and the cybersecurity challenges of the digital economy. ISO/IEC 27091, published in 2023, offers a Privacy Information Management System (PIMS) framework tailored for AI and machine learning systems. It guides organisations in protecting personal data throughout its lifecycle, aligning with privacy regulations like the GDPR.

ISO/IEC 27090, released earlier in 2022, targets the cyber insurance sector, outlining best practices for managing cyber risks. This standard promotes transparency and accountability, helping organisations align with security expectations and assess cyber insurance options effectively.

Then there is the big beast: ISO/IEC 42001:2023, which is the international standard for an Artificial Intelligence Management System (AIMS) (see Table 10.1 for comparing the EU AI Act with this ISO Standard). It involves a structured approach across its ten main clauses.

Table 10.1 Aligning the EU AI Act with ISO 42001, including specific ISO 42001 clauses

Category	*EU AI Act*	*ISO 42001*	*ISO 42001 Clause*	*Alignment*
Scope	Regulates AI systems based on risk levels (Unacceptable, High, Limited, Minimal)	Establishes an AI Management System (AIMS) for organisations to manage AI risks	4.1 (Understanding the Organisation), 4.2 (Understanding Needs & Expectations)	Complementary: EU AI Act sets legal requirements, ISO 42001 provides a framework to meet them
Risk Classification	Defines AI risk categories and strict requirements for high-risk AI	Focuses on risk management principles for AI systems	6.1 (Actions to Address Risks), 8.3 (AI Risk Assessment & Treatment)	Aligned: Both emphasise risk-based approaches
Governance & Compliance	Requires providers and deployers of AI to establish governance mechanisms	Requires organisations to implement AI governance frameworks	5.1 (Leadership & Commitment), 5.3 (Organisational Roles, Responsibilities and Authorities)	Strong alignment: ISO 42001 can help organisations comply with governance obligations in the AI Act
Transparency & Documentation	Requires documentation, logging and explainability for high-risk AI	Promotes transparency, documentation and traceability of AI systems	7.5 (Documented Information), 8.2 (AI System Design & Development)	Aligned: ISO 42001 helps organisations meet AI Act transparency obligations

(Continued)

Table 10.1 (Continued)

Category	*EU AI Act*	*ISO 42001*	*ISO 42001 Clause*	*Alignment*
Accountability & Responsibilities	Assigns accountability to AI providers, deployers and users	Establishes accountability structures for AI governance	5.3 (Roles & Responsibilities), 9.3 (Management Review)	Strong alignment: ISO 42001 provides a framework for accountability required by the AI Act
Human Oversight	Mandates human oversight for high-risk AI systems	Requires organisations to define human oversight in AI governance	8.4 (Human Oversight in AI Systems)	Aligned: Both emphasise human control over AI
Security & Robustness	Requires AI systems to be secure, robust and resilient	Includes security, robustness and resilience as key AI management principles	6.2 (AI Security & Resilience), 8.6 (Monitoring & Response)	Strong alignment: ISO 42001 provides processes to meet AI Act security requirements
Bias & Fairness	Requires mitigation of bias in AI datasets and models	Encourages bias detection and mitigation in AI governance	8.5 (Bias & Fairness in AI)	Aligned: ISO 42001 can help organisations comply with the AI Act's fairness requirements
Monitoring & Continuous Improvement	Requires post-market monitoring and updates to ensure compliance	Emphasises continuous improvement and monitoring of AI systems	9.1 (Performance Evaluation), 10.2 (Continual Improvement)	Strong alignment: ISO 42001 supports ongoing compliance with the AI Act

Key Takeaways:

- ISO 42001 provides structured governance to help organisations meet the EU AI Act's compliance requirements.
- Using ISO 42001 can simplify compliance with the AI Act's requirements for high-risk AI systems.
- Organisations implementing ISO 42001 will have a strong foundation for legal, ethical and operational AI governance.

Clause 1: Scope

This clause defines the standard's purpose, audience and applicability, outlining the boundaries for establishing, implementing, maintaining and continually improving an AIMS. Its implementation steps are:

- Clearly define the scope of your AIMS, specifying which AI systems, processes and activities are included.
- Ensure alignment with organisational objectives and consider factors such as the complexity of AI applications and regulatory requirements.

Clause 2: Normative references

It lists documents that are indispensable for the application of ISO 42001, providing foundational texts for understanding and implementing the standard. Its implementation steps are:

- Review and integrate relevant normative references into your AIMS framework.
- Ensure that your implementation team is familiar with these documents to maintain consistency and compliance.

Clause 3: Terms and definitions

It provides clear definitions of key terms used within the standard to ensure a common understanding among all stakeholders. Its implementation steps are:

- Develop an internal glossary based on this clause to maintain consistency in communication and documentation related to AI management.
- Ensure all stakeholders are educated on these terms to facilitate effective implementation.

Clause 4: Context of the organisation

It emphasises understanding internal and external factors affecting the organisation and how they relate to the AIMS. Its implementation steps are:

- Conduct a thorough analysis of your organisation's context, including market conditions, regulatory environment and technological landscape.
- Identify relevant stakeholders and their expectations regarding AI systems.
- Determine the scope of the AIMS by considering factors such as organisational objectives, the nature of AI systems and compliance obligations.

Clause 5: Leadership

It highlights the critical role of top management in demonstrating leadership and commitment to the AIMS. Its implementation steps are:

- Ensure that senior management actively participates in the development and promotion of AI policies.
- Allocate necessary resources for the effective implementation of the AIMS.
- Establish clear roles, responsibilities and authorities for AI governance within the organisation.

Clause 6: Planning

It focuses on actions to address risks and opportunities, setting objectives and planning changes within the AIMS. Its implementation steps are:

- Identify potential risks and opportunities associated with AI systems through a comprehensive risk assessment.
- Establish clear, measurable objectives for the AIMS that align with organisational goals.
- Develop actionable plans to achieve these objectives, including resource allocation and timelines.

Clause 7: Support

It covers the resources, competence, awareness, communication and documented information necessary for the AIMS. Its implementation steps are:

- Allocate appropriate resources, including personnel, technology and financial support, for the AIMS.
- Ensure staff involved in AI management possess the necessary competence through training and development programmes.
- Maintain open communication channels to promote awareness and understanding of the AIMS across the organisation.
- Establish and control documented information required for the effectiveness of the AIMS.

Clause 8: Operation

It addresses the planning, implementation and control of processes needed to meet AIMS requirements. Its implementation steps are:

- Plan and control the design, development, deployment and monitoring of AI systems to ensure they operate as intended.
- Implement processes to manage changes in AI systems and respond to incidents effectively.
- Ensure that outsourced processes related to AI systems are controlled and aligned with the AIMS requirements.

Clause 9: Performance evaluation

It involves monitoring, measurement, analysis and evaluation of the AIMS performance. Its implementation steps are:

- Establish key performance indicators (KPIs) to assess the effectiveness of the AIMS.

- Conduct regular internal audits to evaluate compliance with ISO 42001 requirements.
- Perform management reviews to ensure the AIMS remains suitable, adequate and effective.

Clause 10: Improvement

It focuses on enhancing AIMS performance through corrective actions and continual improvement initiatives. Its implementation steps are:

- Implement a structured process for identifying nonconformities and taking corrective actions to prevent recurrence.
- Continually seek opportunities to improve the AIMS by analysing performance data and stakeholder feedback.
- Foster a culture of continuous improvement within the organisation to enhance AI management practices.

Annexes A–D

They provide additional guidance and controls for responsible AI development, deployment, monitoring and continual improvement (Table 10.1). Their implementation steps are:

- Refer to Annex A for a comprehensive list of controls related to AI management.
- Utilise Annex B for detailed implementation guidance on these controls.
- Consider the potential organisational objectives and risk sources outlined in Annex C when managing AI-related risks.
- Apply the supplementary information provided in Annex D to enhance understanding and implementation of the standard.

The standards emphasise ethical governance, leadership and transparency. They provide organisations with structured approaches to integrate privacy and cybersecurity into their operational and strategic frameworks. By adhering to these standards, organisations can reduce risks, improve operational resilience and enhance stakeholder trust.

EU Digital Services Act

The EU Digital Services Act (DSA) is a landmark regulation redefining the responsibilities of online platforms. The DSA attempts to address the challenges posed by illegal content, misinformation and targeted advertising. The Act imposes specific obligations on Very Large Online Platforms (VLOPs), requiring them to conduct regular risk assessments, ensure transparency in content moderation and restrict targeted advertising, particularly for minors.

Platforms must also implement user-friendly notice-and-action mechanisms to counter illegal goods and services effectively.

Non-compliance with the DSA can result in significant penalties, reinforcing accountability across digital services. The DSA sets a global precedent for managing online platforms, influencing regulatory approaches worldwide. Furthermore, the Act fosters a balanced digital ecosystem by encouraging innovation while ensuring consumer protection and ethical content dissemination.

ETHICAL IMPLICATIONS AND GLOBAL IMPACT

As AI becomes a global phenomenon, ethical considerations are paramount. Issues such as bias in AI systems, lack of transparency and potential misuse demand attention. Regulatory frameworks like the EU AI Act and ISO/IEC standards attempt to address these challenges by embedding ethical principles into governance structures. However, global disparities in regulatory approaches pose challenges to creating a unified framework.

International cooperation is essential to harmonise AI governance, promoting consistency and reducing compliance burdens for multinational organisations. Initiatives like the Global Partnership on AI (GPAI) exemplify efforts to foster international collaboration, ensuring that AI development aligns with shared ethical values and promotes global stability. At the time of writing, however, there is pushback from various US-based companies and the current USA Administration running contra to these ideals and best practices. It is my hope that a way will be found to overcome these hurdles.

CHALLENGES IN IMPLEMENTATION

Despite the promise of these regulatory frameworks, challenges remain in their implementation. Small and medium-sized enterprises (SMEs) often face resource constraints, making compliance difficult. Additionally, rapidly evolving technologies can outpace regulatory updates, creating gaps in governance.

To address these challenges, regulators must provide clear guidance, resources and support to help organisations navigate compliance requirements. Public-private partnerships can also play a vital role in fostering innovation while ensuring adherence to ethical standards.

And speaking of public-private partnerships, a leading light of this in the world of security standards is the National Institute of Standards and Technology (NIST) Cybersecurity Framework (CSF). Let's dive back.

EXPLORING NIST CSFs AND STANDARDS

The NIST plays a pivotal role in shaping practices by offering comprehensive frameworks and guidelines. This section explores the NIST CSF, its latest developments and other key NIST standards that help organisations address cybersecurity risks effectively.

NIST Cybersecurity Framework (CSF): An overview

The NIST CSF, first introduced in 2014, was designed to enhance cybersecurity for critical infrastructure sectors. As a voluntary framework, it provides a structured approach for organisations to understand, manage and mitigate risks. The framework's popularity stems from its flexibility, making it applicable across industries and organisational sizes. Version 2.0 of the NIST CSF builds on the original framework, incorporating significant updates to address emerging threats and challenges. It offers enhanced usability and aligns more closely with international standards, further solidifying its relevance in the global cybersecurity landscape.

The framework is organised around five core functions: Identify, Protect, Detect, Respond and Recover. These functions provide a comprehensive and scalable foundation for organisations to manage cybersecurity risks effectively. The framework's flexibility ensures it remains relevant to organisations of varying sizes and industries, from small enterprises to large multinational corporations.

Key updates in NIST CSF Version 2.0

Version 2.0 introduces notable changes aimed at improving the framework's practicality and scope. These updates include expanded guidance on framework use, providing organisations with detailed instructions on integrating the framework with other risk management processes. Enhanced implementation tiers have been increased from four to seven, enabling more granular assessments of cybersecurity maturity. The inclusion of a privacy framework emphasises the intersection of privacy and security, aligning data protection measures with organisational security goals.

Furthermore, the updated framework incorporates new categories addressing supply chain risk management, recognising the growing reliance on third-party services. Updates to the Identity Management and Access Control category also introduce enhanced concepts for authentication and identity proofing. Additional guidance on vulnerability disclosure and governance reinforces transparency and accountability, equipping organisations to manage cybersecurity incidents more effectively.

The increased emphasis on supply chain risk management reflects the evolving threat landscape, where vulnerabilities in third-party systems can have cascading effects on organisations.

Governance in NIST CSF

NIST CSF incorporates governance elements, although it does not prescribe a formal ISMS like ISO 27001. Key governance features in Version 2.0 include the establishment of roles and responsibilities within the Identify Function, which calls for clear assignment of cybersecurity roles across the organisation. The framework encourages the development of policies and procedures to manage regulatory, legal and risk requirements, integrating governance oversight into information-sharing processes. Strategic goal setting is also recommended to align cybersecurity objectives with broader business priorities.

Comparing NIST CSF with ISO 27001

While NIST CSF and ISO 27001 are widely recognised in information security, they differ in scope, structure and application. NIST CSF is a US-developed framework focusing on critical infrastructure, whereas ISO 27001 is an international standard for security management systems implementation. Structurally, NIST CSF employs a flexible framework with categories and subcategories, while ISO 27001 provides formal requirements and controls. ISO 27001 mandates extensive documentation and internal/external audits for certification, whereas NIST CSF focuses on voluntary guidance without certification processes.

Despite these differences, many organisations combine both standards to leverage their complementary strengths. NIST and ISO's adaptive approaches can be tailored to address specific organisational needs, providing comprehensive cybersecurity coverage and aligning with regulatory expectations.

Other key NIST publications and their applications

Beyond the CSF, NIST offers an extensive catalogue of publications addressing various cybersecurity aspects. Notable standards include NIST SP 800-53, which provides a comprehensive list of security and privacy controls for federal information systems. This publication's defence-in-depth approach encompasses technical, operational and management-level controls, supporting organisations in meeting compliance requirements like FISMA, HIPAA and Payment Card Industry Data Security Standard (PCI-DSS).

NIST SP 800-61, the Computer Security Incident Handling Guide, offers detailed guidance on preparing for and responding to cybersecurity incidents, helping organisations build robust incident response capabilities. NIST SP 800-34 focuses on contingency planning, outlining strategies for IT service recovery during disruptions to ensure business continuity. Additionally, NIST SP 800-86 integrates forensic techniques into incident response processes, aiding organisations in investigating security incidents and operational issues.

NIST SP 800-171 addresses the protection of Controlled Unclassified Information (CUI) in non-federal systems, providing specific guidelines for contractors working with government agencies. These standards collectively provide organisations with a robust toolkit for managing diverse cybersecurity challenges, enhancing resilience against ever-evolving threats.

Benefits of adopting NIST standards

Implementing NIST standards offers numerous advantages. Enhanced security posture is a key benefit, as organisations can systematically identify and mitigate risks, improving resilience against cyber threats. Alignment with NIST standards also supports regulatory compliance with various legal and regulatory requirements. Additionally, streamlined processes and clear guidance reduce inefficiencies, improving response times during incidents. The strengthened alignment with international standards like ISO 27001 facilitates collaboration and consistency across borders, positioning organisations to operate confidently in the global cybersecurity landscape.

Challenges and future directions

While NIST standards provide robust guidance, challenges remain in their implementation. Resource constraints, particularly for small and medium-sized enterprises (SMEs), can hinder adoption. Rapidly evolving threats may also outpace updates to standards, creating governance gaps. To address these challenges, organisations should leverage public-private partnerships and explore innovative solutions like AI-driven threat detection and advanced monitoring systems. NIST's ongoing updates and collaborations with international bodies aim to ensure its frameworks remain relevant and effective.

Future directions for NIST standards include increased emphasis on AI and machine learning security, as these technologies become more prevalent. Enhancements in cloud security guidelines, tailored recommendations for Internet of Things (IoT) devices and strategies to address quantum computing threats are also likely areas of focus. By staying at the forefront of these developments, NIST will continue to provide organisations with actionable tools to address emerging cybersecurity challenges.

TISAX: A STANDARD FOR THE AUTOMOTIVE INDUSTRY

TISAX (Trusted Information Security Assessment Exchange) was developed specifically for the automotive industry to enhance information security across supply chains. Rooted in ISO 27001, TISAX aligns with cybersecurity requirements such as those outlined by the EU DORA. However, its scope is narrower, focusing on automotive-specific risks.

Key features of TISAX include mandatory cyber risk assessments, defined sets of information security controls and independent audits to verify compliance. It emphasises supply chain security, ensuring that third-party vendors maintain robust cybersecurity measures. While TISAX supports DORA's goals in areas like risk management and supply chain oversight, it lacks cross-sectoral applicability and comprehensive regulatory mechanisms like EU-wide incident reporting and governance frameworks.

For automotive companies, adopting TISAX provides a structured way to demonstrate commitment to security and regulatory compliance. It streamlines security practices across the supply chain, ensuring consistent application of standards among vendors and partners. However, organisations operating across multiple sectors must address broader requirements to ensure comprehensive compliance with varying regulatory expectations.

PCI-DSS: PAYMENT CARD DATA

PCI-DSS was designed to ensure that organisations handling payment card information maintain a secure environment. This standard applies to merchants, payment processors and service providers involved in storing, processing or transmitting cardholder data.

PCI-DSS focuses on six core objectives: building and maintaining a secure network through firewalls and encryption, protecting cardholder data by masking sensitive information and securing stored data, maintaining a vulnerability management programme with regular updates and secure configurations, implementing strong access controls to restrict and monitor data access, regularly monitoring and testing networks through log reviews and penetration tests and maintaining an information security policy to outline roles and responsibilities.

Compliance validation for PCI-DSS varies based on transaction volume, with organisations completing either self-assessment questionnaires or formal audits. Organisations that achieve PCI-DSS compliance not only meet industry requirements but also enhance customer confidence by demonstrating their commitment to data protection.

Recent updates to PCI-DSS, such as Version 4.0, have introduced enhanced controls and a more flexible risk-based approach to compliance. This version addresses evolving payment technologies, emphasising continuous monitoring and stronger authentication methods. These changes ensure that the standard remains relevant in the face of emerging threats and technological advancements.

SOC 2

SOC 2 audits evaluate the controls organisations implement to protect information security, availability, processing integrity, confidentiality and privacy. Unlike PCI-DSS, which focuses on payment security, SOC 2 provides a broader assessment of IT controls and is widely used by cloud services, SaaS providers and technology organisations.

SOC 2 reports are divided into two types: Type 1 evaluates controls at a specific point in time, while Type 2 assesses controls over an extended period, providing greater assurance of operational effectiveness. SOC 2 audits are based on the Trust Services Criteria, which encompass security, availability, processing integrity, confidentiality and privacy. The process involves scoping, documentation, self-assessments and rigorous testing. Although SOC 2 does not provide formal certification, completing the audit demonstrates an organisation's commitment to maintaining robust IT controls.

For service providers, undergoing a SOC 2 audit is often essential for gaining customer trust and differentiating themselves in competitive markets. The Type 2 report, in particular, serves as a benchmark for demonstrating long-term control effectiveness. Organisations that adopt SOC 2 often report enhanced operational transparency and streamlined processes, fostering trust among stakeholders and reducing the risk of security breaches.

ISO 9001: THE QUEST FOR QUALITY

ISO 9001 is the gold standard for quality management systems (QMS), applicable across industries. Its principles revolve around continuous improvement, customer satisfaction and process management. To achieve ISO 9001 certification, organisations must implement documented procedures, set quality objectives, conduct internal audits and address nonconformities through continual improvement.

Certification under ISO 9001 involves an independent audit that assesses compliance with the standard's requirements. This rigorous process ensures that organisations meet customer and regulatory expectations related to quality. By achieving ISO 9001 certification, businesses signal their commitment to excellence, operational efficiency and stakeholder trust.

ISO 9001 also serves as a foundation for integrating other standards, enabling organisations to build cohesive management systems that address both quality and security. Companies often leverage ISO 9001 as a strategic tool for fostering innovation, improving customer retention and aligning operational goals with long-term business strategies.

INTEGRATING STANDARDS FOR COMPREHENSIVE COMPLIANCE

Organisations often adopt multiple standards to meet diverse regulatory, operational and customer requirements. A cloud service provider might combine SOC 2 to demonstrate IT security with ISO 9001 to showcase quality management. Similarly, a retailer handling payment card transactions might implement both PCI-DSS for payment security and ISO 27001 for broader information security management.

Integrating standards offers numerous benefits, including streamlined processes, reduced duplication of efforts and enhanced cross-departmental collaboration. When standards are effectively integrated, organisations can achieve operational efficiencies, ensuring that compliance initiatives align with broader strategic objectives. However, successful integration requires careful planning, alignment of objectives and ongoing monitoring to ensure compliance across all frameworks.

Organisations can use unified dashboards to monitor compliance metrics across different standards, providing real-time insights into performance and potential vulnerabilities. This approach fosters a proactive compliance culture, where continuous improvement is embedded into daily operations.

CHALLENGES AND BEST PRACTICES

While implementing these standards offers significant advantages, organisations often face challenges such as resource constraints, complexity in aligning multiple standards and staying updated with evolving requirements. To overcome these challenges, investing in training equips employees with the knowledge needed to understand and implement standards effectively. Training programmes tailored to specific roles and responsibilities ensure that employees at all levels contribute to compliance efforts.

Leveraging technology can streamline compliance management through automated monitoring, reporting and audit processes. Regular reviews of compliance efforts help identify gaps and ensure continuous improvement. By conducting periodic audits and benchmarking against industry best practices, organisations can adapt their compliance strategies to address emerging risks and regulatory changes. This proactive approach positions organisations to thrive in dynamic regulatory environments.

Beyond meeting regulatory requirements, implementing compliance standards delivers broader organisational benefits. Adherence to standards enhances brand reputation, fostering trust among customers, investors and partners. It also strengthens operational resilience, ensuring that organisations can withstand disruptions and recover efficiently.

Compliance standards play a critical role in enabling organisations to expand into new markets. Certifications like ISO 9001 and PCI-DSS demonstrate adherence to international benchmarks, facilitating global partnerships and cross-border collaborations. Moreover, organisations that prioritise compliance are better positioned to attract top talent, as they create work environments grounded in accountability, transparency and ethical practices.

UK's Cyber Security and Resilience Bill

The UK Cyber Security and Resilience Bill, introduced following the July 2024 King's Speech and supported by a policy statement published in April

2025, is intended to modernise and strengthen the UK's cyber security framework. It builds upon the existing Network and Information Systems (NIS) Regulations 2018, while also incorporating elements of the EU's NIS2 Directive, adapted to fit the UK's national context. The bill forms part of the government's wider strategy to protect critical national infrastructure and improve the overall cyber resilience of both public and private sector organisations.

One of the central aims of the bill is to expand the scope of the existing NIS Regulations. It proposes to include a broader range of entities, particularly those that play a crucial role in the UK's digital supply chain. This includes managed service providers (MSPs) and data centres, recognising their significance in supporting essential services. The proposed legislation also gives greater regulatory powers to authorities such as the Information Commissioner's Office (ICO), particularly in terms of enforcement and information gathering.

A key change introduced by the bill is a more rigorous approach to incident reporting. Under the proposed framework, organisations will be required to notify their sector regulator and the National Cyber Security Centre (NCSC) of a significant cyber incident within 24 hours. A more detailed incident report must then follow within 72 hours. This move aims to improve the speed and effectiveness of the UK's response to cyber threats.

The bill also addresses the need for international alignment, despite the UK no longer being part of the EU. While it does not directly implement the NIS2 Directive, it seeks to remain compatible with it in key areas to support cross-border cooperation and maintain international credibility.

A significant feature of the bill is its formalisation of the NCSC's Cyber Assessment Framework (CAF). The CAF is a widely respected tool that helps organisations assess and improve their cyber resilience. Under the new legislation, use of the CAF will become more structured and potentially mandatory for regulated sectors. This integration is intended to drive consistent standards and ensure a common understanding of good cybersecurity practice across industries.

The Bill marks a significant development in the UK's approach to digital security. It aims to future-proof the existing regulatory framework, better protect critical infrastructure and embed good security practices across the UK economy (Table 10.2).

UNDERSTANDING REGULATORY BODIES AND SECURITY OBLIGATIONS

As the global digital ecosystem continues to expand, the need for robust cybersecurity governance has become increasingly evident. Various regulatory and advisory bodies across the world have been established to develop policies,

Table 10.2 Summary Table

Aspect	Current NIS Regulations (2018)	Proposed Cyber Security and Resilience Bill
Scope	Operators of essential services and relevant digital service providers	Includes MSPs, data centres and broader supply chain entities
Regulatory powers	Limited	Enhanced powers for regulators like the ICO
Incident reporting	Basic requirements	Mandatory two-stage reporting within 24 and 72 hours
Alignment with EU	Based on original NIS Directive	Aligns with NIS2 where appropriate
Use of NCSC CAF	Voluntary guidance	Formalised within regulatory framework

enforce compliance and coordinate information security efforts. Let's briefly explore key regulatory entities, their roles and the obligations they impose on organisations, focusing on Europe, Asia, Australia and Africa.

European Regulatory Bodies and frameworks

In the European Union, several institutions and initiatives are dedicated to strengthening information security across member states. ENISA, the European Union Agency for Cybersecurity, leads efforts to develop expertise in cybersecurity, support policy implementation and promote cooperation across the EU. By providing resources, guidelines and training, ENISA helps organisations build resilience against evolving cyber threats. Europol's European Cybercrime Centre (EC3) focuses on combating cybercrime through cross-border operations, threat intelligence sharing and research. It collaborates with law enforcement agencies across the EU to address cybercriminal activities effectively.

CERT-EU, the Computer Emergency Response Team for EU Institutions, protects EU institutions from cyber threats by providing incident response services, threat intelligence and alerts. Its role is crucial in ensuring the operational continuity of EU bodies. Similarly, the European Cyber Security Organisation (ECSO) fosters public-private cooperation, supporting research, market development and skills enhancement in information security across the EU. There is a group under the NISs Directive which facilitates strategic collaboration between member states, playing a key role in the security of network and information systems across the EU. Other notable entities include the European Data Protection Board (EDPB), which oversees the consistent application of GDPR, and Europol's Joint Cybercrime Action Taskforce (J-CAT), which focuses on complex cybercrime investigations.

Regulatory bodies in Asia, Australia and Africa

Across Asia, Australia and Africa, nations have also established regulatory bodies to address cybersecurity challenges and support digital growth. In Singapore, the Cyber Security Agency oversees national strategies, policies and coordination efforts. In India, CERT-In (Indian Computer Emergency Response Team) serves as the nodal agency for cybersecurity threat response. In China, the Cybersecurity Administration governs cyber strategies, security reviews and data regulation.

In Australia and New Zealand, agencies like the Australian Cyber Security Centre (ACSC) and CERT NZ lead efforts in threat response and preparedness. Collaborative initiatives such as ACSC's Joint Cyber Security Centres foster regional cooperation. In Africa, the regulatory landscape is evolving with the establishment of national and regional bodies. The African Union (AU)'s Convention on Cyber Security and Personal Data Protection provides a framework for member states to develop legal and regulatory structures. The Economic Community of West African States (ECOWAS) has created a legal framework to combat cybercrime and established a regional CSIRT. While progress has been made, challenges such as resource constraints and policy fragmentation persist, requiring continued investment in capacity building and harmonisation.

THE FUTURE OF CYBERSECURITY REGULATIONS

The regulatory landscape is expected to continue evolving in response to emerging technologies, geopolitical dynamics and shifting societal expectations. As AI becomes more pervasive, regulatory bodies are likely to introduce specific guidelines addressing ethical and security considerations. Increased cross-border cooperation and harmonisation of standards will be essential to address global cyber threats effectively. Governments are placing greater emphasis on securing critical infrastructure sectors, such as energy, healthcare and finance. Organisations that remain agile and forward-looking will be better equipped to navigate these changes and thrive in a dynamic regulatory environment.

DISCUSSION – BESPOKE FRAMEWORK

By now I will be hearing you say there are many organisations who build or wish to build their own bespoke framework and you want to know the implications. So, lets discuss building a bespoke security control framework aligned with NIST, ISO 27001 and data privacy regulations to drive strategic business objectives.

Building a suitable integrated approach that not only protects the enterprise but also aligns with broader business goals means you need a control framework which works for you serving your company's strategic objectives, enabling innovation, trust and resilience. Given the prevalence of standards and frameworks out there, it raises an important question: Why build a bespoke framework?

Security leaders are often caught between multiple frameworks, compliance mandates and internal priorities. Off-the-shelf models, while foundational, rarely fit neatly into unique operational contexts for due to contextual reference, redundancy avoidance and strategic alignment reasons. You need to prioritise operational efficiency to reduce control and audit fatigue, and inconsistent reporting; enhance risk transparency and strategic clarity; regulatory flexibility as you can adapt to new compliance regimes without needing to reinvent the wheel and continuous improvement with agility and adaptability.

Before diving straight into controls, map out your corporate strategy. What are your top priorities: Customer acquisition? Regulatory market entry? Cloud migration? Digital transformation?

Next, align your risk appetite with those objectives. Not all risks are equal. Some can be accepted; others must be actively managed. This step ensures your framework supports, not hinders, growth.

Pull in controls from each framework and regulation:

- *From NIST CSF*: Functions, categories and subcategories (e.g., asset management, identity protection, threat detection)
- *From ISO 27001*: Annex A controls (e.g., access control, cryptography, supplier relationships)
- *From GDPR/CCPA*: Requirements around consent, breach notification, DPIAs and data subject rights

Identify overlaps and areas of unique emphasis. Build a consolidated control matrix that breaks down each control into its source, purpose and strategic impact.

Now tailor controls to your environment and prioritise controls based on risk impact and business enablement.

- Consolidate duplicates (e.g., access controls appear in both NIST and ISO)
- Adapt wording to your operational context
- Eliminate non-applicable requirements
- Augment with internal best practices or industry-specific needs (e.g., PCI-DSS, SOC 2, HIPAA)

Align your controls with strategic goals. Every control should map to at least one business outcome. Use this linkage to demonstrate the value of security to executives and secure ongoing investment, for example:

- Protecting brand trust → Privacy controls, breach response
- Enabling scalability → Identity and access management, cloud governance

- Demonstrating compliance → Documentation, audit readiness
- Enabling partnerships → Third-party risk management, certifications

Next, develop or leverage existing processes for:

- Control ownership and accountability
- Measurement and metrics (e.g., time to detect/respond, control effectiveness)
- Automation where feasible (especially for detection and response)
- Audit readiness (internal or external)

Building a framework is only half the challenge. Governance makes it sustainable. The steps are:

- Establish a cross-functional Security Steering Committee to own the framework
- Define control ownership within departments (e.g., HR owns onboarding controls)
- Align security with privacy, legal and risk teams
- Encourage a security-aware culture, not just awareness training

Be under no illusion though, there are challenges and multiple considerations to take into account. There is complexity in mapping from your bespoke framework, as manually cross-referencing standards can be labour-intensive. You will need to convince your business' leadership of the value of creating your own instead of a variation of an existing, proven Standard. You will run the risk of over-customisation, as you could stray too far from best practices and hinder auditability.

CONCLUSION

Regulatory bodies and frameworks play a crucial role in shaping the cybersecurity landscape. From the EU's coordinated approach to Asia's dynamic regulatory developments, these efforts reflect a global commitment to protecting digital infrastructure.

Mainstream standards and frameworks like TISAX, PCI-DSS, SOC 2, NIST and ISO 9001 play pivotal roles in enhancing security, ensuring quality and building trust. These frameworks provide structures and best practice guidance that organisations can address diverse risks, meet regulatory requirements and position themselves as industry leaders. The integration of these standards not only ensures compliance but also, when used correctly, fosters innovation, operational excellence and long-term growth.

Chapter 11

Exploring career pathways

In today's dynamic professional landscape, a career in Governance, Risk and Compliance (GRC) and Data Privacy is not only rewarding but also critical to the sustainability and ethical operation of organisations. This chapter provides an overview of career pathways, the skills and qualifications needed and strategies for success.

These professionals play a vital role in helping organisations navigate the complexities of today's regulatory environment. They contribute to organisational growth and profitability by protecting assets and fostering a culture of compliance and accountability, which enhances trust among stakeholders. Moreover, they must adapt strategies to fit local nuances and regulatory landscapes, ensuring that global enterprises remain compliant across multiple jurisdictions.

They are responsible for developing and implementing policies and procedures that ensure compliance with regulatory requirements. They conduct risk assessments, identify potential threats and develop strategies to mitigate risks. Their work involves close collaboration with various departments, including legal, finance and operations, to ensure a cohesive approach to risk management and compliance. Their work directly impacts organisational success by safeguarding assets, maintaining regulatory compliance and fostering a culture of accountability. They help build trust with stakeholders, including customers, investors and regulators, by ensuring that organisations adhere to legal and ethical standards. This trust is essential for long-term sustainability and growth.

COMMON STRATEGIES FOR SUCCESS

While specific career paths in GRC may differ, several strategies are universally beneficial for those pursuing roles in this field. Obtaining a relevant academic degree and professional certifications demonstrates expertise and enhances credibility. Certifications such as Certified Information Systems Auditor (CISA), Certified Information Security Manager (CISM) and Certified in Risk and Information Systems Control (CRISC) are

DOI: 10.1201/9781003543992-12

highly valued. For Data Privacy, the International Association of Privacy Professionals (IAPP) offers the Certified Information Privacy Professional (CIPP) range for Europe, the USA and Canada, which is globally applicable given the alignment of many data privacy laws with the General Data Protection Regulation (GDPR).

The landscape evolves rapidly with emerging regulations, risks and best practices. Staying updated through training programmes, webinars and industry publications is essential for professional growth. Practical experience in areas such as compliance monitoring, auditing or risk assessment is crucial. Entry-level roles, internships and volunteer opportunities provide practical exposure and help build foundational skills. Strong analytical and problem-solving skills are essential to analyse complex information, identify risks and propose effective mitigation strategies. Effective communication and collaboration are critical for working across departments, gaining stakeholder buy-in and ensuring the successful implementation of policies. A deep understanding of the industry or sector in which an organisation operates provides valuable context for managing risks and compliance requirements. Engaging with the GRC community through conferences, forums and associations opens doors to mentorship, resources and job opportunities.

To illustrate these strategies, let's explore some fictional case studies and examples. In one case, a multinational corporation faced significant challenges in managing risks across its diverse operations. The GRC team implemented a comprehensive risk management framework that included regular risk assessments, employee training programmes and the development of robust policies and procedures. The organisation successfully mitigated potential threats and enhanced its overall resilience by adopting a proactive approach to risk management. In another example, a financial institution needed to comply with stringent data privacy regulations, including GDPR. The Data Privacy team conducted a thorough assessment of the organisation's data handling practices and implemented measures to ensure compliance. This included updating privacy policies, conducting regular audits and providing training to employees. As a result, the institution achieved full compliance and strengthened its reputation for protecting customer data.

BUILDING A SUCCESSFUL CAREER

Achieving success involves a combination of technical skills, strategic thinking and adaptability. You should actively seek opportunities for growth and development. Developing soft skills, such as interpersonal and communication abilities, is essential for building relationships, influencing decisions and fostering collaboration. Seek mentorship from experienced professionals who can provide valuable insights and guidance. Mentors can offer advice on career development, share industry knowledge and help navigate challenges. Networking with peers and industry experts through conferences, forums and professional associations can also open doors to new opportunities and resources.

Gaining experience in different areas of an organisation can enhance understanding of its operations and dynamics. This exposure can be achieved through rotational programmes, project assignments or collaboration with other departments. Cross-functional experience broadens skill sets and prepares professionals for leadership roles. Familiarity with GRC tools and platforms is also essential for efficiency and effectiveness. You should seek training in relevant software and technologies. This includes GRC software, data privacy management tools and audit management systems.

BUILDING A STRONG PERSONAL BRAND

Establishing a strong personal brand is essential for professional growth and recognition. Your personal brand represents how you present your skills, values and unique perspectives to the world. It highlights what sets you apart and positions you as a trusted expert in your field. A well-crafted personal brand not only helps you stand out but also creates opportunities for meaningful connections and career advancement.

To build a strong personal brand, start by defining your unique value proposition. Reflect on your strengths, skills and experiences that set you apart from others. Consider how you can add value to organisations or solve specific challenges they face. For example, pursuing additional qualifications, such as an MBA, can provide business-oriented skills that distinguish you in a competitive field. Your online presence should align with the brand you want to project. This includes maintaining a professional image on LinkedIn, personal websites and professional profiles. Ensure that your profiles are up-to-date and reflect your expertise and achievements. High-quality content, such as articles, presentations and social media posts, can help build your reputation and establish credibility.

Engagement is key to building and maintaining a strong brand. Actively respond to comments, participate in discussions and network to expand your professional reach. Social media platforms amplify your voice: share industry news, engage in trending discussions and use relevant hashtags to increase visibility. Additionally, public speaking opportunities at industry conferences can help you showcase your knowledge, strengthen your professional network and enhance your credibility.

THE POWER OF TRANSFERABLE SKILLS

Transferable skills are versatile abilities that can be applied across roles, industries and disciplines. They are the foundation of adaptability, allowing professionals to thrive in diverse environments and meet new challenges with confidence. The professionals often work with diverse teams and stakeholders, requiring strong interpersonal skills to build trust, facilitate communication and resolve conflicts. These skills are also important for negotiating with regulators, vendors and other external parties. Technical proficiency and digital literacy have become indispensable in the modern workplace. Nearly every profession now requires familiarity with digital tools and technologies.

Effective communication is essential in virtually every role. Whether it's writing clear reports, delivering compelling presentations or facilitating meetings, strong communication skills enable professionals to convey complex information clearly and persuasively. In GRC and Data Privacy roles, communication is crucial for explaining regulatory requirements, presenting risk assessments and gaining stakeholder buy-in for compliance initiatives. Critical thinking involves analysing information, identifying patterns and making informed decisions. Problem-solving skills enable professionals to tackle complex challenges and implement effective solutions. In GRC, these skills are vital for assessing risks, developing mitigation strategies and ensuring compliance with regulations.

THE FUTURE OF GRC AND DATA PRIVACY

The fields of GRC and Data Privacy are continuously evolving, driven by emerging trends, technological advancements and changing regulatory landscapes. Understanding the future of these fields is essential for professionals seeking to build successful and sustainable careers.

One of the key trends shaping the future of GRC is the increasing focus on environmental, social and governance (ESG) factors. Organisations are recognising the importance of ESG considerations in their risk management and compliance strategies. This includes addressing environmental risks such as climate change, promoting social responsibility and ensuring good governance practices. GRC professionals must develop expertise in ESG issues and integrate them into their GRC frameworks.

As stated in other chapters, the rise of artificial intelligence (AI) and machine learning (ML) is transforming the way organisations manage risks and ensure compliance. AI and ML technologies enable organisations to analyse vast amounts of data, identify patterns and predict potential risks. This allows for more proactive and data-driven approaches to risk management and compliance. You must stay abreast of these technological advancements and develop the skills to leverage AI and ML in their work.

The increasing complexity of global supply chains presents new challenges. Organisations must manage risks and ensure compliance across multiple jurisdictions, ensuring that their operations comply with local regulations and standards. This requires a deep understanding of the regulatory landscapes in different countries and the ability to navigate complex legal requirements. You must develop strategies to manage risks and ensure compliance across global supply chains, including conducting regular audits, implementing robust policies and collaborating with local experts.

The growing importance of data privacy is another trend shaping the future of GRC. As individuals become more aware of their rights and the potential misuse of their personal information, organisations must prioritise data privacy and protection. This includes complying with regulations such as GDPR and CCPA, implementing strong security measures and ensuring transparency in data handling practices. Data privacy professionals must stay updated on the latest developments in privacy regulations and technologies to effectively protect personal data.

CONCLUSION

Practical experience is essential for building successful careers in GRC and Data Privacy. Entry-level roles, internships and volunteer opportunities provide practical exposure and help build foundational skills. Entry-level roles in GRC and Data Privacy offer opportunities to learn the basics. These roles involve tasks such as conducting risk assessments, monitoring compliance activities and managing data privacy programmes. Entry-level roles provide hands-on experience and help professionals develop the skills needed for more advanced positions.

Internships offer valuable opportunities for practical experience and skill development. Interns work closely with experienced professionals, gaining insights into the day-to-day operations of GRC and Data Privacy programmes. Internships provide exposure to real-world challenges and allow professionals to apply their knowledge and skills in a practical setting. This experience is invaluable for building a strong foundation and preparing for advanced roles.

A deep understanding of the industry or sector in which an organisation operates provides valuable context for managing risks and compliance requirements. Industry knowledge enables professionals to develop strategies that address the specific challenges and opportunities of their sector. This includes understanding the regulatory landscape, identifying industry-specific risks and developing tailored compliance programmes.

Industry knowledge involves understanding the regulatory requirements, risks and best practices of a specific sector. In GRC and Data Privacy, professionals must stay updated on the latest developments in their industry, including regulatory changes, emerging risks and technological advancements. This knowledge enables professionals to develop strategies that address the unique challenges and opportunities of their sector. To end this chapter, I strongly encourage you to read the book *EMTech Anthropology*, which will broaden your outlook on the possibilities.

Chapter 12

Drawing it all together

Security by itself is *not* a Top 10 business topic. This is a strange sentence to write at the end of a book all about how to be a better security practitioner. It is, however, reality. Risk is. Safety is. Quality is. Resilience is. Efficiency is. Your job is not about preventing breaches. It is about brand reputation, customer trust and the financial stability of your company. It is up to you as the practitioner to hitch your wagon to these bigger issues and you will address security through Secure By Design. Ultimately, security is about business outcomes. Protection of assets is an outcome of the actions we take relative to the business' risk appetite and understanding of its own value. Businesses want maximum uptime. They want to innovate faster or, in organisations in critical national infrastructure like the nuclear industry to safely move forward in a risk adverse-calculated manner. And they want the assurance they can do so.

Ask yourself, what are the activities which will have the biggest impact to improve business operations and the financial bottom line. This is a question which is not a "stop the bad guys" technology question. Like Enterprise Architecture, and indeed some other departments such as Finance, there is a need in security to map the business processes and correlate impact against those processes with business-derived KPIs. Effectively, this is about how do we help the business maximise its value, which includes and goes beyond protective actions against malicious behaviours to assisting the business achieve its targets. You will commonly hear, be a business enabler. You will also hear that this is just talk. I'll give an example to show that it is not just talk. One company I worked for wanted to diversify its sales and distribution mechanisms to include channel partners. One channel partner's compliance function had the ability to potentially block the deal. Through a series of meetings between myself and the other company's representative, we ran through everything, cleared any potential hurdles and enabled the authorisation for the deal to proceed if the respective executives wished.

It should be clear by now that while data security, IT security, Information Security and Data Privacy security are overlapping, Information Security and Data Privacy are broader in scope. They take in the protection of information regardless of format or location. The same goes with strategies, concepts, creative ideas and more. The IT element is just that, one component.

DOI: 10.1201/9781003543992-13

Central to GRC is human behaviour. Taking this down to a process and a technology level, this is the flow of data related to human behaviour. What you must never do is disrupt employee productivity. Think of a scale and zoom in or out on different roles. In an idea world, you should have the capacity and capability to look through the lens of risk differentials according to the role; through you, you start treating the holder of the role more personally instead of using a blunt hammer approach across your company. Strait jackets and not removing friction do not work, as anyone with teenagers would know and they are the workers of the future.

Businesses ultimately need to retain their data. In the European Union with DORA, there are fines for executives and yet AI could potentially help automation for companies to demonstrate their compliance to the regulators. Yet, who guards the AI. What are, to use government and civil service terminology, the guardrails. The EU AI Act is a start but changes are outpacing the ability of legislators to keep up. Companies are having to develop a lot of their own guardrails or safeguards, outside of subscribing to say Microsoft's business Co-Pilot and relying on the large companies' assurance there is proper segmentation in place between different instances. This will become more critical as AI agents are deployed alongside personnel first responders to security incidents, and as such agents are developed to assist with post-mortems.

Digital assistants have increasingly become involved in triaging evaluations and must be accompanied by human oversight. From a business perspective, there is a need to create differentiation against competitors, which has capital investment implications and therefore needs to have robust levels of review assurance processes. If a company strikes the right balance for that moment in time, excellence could lead to operational excellent. This is another way in which security could positively influence business direction and value generation.

How we plan for the unplanned comes back to having a resilience function needing substantial data points aligned with the assets that matter to your company. Ask yourself, "What kind of capabilities do I want to develop or bring in?" There is a cost implication to the state of readiness. Build automated workflows into your resilience process. Such workflows can take numerous forms, from "if X occurs, do y" to standing up a clone of a technical function (e.g., activating a cold Cloud datacentre) while the technical incident response team gets to work.

You may in your career encounter a CEO who says they understand information security, but who in reality does not know as much about security relating to business processes and objectives as they think. By contrast, they may come at it instead from the perspective of IT over data minimisation and system sprawl. I recommend arranging for gamification training for the Executive and/or Board. Draw upon your Business Canvas Model and conversations with stakeholders to delineate the top ten business risks and revenue drivers. Align your recommendations with the overall business strategy to enhance the resiliency and transparent financial costings; these include:

choices inclusive of competing or complimentary operating models, talent and capability, market engagement and innovation. For the presentation to the Executive and/or Board, I personally have 10–13 slides and no more covering: Current state, effectiveness of the existing business controls, lessons learnt, agreed risk indicators (in partnership with the Enterprise Risk Management function and the CFO), the threat landscape appropriate to your industry and the impact against the top ten business revenue drivers, privacy impact and options on improvement programmes to reach the desired future state. The desired future state needs to be set by them in partnership with your as an advisor according to their risk appetite. A useful tip is to approach this as business risk reduction through quality management, which also develops business capabilities.

Now I have mentioned the Business Canvas Model a few times. You can actually start building this out before starting your role as well as any time in your role. For interviews, you can do open-source intelligence, the company's website and go to Companies House to obtain a copy of the latest business financial statement which will give you a good idea of the financial health of the company as well as what it publicly regards as its key drivers. When you're in a company, couple these with your conversations with senior leadership. You may be surprised at how open senior leaders are to discuss their areas of interest, focus and priorities. You may also be surprised at how open people are to improving their processes, which can be done by embedding security into projects and operations, looking at localised risk registers and being a conduit to resolving any risk mitigation issues they may encounter. Such activities will increase the relevant departments' assurance and help create security champions without further direct cost to your department.

This information is what underpins your highest level Information Security Policy, or Enterprise Security Policy. This policy establishes the overarching framework for information security within your company. It defines your company's commitment to security, high-level objectives and governance structure. It has a number of key characteristics:

- It focuses on the security vision, principles and commitment
- It defines governance structures, including roles and responsibilities
- It covers all departments, employees, third parties and digital systems
- It establishes the foundation for risk assessment, mitigation and resilience
- It acts as the parent document to more detailed policies and standards, e.g., the Access Control Policy, the Data Protection Policy.

For operationalising what we have discussed, it is necessary to create formal delivery and operating models aligned to your company's governance framework, to ensure consistency of approach. A security function can either centrally provide all the services or it can be federated. An example of federation, with oversight control, could be Enterprise Security Architecture where new projects have to provide funding to bring in a project security architect reporting to both the project owner and the ESA management team. ESA provides architectural, design and engineering best practice requirements alongside governance and assurance to ensure that all services both existing and new are fit for purpose. These services are designed to meet user needs, aligns with the organisation's strategic direction and principles and complies with legal, regulatory and safety standards. Utilising ESA means it acts as a custodian of the digital landscape by preventing avoidable issues, setting a clear direction, crafting effective strategies and defining actionable roadmaps.

Develop your roadmap to enhance your capabilities and capacity over not just the next financial year but a couple of years into the future. Have a Playbook for your security function, undertake wider stakeholder engagement, a capability roadmap for projects and operations, have a skills matrix and enhance your security testing provision beyond penetration testing. In Europe, you will have regulatory requirements and remediation programmes against those requirements. Accordingly, what you will have to construct are Non-functional Requirements, which are criteria that define how a system should operate from a security perspective, focusing on aspects like performance, availability, maintainability and scalability, rather than specific functionalities.

Let's take the Playbook. It is a comprehensive guide that outlines standardised procedures, best practices and methodologies for designing, implementing and managing your security function. It includes detailed instructions, templates and frameworks to support consistent security practices. Its purpose is to ensure that your company's security architecture is robust, consistent and aligned with industry standards. This will greatly assist you in the creation of service provision metrics (KPIs), and management products and operating manuals. We'll briefly discuss both.

The Service Provision Metrics Report is a detailed document that tracks and analyses key performance indicators related to the delivery of services. Its purpose is to evaluate the performance of services and ensure accountability. It helps stakeholders understand the effectiveness of security initiatives, identify areas for improvement and undertake strategic planning to enhance your company's overall security posture.

The management products and operating manuals are comprehensive documents that provide detailed instructions and guidelines for the operation, maintenance and processes for the managed service. They include the lessons learnt log and collaboration strategy. Their purpose is to ensure consistent and efficient operation of security systems and processes. They serve as a reference for team members to understand procedures and enhance operational effectiveness.

Accordingly, you should develop an integrated RACI supported by governance and reporting processes linked to your organisation's digital demand process and technical design groups in sync with wider governance. The RACI should outline your role and your team's role across the relevant governance and operational meetings, ensuring clarity in ownership and decision-making processes. There should be a front door to your function or team with clear links to the governance processes. There may be dependencies, such as governance and reporting processes outside of security and you need to keep in mind that modifications may be needed. What it will give you is an established security governance and reporting view across the Executive, Strategic, Management, Operational and Delivery levels for efficient escalation and information dissemination. It ensures consistency, reduces duplication and streamlines decision-making.

Breaking down governance level meeting levels:

- *Executive*: Organisation direction, decision-making, oversight, risk appetite
- *Strategic*: Oversight and direction. Monitoring of operational services, aiding with high risk, high impact decisions and providing assurance that teams are focusing on the right priorities in line with the Business Strategy
- *Management*: Cross-functional boards for business and technical steer, portfolio management and solution direction for operational services and products spanning all lifecycle stages
- *Operational*: Services portfolio governance for setting out the functional and technical requirements for the service. Decision-making on end-to-end service lifecycle and ensuring teams are delivering as per the objectives for the services portfolio
- *Delivery*: Product and programme boards overseeing the delivery roadmap and decision-making on delivery and low-level considerations

The following forms part of the structured view of the governance and decision-making forums to ensure clarity, alignment and efficiency in leadership engagement, strategic discussions and investment approvals:

- *Meeting Purpose and Scope*: Strategic focus, objectives and decision-making responsibilities
- *Cadence and Ownership*: Frequency, meeting lead and key stakeholders
- *Inputs and Outputs*: Required materials, decision-making criteria and expected outcomes
- *Inter-dependencies*: How each meeting feeds into broader governance frameworks

Moving inwards, consider constructing an alignment matrix for the information security function. This will align initiatives with requirements, both within your specific team as well as between teams. The purpose is to ensure that security strategies and actions are directly contributing to the achievement of your organisation's objectives. An important component is an Assurance Schedule, which is a timetable outlining the planned activities, assessments and reviews related to Information Security assurance. It includes the scheduling of regular security audits, vulnerability assessments, compliance checks and other assurance activities managed by your team. The purpose of an Assurance Schedule is to ensure that all activities are systematically planned and executed. It helps maintain a consistent security posture, ensures compliance with relevant standards and regulations, identifies and mitigates risks in a timely manner and supports continuous improvement.

When you go down a layer deeper to construct processes, look at usability, interoperability, integration, supportability, development costs and speed, scalability, re-usability and what business-as-usual looks like. You have to ask if your actions are proportionate, aligned and comprehensive; if your actions are in relation to managing risk, add embedded and dynamic. To be effective, you must have or develop interpersonal skills. These skills are: Motivation, flexibility, ability to network, emotional intelligence which feeds into self-awareness, conflict negotiation and collaboration.

When you are talking with stakeholders from other teams or with your senior leadership, structure your communications around the STAR method. It is a structured approach used to convey information clearly and effectively. It stands for Situation (the context of the event, problem or task), Task (the specific role, objective or challenge being addressed), Action (what is being recommended or undertaken) and Result (outcome or resolution, including key takeaways or impact).

Let us take the management of supply chain risk as an example. You need to know who the vendors are and categorise them into risk tiers. For new vendors, you need an appropriate selection and due diligence process. You weave this into understanding your specific company's value-at-risk. You also need an ongoing assurance process looking at the risk management, strategic focus, finances and resilience factors, which should be mature enough to identify anything problematic at an early enough stage.

To take another example of reporting upwards on risk from external threat actors: Reframe the discussion to the types of threat actors in your industry vertical, the methods they are known to use (resulting in categories and patterns against which protection measures can be initiated), the controls used to minimise their impact are XYZ, the assurance of their coverage and effectiveness is ABC and the results from resilience simulations are <insert>. It is a good idea to have gamification activities internal to the Information Security and Data Privacy functions as well as at the senior executive level.

In a similar vein, it is a good idea to create a centre of excellence looking to the future. This would be a convergence of security, safety, resilience and quality wrapped up in partnerships with academia, other appropriate collaborators and your supply chain to build future capabilities. This envelops your within a wide network of contacts and drives value outwards from your business as well as ensuring access to learning from elsewhere can be adapted and applied to yours.

In terms of operational excellence, it is a good idea to draw up high-level design documents and low-level design documents. Having two sets of documents isn't strictly necessary in smaller organisations. Larger organisations used both sets to validate the security requirements at conceptual, approval and implementation levels. Blueprints arise out of these, some examples of which are: dataflow diagrams, audit checklists, impact assessments, security accreditations, gap analyses, threat models, risk registers, usability tests and functional tests. The operational security plan must be aligned with any broader Secure By Design programmes and security management frameworks.

Within organisations, there is a common theme that security teams understand and grasp threats, but that wider departments may not. Communication is important, as has been repeatedly stressed throughout this book. While the business owns the risk, the need to quantify risk is Security's. For example, Security does not own ISO 27001/SOC/DORA/NIS(2) as the business or appropriate business department does. The issue is that being constantly bombarded with risk makes departments feel powerless. We as practitioners must always work on solutions and not just problems when we communicate risk.

There is also the perennial issue of different forms of federation or centralisation of the Security function, recognising the scale and complexity within each business. Most security teams are not responsible for a business' operational technology, nor does the responsibility for it sit with the Chief Information Security Officer. Proposed models must consider business complexities, while recognising the need for governance and visibility. In terms of operationalisation, the model for how security is constituted in a company must be defined with the flexibility required for operational needs. Otherwise, there is a risk of distractions, duplication of effort and potential incompatibility (including with regulations and directives). Try not to engage in increased reporting without it leading to risk reduction.

RETURNING TO ACADEMIA IN INFORMATION SECURITY

I am not intending to repeat information for the sake of repetition. It is to re-emphasise a factor which is becoming more prevalent. I've already mentioned Sarah Armstrong-Smith's book. There is also the fantastic co-edited book called EMTech Anthropology, which has a number of valuable references to published journals and books worth looking at. One may think companies are hierarchical, but actually the social dynamics are complex. Think fluid mixes of hierarchy and heterarchy. Heterarchy is where different entities or people exist in a more flexible, interconnected structure; they interact in various ways without a fixed chain of command. Examples include decentralised networks, collaborative work environments and certain types of social structures. How hierarchy and heterarchy come together or pull apart depend on specific contexts, and you need to learn to recognise the signs and adapt accordingly.

You must also cultivate a leadership style that suits you, keeping in mind that leadership and management are distinct. This approach will highlight various aspects of political and social capital depending on the context. By doing so, you will gain a deeper understanding of strategies for reshaping inter-departmental dynamics, removing obstacles and strengthening stakeholder engagement.

What does this mean I reality? Let's dive back in: Enterprise architecture (EA) frameworks help organisations design and manage complex IT and business environments. Two widely adopted frameworks are SABSA (Sherwood Applied Business Security Architecture) for Enterprise Security Architecture and TOGAF (The Open Group Architecture Framework) for Enterprise IT Architecture. Both frameworks establish a set of principles that guide organisations in structuring their enterprise security and governance alignment.

Understanding these principles and their applications goes beyond technical implementation. Anthropology, which studies human societies and cultures, plays a crucial role in shaping EA. EA is not just about technology but also about human behaviour, decision-making and organisational dynamics. This sub-section runs the roost over:

1. *SABSA Principles*: How SABSA ensures security is embedded in EA through a business-driven approach.
2. *TOGAF Principles*: The foundational guidelines that drive consistency, flexibility and alignment in EA.
3. *Links with Anthropology*: How anthropology's focus on human behaviour, culture and organisational dynamics informs EA principles and implementation.

SABSA principles

SABSA is a risk-driven security framework that integrates security into EA using a layered model. It follows a business-driven approach, ensuring that security aligns with organisational goals rather than being an afterthought.

The SABSA model is structured into six layers, each corresponding to a different aspect of security and business requirements.

1. *Contextual Layer* (*Why?*): Business goals, strategies and security objectives.
2. *Conceptual Layer* (*What?*): Security concepts, risk management strategies and policies.
3. *Logical Layer* (*How?*): Logical security models, risk controls and security services.
4. *Physical Layer* (*With What?*): Specific technologies and infrastructure implementing security.
5. *Component Layer* (*Where?*): Deployment of security mechanisms in IT systems.
6. *Operational Layer* (*Who & When?*): Real-time security operations and monitoring.

Each layer ensures that security is integrated from the top-down, rather than added after technical solutions are already in place. There are a number of key Principles embedded across these layers:

Business-Driven Security: SABSA emphasises that security decisions should be based on business needs and risks rather than purely technical concerns.

Risk Management Focus: Security controls are selected based on risk assessments, ensuring that investments in security are aligned with the most critical risks.

Policy-Driven Approach: Policies define security requirements across all layers of the architecture, ensuring consistency and enforceability.

Layered Security Architecture: By aligning security with different levels of abstraction (business, logical, technical), SABSA ensures comprehensive coverage.

Continuous Assurance: Security is not a one-time implementation but an ongoing process requiring monitoring, adaptation and improvements.

Stakeholder-Centric Design: Security should consider the needs of various stakeholders, including executives, employees, customers and regulators.

TOGAF principles

TOGAF is a widely used EA framework that provides structure for designing, implementing and managing IT systems in alignment with business goals.

TOGAF consists of several key components:

- *Architecture Development Method (ADM)*: A step-by-step process for creating an EA.
- *Enterprise Continuum*: A classification system for architecture assets and solutions.
- *Reference Models*: Standardised architectures that organisations can adopt or adapt.
- *Governance and Compliance*: Ensuring that architecture aligns with business policies and regulatory requirements.

TOGAF establishes principles that guide EA design. These principles fall into three broad categories:

1. *Business Principles*: Ensure alignment between IT and business goals.
2. *Data Principles*: Govern data management and accessibility.
3. *Technology Principles*: Provide guidance on infrastructure and application development.

Let's break these down.

Business principles

- *Primacy of Business Needs*: IT decisions must support business objectives.
- *Maximise Reuse*: Reuse existing assets to reduce costs and complexity.
- *Compliance with Regulations*: Ensure adherence to legal and industry standards.
- *Simplification and Standardisation*: Reduce complexity to enhance agility.

Data principles

- *Data is an Asset*: Data is a valuable resource that must be managed effectively.
- *Common Data Definitions*: Standardised data definitions ensure consistency.
- *Data Security*: Data should be protected based on risk levels.

Technology principles

- *Technology Independence*: Avoid vendor lock-in by adopting open standards.
- *Interoperability*: Systems should be compatible and capable of seamless integration.
- *Scalability and Flexibility*: Architectures should support future growth and changes.

Links between Enterprise Architecture and Anthropology

EA is not just about technology: it is deeply human-centric. Anthropology provides insights into organisational culture, human behaviour and decision-making, all of which influence how EA frameworks like SABSA and TOGAF are implemented.

Pierre Bourdieu's 1986 work "The Forms of Capital" outlines three primary types of capital that influence social stratification and power dynamics:

1. *Economic Capital*: Material wealth, financial resources and assets that can be directly converted into money (e.g., income, property, investments).
2. *Cultural Capital*: Non-financial social assets that contribute to social mobility, including education, knowledge, skills and cultural tastes. Bourdieu further divides cultural capital into three forms:
   - Embodied (e.g., language, mannerisms, knowledge acquired through socialisation).
   - Objectified (e.g., books, artwork, instruments).
   - Institutionalised (e.g., academic degrees and credentials).

3. *Social Capital*: The network of relationships, connections and social ties that provide access to resources and opportunities. It includes group membership and the ability to mobilise social networks for personal or collective gain.

Bourdieu argues that these forms of capital can be converted into one another (e.g., using social capital to gain economic capital) and that they play a crucial role in maintaining social hierarchies and reproducing power structures.

It is a fascinating exercise applying Bourdieu's Forms of Capital to Information Security Risk Management. Pierre Bourdieu's theory of capital provides a useful lens for understanding how different types of resources – economic, cultural and social – shape an organisation's ability to manage information security risks. Below is a deeper exploration of how each form of capital influences cybersecurity risk management and how they interact in practice.

Economic capital: Financial resources and security investments

Economic capital refers to an organisation's financial resources, which are critical in determining its ability to implement and sustain cybersecurity measures. Organisations with high economic capital can afford:

- Advanced security technologies (e.g., firewalls, SIEM systems, endpoint protection).
- Skilled cybersecurity professionals (e.g., hiring CISOs, security analysts).
- Regular penetration testing, audits and compliance monitoring.
- Cyber insurance to mitigate financial losses in case of breaches.
- Organisations with low economic capital may struggle to:
- Implement comprehensive security controls, leaving gaps in protection.
- Retain skilled cybersecurity talent, leading to reliance on outsourced services or untrained personnel.
- Stay compliant with security regulations, increasing legal and reputational risks.

Cultural capital: Knowledge, skills and security awareness

Cultural capital encompasses the security-related knowledge and competencies within an organisation. This includes both technical expertise and security awareness among employees. There are three Forms of Cultural Capital:

1. *Embodied Cultural Capital* (*Personal Security Knowledge & Behaviour*): There are employees' cybersecurity awareness, habits and vigilance against threats like phishing, social engineering and weak passwords.

2. *Objectified Cultural Capital* (*Security Tools & Policies*): These are security frameworks, policies and documentation (e.g., ISO 27001, NIST cybersecurity framework), as well as ownership of cybersecurity tools, encryption software and security infrastructure.
3. *Institutionalised Cultural Capital* (*Certifications & Credentials*): These are certifications (e.g., CISSP, CISM, CEH) that validate expertise as well as industry standards compliance (e.g., GDPR, HIPAA, PCI-DSS) that reinforce security best practices.

High cultural capital leads to:

- Better internal cybersecurity governance and employee adherence to security policies.
- Well-trained IT teams capable of identifying and mitigating threats effectively.
- Stronger regulatory compliance and security certifications that enhance trust with stakeholders.

Low cultural capital results in:

- Weak security awareness, making employees easy targets for cybercriminals.
- Poorly defined or outdated security policies, increasing exposure to threats.
- Ineffective incident response due to a lack of trained personnel.

Social capital: Networks, partnerships and threat intelligence sharing

Social capital represents the relationships and connections that an organisation has within the cybersecurity ecosystem. This includes collaborations with industry peers, government agencies, regulatory bodies and cybersecurity communities.

Strong social capital enables:

- Access to threat intelligence from cybersecurity communities (e.g., ISACs, government agencies).
- Collaboration with industry peers to share best practices and security insights.
- Faster incident response through partnerships with cybersecurity firms and experts.
- Influence on security policies and regulatory frameworks.

Weak social capital leads to:

- A lack of awareness about emerging cyber threats.
- Difficulty in obtaining external support during security incidents.

- Increased regulatory risks due to limited interaction with compliance authorities.
- Interplay Between the Forms of Capital in Cybersecurity

Bourdieu's concept of capital conversion is particularly relevant in security risk management. Different forms of capital influence each other:

- Economic capital → Cultural capital:
  - Organisations with high financial resources can invest in security training (cultural capital) to enhance workforce cybersecurity awareness.
- Cultural capital → Social capital:
  - Skilled cybersecurity professionals (institutionalised cultural capital) build strong networks, increasing an organisation's access to external expertise (social capital).
- Social capital → Economic capital:
  - Strong partnerships with cybersecurity firms and regulators help reduce financial losses by improving risk mitigation strategies.

Bourdieu's framework provides a multidimensional perspective on security risk management, showing that security is not just about technology but also about financial resources, knowledge and relationships. To build a resilient security posture, organisations must:

1. Strengthen economic capital by allocating adequate budgets for security investments.
2. Develop cultural capital by promoting security awareness, training and adherence to best practices.
3. Leverage social capital by fostering collaborations and engaging in threat intelligence sharing.

By balancing these three forms of capital, organisations can create a comprehensive, sustainable approach to cybersecurity risk management, reducing vulnerabilities and enhancing overall resilience in the face of evolving threats. They can interweave this with ESA. EA initiatives require buy-in from multiple stakeholders (executives, employees, IT teams, regulators). Anthropology helps in understanding different stakeholder perspectives and developing effective communication strategies. EA should consider the human impact of technology decisions: User experience (UX) principles, rooted in anthropology, influence how EA solutions are designed and adopted.

Many organisations struggle with digital transformation due to cultural resistance. SABSA and TOGAF provide structured approaches to enterprise security and architecture, ensuring that IT supports business goals. However, their success depends on human factors, making anthropology a crucial field for understanding culture, risk perception, governance and organisational behaviour. By integrating anthropological insights, organisations can improve EA adoption, enhance security awareness and design systems that truly align with human needs. Anthropological methods such as ethnographic research help EA teams understand organisational dynamics and design solutions that align with employee behaviours and expectations. In the future, we will hopefully see greater interdisciplinary collaboration between EA professionals and anthropologists to develop more adaptive, human-centred EAs.

HOW GRC, DATA PRIVACY AND SECURITY ARCHITECTURE COME TOGETHER

In an era where data breaches, regulatory changes and rapidly evolving technological landscapes are the norm, organisations can no longer treat GRC, Data Privacy and ESA as independent silos. Instead, these disciplines must be integrated into a unified strategy that protects information assets, ensures business resilience and meets compliance obligations.

What this sub-section attempts to do is briefly discuss the convergence of these fields, outline why integration matters and detail practical methods for achieving alignment across the board. This, in turn, will help organisations develop holistic strategies that address external threats, regulatory pressures and internal vulnerabilities. We will start off by exploring each of these components in depth before examining their intersections, challenges and strategic benefits. Whether you are an executive, a security architect or a compliance officer, the principles detailed herein can be adapted to your unique context and help shape robust policies for today and tomorrow.

The evolution of GRC in today's business environment

The concept behind GRC is that by interlacing strategic governance with hands-on risk management and rigorous compliance efforts, organisations can better prioritise investments, improve operational efficiency and foster a culture of accountability. This integrated framework not only reduces the likelihood of security incidents but also ensures that a company's risk posture remains aligned with its overarching business goals.

GRC has matured significantly over the last decade. Frameworks such as COSO (Committee of Sponsoring Organizations), ISO 31000 for risk management and COBIT (Control Objectives for Information and Related Technology) for governance have become instrumental in guiding organisations. These frameworks provide well-defined processes and metrics that organisations can configure to match their operational realities. Furthermore, new GRC solutions built on emerging technologies have enabled improved data analytics, better risk reporting and automation of compliance monitoring.

The success of a GRC initiative depends not only on processes and technology but significantly on leadership. Executive management must champion the cause, ensuring that risk management and compliance are woven into the corporate culture. CEOs, CISOs and other senior executives need to empower teams, set an example through transparency and invest in employee training and technology that reinforces these principles. Strong leadership can transform a fragmented security posture into a strategically integrated system that permeates every aspect of the organisation.

Data Privacy: The new frontier of trust and regulation

Data privacy refers to the rights and practices that protect personal and sensitive information from unauthorised access, use or disclosure. With the advent of digital transformation, enormous volumes of data are generated daily – data that includes personal identifiable information (PII), financial data and proprietary business information. Regulations such as the General Data Protection Regulation (GDPR) in Europe, the California Consumer Privacy Act (CCPA) and other country-specific legislations have imposed strict requirements on how this data is managed and protected. For many enterprises, data privacy is not just about legal compliance; it is a cornerstone of trust. Customers, partners and employees expect that their information will be safeguarded. Ensuring data privacy requires a combination of clear policies, robust technical safeguards and continuous monitoring and assessment to prevent breaches and unauthorised use.

Data privacy regulations come with a heavy compliance burden that has only grown in complexity over time. Organisations must establish data handling and processing protocols that comply with multiple jurisdictional requirements. This involves not only implementing technological protections but also creating comprehensive privacy policies, conducting regular audits and ensuring transparency in data utilisation.

Data privacy is not a "bolt-on" feature; it must be integrated into the fabric of every organisational process, from vendor management to product development. Key trends include the use of artificial intelligence (AI) for detecting anomalous data access, the implementation of blockchain for secure data transfer and an increased focus on consumer-driven data rights. Moreover, regulatory bodies are increasingly demanding transparency and accountability, forcing companies to invest in advanced cybersecurity measures that align with evolving legal expectations. This evolving landscape makes it critical for organisations to adopt dynamic, broad-spectrum solutions that can adapt to new requirements.

Enterprise Security Architecture: Building the resilient foundation

ESA is the practice of designing and optimising an organisation's security posture through a holistic view of its networks, systems, applications and data. An effective ESA is built on several core pillars:

1. Risk Assessment and Management
2. Security Controls and Policies
3. Incident Response and Recovery
4. Security Governance

These pillars guide the continuous improvement of an organisation's security landscape. ESA is not a one-time project but a perpetual cycle of assessment, design, implementation and reassessment. Successful ESA is one that dovetails seamlessly with business processes. It must enable business agility while not compromising on security. This requires two intertwined approaches. First, security must be designed into systems from the outset – commonly referred to as "security by design" – ensuring that it is an essential part of the system development life cycle (SDLC). Second, security policies and controls must be adaptive and scalable, accommodating the dynamic nature of modern business operations.

A robust ESA framework ensures that all layers of the organisation work together to form an impenetrable defence.

The convergence: Where GRC, Data Privacy and ESA intersect

As has been repeatedly iterated, the rapid evolution of cyber threats and compliance landscapes demands that organisations break down internal silos. An integrated model brings several advantages:

1. *Risk Reduction*: Overlapping functions ensure that vulnerabilities are not missed. For instance, if a data privacy risk is identified, it can be immediately addressed through improved security architecture while also informing compliance checks.
2. *Cost Efficiency*: Consolidating these functions reduces redundancy, streamlines reporting processes and creates efficiencies in both resource allocation and operational oversight.
3. *Enhanced Agility*: A unified approach allows organisations to rapidly adapt to regulatory changes and emerging threats by switching from a reactive stance to a proactive one.
4. *Cultural Shift*: Embedding security and compliance into the organisational culture reinforces the idea that every member is responsible for protecting the enterprise.

The first step in achieving integration is to align the principles of GRC with every element of the enterprise's security architecture, including ESA's own principles. This means:

1. *Embedding Compliance Requirements*: Security architecture must incorporate controls that meet industry standards and regulatory mandates, such as encryption protocols, access logging and incident reporting frameworks.
2. *Risk Management Integration*: Risk assessment outcomes should drive the design of security architectures. For example, determining the value of data assets and their exposure to threats can dictate the level of technical controls and monitoring systems required.
3. *Governance and Continuous Oversight*: Establishing a continuous feedback loop between governance committees and security teams ensures that architectural changes are reviewed regularly. This not only aligns with regulatory requirements but also stays ahead of emerging threats.

Intriguingly, as it may come as a surprise to some but not to others, data privacy plays a pivotal role as a bridge between GRC and ESA. By defining how data should be collected, processed, stored and shared, data privacy policies create benchmarks that security architectures must meet. Privacy-driven requirements may necessitate data encryption at rest and in transit, strict access controls and granular monitoring of data access attempts. Data privacy initiatives thus inform both risk assessments and security policies and help organisations build architectures that are inherently privacy-conscious.

Operationalising the unified model

Operationalising this unified model involves several best practices:

1. *Cross-Functional Teams*:** Assemble teams that include representatives from risk management, compliance, IT security and legal departments. These teams can collaborate on policies, incident response plans and continuous monitoring initiatives.
2. *Technology Integration*: Bring together representatives from the different areas of the business owning and/or overseeing digital services. Create working groups where quality and risk management deep dives can be done on the end-to-end lifecycle of the service. Feed the information up into the GRC risk register and the Enterprise Risk Management risk register.
3. Leverage modern tools that unify data flows from GRC systems, privacy management platforms and security information event management tools. Data dashboards that provide at-a-glance health metrics can drive rapid decision-making.
4. *Automated Controls and Analytics*: Automation helps bridge the gap between policy and practice. Use automated risk assessments, continuous monitoring and advanced analytics to correlate data privacy incidents with broader security events.

5. *Policy Alignment*: Regularly update policies to reflect new regulatory changes and emerging security threats. Ensuring that the language of GRC documents, data privacy protocols and security architecture guidelines is harmonised reduces confusion and enforces a uniform security posture.

BEST PRACTICES ACROSS INDUSTRIES

Across industries, common success factors include:

- *Strong Executive Sponsorship*: Leaders must commit to integrating these disciplines and providing the necessary resources.
- *Holistic Risk Views*: A unified control dashboard that aggregates risk data, privacy incidents and security events helps decision-makers.
- *Regular Training and Awareness*: Employees should be trained on cross-functional processes that explain how their actions affect overall security, compliance and privacy.
- *Iterative Improvement*: Adopt continuous monitoring and improvement cycles to ensure that all systems remain robust and compliant in the face of evolving threats.

Integrating GRC, data privacy and ESA begins with a clear strategic roadmap. Organisations must articulate specific short-term and long-term objectives, such as reducing audit findings, mitigating potential breaches or improving data accountability. This roadmap should be developed collaboratively by all stakeholders, ensuring that every perspective – from legal and compliance to IT and risk management – is expressed and incorporated.

A successful integration strategy involves:

- *Baseline Assessments*: Conduct comprehensive audits to understand the current state of governance, data handling practices and security architecture.
- *Defining Key Performance Indicators (KPIs)*: Establish metrics that allow ongoing measurement of integration success ranging from incident response times to compliance audit scores.
- *Risk Prioritisation*: Map out the most critical data assets and assess the external and internal threats associated with them.
- *Resource Allocation*: Allocate budgets and human resources to address identified gaps and monitor progress towards integration.

Beyond technology, the human and process elements play a critical role. Integration requires that communication channels between disparate teams are open, with clearly delineated roles and responsibilities. Cross-disciplinary working groups can serve as the bridge between data privacy officers, IT security managers and GRC leaders. Formalised meetings, joint audits and shared reporting frameworks foster a culture of accountability and transparency. Moreover, developing clear Standard Operating Procedures (SOPs) that detail how findings in one domain trigger assessments in another helps create a seamless operational flow. For instance, if a data privacy audit reveals gaps in data access controls, that information must immediately flow to the security architecture team for remediation. Equally, risk management assessments should inform the updating of privacy policies and governance tests, ensuring that every domain supports the others in a continuous loop of improvement.

One of the most significant challenges to integration is cultural resistance within organisations. Departments that have historically operated in silos may be reluctant to change established processes. Security architects might view compliance as a bureaucratic burden, while compliance officers might see technical controls as overly technical or inaccessible. Overcoming these barriers demands strong leadership, clear communication and a robust change-management strategy.

Regulations around data privacy and cybersecurity are in constant flux. What works for today may not suffice tomorrow. A unified model must be capable of rapid adaptation to regulatory changes, necessitating continuous review cycles and built-in flexibilities within the security architecture. Failing to anticipate changes can result in non-compliance, exposing the organisation to fines and reputational damage.

Implementation challenges are often exacerbated by resource limitations. Integrating three extensive domains requires not only a financial commitment but also access to experienced personnel who understand both the technical and regulatory nuances. Balancing day-to-day operational needs with strategic integration efforts can be a juggling act that many organisations find daunting. Strategic planning, however, can help allocate resources more effectively and create phased integration plans that are viable even with budgetary and personnel constraints.

Integration is not a "set-once" project but a journey of continual improvement. Implementing feedback loops is essential for adapting processes, technologies and policies based on real-world experience. Regular cross-departmental review sessions, updated risk assessments and adaptive policy revisions create an ecosystem that continuously learns and evolves. Industry case studies reveal that organisations that have successfully integrated these domains often share common practices such as:

- Developing clear, documented processes for cross-functional collaboration.
- Investing early in adaptive technologies that ensure interoperability.
- Creating a culture where security, compliance and privacy are seen as everyone's responsibility.

As international commerce continues to grow, governments and regulatory bodies are moving towards a more harmonised approach to data privacy and cybersecurity regulations. Future trends point towards standardised frameworks that can be applied globally, reducing complexity for multinational organisations. Harmonised regulations will further stress the importance of integrating GRC and security architectures, as organisations will need a consistent way to navigate different regional regulatory environments.

Organisations can respond more quickly to both regulatory changes and emerging security threats by dissolving silos and fostering cross-departmental collaboration. This integrated approach empowers organisations to reduce risks, cut operational costs and build a resilient security posture that aligns with long-term strategic objectives. A unified framework has the potential to transform how organisations interact with technology, manage risk and engage with customers, regulators and business partners alike. Through leveraging technology, aligning processes and nurturing an organisational culture that values transparency and continuous improvement, enterprises can not only meet the challenges of today but also adapt to the uncertainties of tomorrow. As information security threats and regulatory requirements evolve, the integration of GRC, data privacy and ESA will remain at the heart of a resilient and forward-thinking business strategy.

By continuously refining strategies through ongoing feedback, cross-industry collaboration and emerging best practices, organisations can stay ahead of challenges and leverage integration as a competitive advantage. The convergence of GRC, data privacy and ESA represents a holistic paradigm that appeals to every stakeholder from the boardroom to frontline employees. The journey is complex and requires careful planning, robust technological support and an unwavering commitment to fostering a culture of vigilance and collaboration. However, the rewards are substantial: reduced risk exposure, enhanced trust with customers and a resilient operational model capable of weathering the storms of modern cyber threats and regulatory disruption. This framework is designed to spark further ideas, initiate discussions among cross-functional teams and ultimately empower your organisation to create an integrated, secure and compliant future.

—

I trust you will use the information provided in this book to increase your working effectiveness in your organisation through your team, individual behaviour and engagement. Some of what I was taught growing up in South Africa was fundamentally wrong: We were often told to work in silence and let your work do the talking. There was a sense of a strict hierarchy and an expectation by some segments of society of meekness on the part of others, regardless of skin colour and cultural backdrop. It took me a long time to start speaking up in such a way that I was not ignored, pushing myself into higher visibility and consequential projects. I had to confront my own flaws and find mechanisms to bypass other people's perceptions and intentions when these were harmful. This is the power of emotional intelligence and self-awareness.

You are now appropriately armed to increase your strengths and address your weaknesses, to engage confidently in internal processes and to realise the risks and benefits of decisions. Through this, you can help shape human responses to change and increase the resiliency of your organisation. I wish you all the very best for your career.

Bibliography

Allen, B., Bapst, B. and Hicks, T. 2023. *Building a Cyber Risk Management Program: Evolving Security for the Digital Age*. Sebastopol: O'Reilly Media, Inc.

Artz, M. and Koycheva, L. 2024. *EmTech Anthropology: Careers at the Frontier (Anthropology & Business)*. London: Routledge.

Bonney, B., Hayslip, G. and Stamper, M. 2018. *CISO Desk Reference Guide: A Practical Guide for CISOs*. San Diego: CISO DRG Joint Venture Publishing.

Brown, J. 2021. *The Security Leader's Communication Playbook: Bridging the Gap between Security and the Business*. Boca Raton: CRC Press.

Crask, J. 2021. *Business Continuity Management: A Practical Guide to Organizational Resilience and ISO 22301*. London: Kogan Page.

Geary, J. 2025. *How to be a Chief Risk Officer: A handbook for the modern CRO*. Kindle Direct Publishing.

Graeber, D. 2015. *The Utopia of Rules: On Technology, Stupidity, and the Secret Joys of Bureaucracy*. London: Melville House.

Graeber, D. 2018. *Bullshit Jobs: A Theory*. London: Allen Lane.

Graeber, D. and Wengrow, D. 2021. *The Dawn of Everything: A New History of Humanity*. London: Allen Lane.

Hasib, M. 2014. *Cybersecurity Leader*. Createspace Independent Publishing Platform.

Hasib, M. 2020. *Bring Inner Greatness Out*. Tomorrow's Strategy Today, LLC.

Hopkin, P. 2018. *Fundamentals of Risk Management: Understanding, Evaluating and Implementing Effective Risk Management*. London: Kogan Page.

Hubbard, D. and Seiersen, R. 2023. *How to Measure Anything in Cybersecurity Risk*. New Jersey: Wiley.

IAPP. European Data Protection, Third Edition.

Knibbs, C. and Hibberd, G. 2023. *A Practitioner's Guide to Cybersecurity and Data Protection: How to Ensure Client Confidentiality*. London: Routledge.

Oberlander, M. 2020. *Global CISO – Strategy, Tactics and Leadership: How to Succeed in InfoSec and Cybersecurity*. Independently Published.

Oberlander, M. 2024. *Premier CISO – Board & C-Suite: Raising the Bar for Cybersecurity*. Independently Published.

Room, S. 2021. *Data Protection and Compliance*, Second edition. London: BCS, The Chartered Institute for IT.

Sharp, M. and Lambros, K. 2022. *The CISO Evolution: Business Knowledge for Cybersecurity*. New Jersey: Wiley.

van der Wens, C. 2023. 2019. *ISO 27001 ISMS Handbook: Implementing and Auditing an Information Security Management System in Small and Medium-sized Businesses*. Independently Published.

Zongo, P., Argyle, D. and Schreuder, J. 2024. *The Cyber Leadership Imperative: Powerful Strategies to Unlock Your Potential and Become an Exceptional Cybersecurity Executive*. Sydney: Cyber Leadership Institute.
Zongo, P. 2018. *The Five Anchors of Cyber Resilience: Why Some Enterprises are Hacked into Bankruptcy, While Others Easily Bounce Back*. Sydney: Broadcast Books.

Index

Note: *Italic* and **Bold** page numbers refer to *figures* and **tables**.

For Product Safety Concerns and Information please contact our EU representative GPSR@taylorandfrancis.com Taylor & Francis Verlag GmbH, Kaufingerstraße 24, 80331 München, Germany